Unconquered

Unconquered
The Iroquois League at War in Colonial America

•

Daniel P. Barr

Modern Military Tradition
Jon L. Wakelyn, Series Editor

Westport, Connecticut
London

Library of Congress Cataloging-in-Publication Data

Barr, Daniel P., 1971–
    Unconquered : the Iroquois League at war in colonial America / Daniel P. Barr.
        p. cm.—(Modern military tradition, 1553–7196)
    Includes bibliographical references and index.
    ISBN 0–275–98466–4 (alk. paper)
    1. Iroquois Indians—Wars. 2. Iroquois Indians—Warfare. 3. Five Nations—History.
4. Six Nations—History. 5. Great Britain—Colonies—America. 6. Indians of North
America—History—Colonial period, ca. 1600–1775. 7. United States—Politics and
government—To 1775. 8. United States—History—Colonial period, ca. 1600–1775.
I. Title. II. Series.
E99.I7B22   2006
974.7004'9755—dc22   2005030018

British Library Cataloguing in Publication Data is available.

Library of Congress Catalog Card Number: 2005030018
ISBN: 0–275–98466–4
ISSN: 1553–7196

First published in 2006

Praeger Publishers, 88 Post Road West, Westport, CT 06881
An imprint of Greenwood Publishing Group, Inc.
www.praeger.com

Printed in the United States of America

The paper used in this book complies with the
Permanent Paper Standard issued by the National
Information Standards Organization (Z39.48–1984).

10 9 8 7 6 5 4 3 2 1

For Delaney and Coldan,
whose father spent far too many sunny summer days
lost in the Iroquois wars when he should have been with them.

Contents

Foreword

In *Unconquered: The Iroquois League at War in Colonial America*, Daniel Barr has both written an excellent synthesis of nearly two hundred years of Indian warfare on the New York frontier and shed new light on that early contest among Indians and colonists for preservation of power and native land. He has combined the best of the secondary literature with new insight into how to study warfare. This is indeed a tricky shoal, for original materials are hard to come by, and when found they are often biased and confused. Through expert understanding of Indian culture and keen analysis of political organization, Barr recounts the story of how the six nation Iroquois League formed, fought and defended itself, was nearly destroyed, but because of its unity came through the American Revolution and subsequent peace intact, and continued to thrive in western New York down to now. Barr's work is at once a brilliant reconstruction of colonial warfare and a timely lesson on how organization for mutual defense produced lasting survival.

The book begins with a deft study of how culture, geography, societal structure, and politics formed the Iroquois League. Barr is especially skillful at using legends and myths to draw conclusions about concrete organization. He focuses on how the Iroquois used river and lake navigation to organize military defense as well as grain access to trading lanes along the St. Lawrence River. Barr then describes how the Indians organized their lives, as hunters and fishers and farmers, developing large village life around the longhouse, surrounding smaller economic villages, and hunting and fishing camps. The longhouse were essential to family existence and led to active decision making for the women, patterns of leadership development for the young men, and a means to unite into a league of likeminded people. At first, says Barr, those Iroquois tribes fought one another, but their cultural and political traits united them in mutual defense against Indian foes on all sides, as well as French, English (sometime allies), and colonial Americans bent on spreading into and beyond present New York state.

Through a careful reading of Iroquois political organization, Barr describes how these tribes created mutual defense. He well understands that a study of warfare today requires cultural and political analysis. To preserve their cultural values, individual Indian families sought revenge against enemies, Indian and European alike. By recounting their own creation myth stories, Iroquois leaders came to understand that political unity was crucial to mutual defense. Respecting individual longhouse family structure and the interests and desires of different tribes, the leaders developed a political system deferential to single tribal decisions. They formed their league based on the confederation principle that gave each tribe an absolute veto over plans for joint defense. Thus any collective action required negotiation and compromise among the six tribes. Through their individualism, says Barr, they became even stronger and better able to defend themselves.

Barr ends the volume by telling of the British betrayal of the league in the treaty of 1783, in which the Iroquois lands were deeded to the Americans. Having already been forced to take up residence in western New York around present day Buffalo, the league members faced the fate, like other Indian tribes, of being forced ever westward into the cruel wilderness. But through the unity forged from the confederation principle, the Iroquois held together and struck a series of bargains and treaties with the Americans that allowed them to continue to live in central and western New York.

The Iroquois League experience of war and peace offers a useful lesson for other peoples of similar cultural values and language to organize as political confederations. The politics and culture of Iroquois League warfare that Barr has reconstructed from many disparate sources is as timely for present analysis of divisive warfare as it is for understanding the past survival of those Indian tribes. The lesson is that out of unity of purpose, along with the willingness to protect individual interests, emerges the strength found in collective military defense.

—*Jon L. Wakelyn, Series Editor*

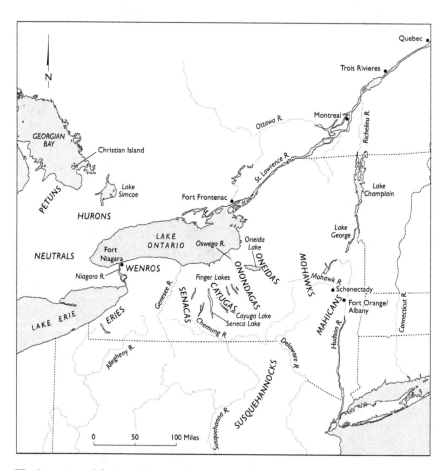

The Iroquois and their neighbors in the seventeenth century. Created by Bill Nelson.

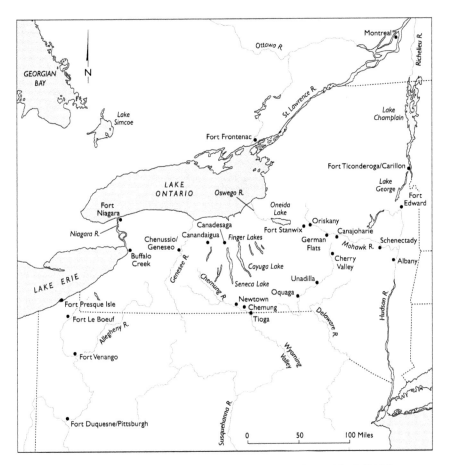

The Iroquois and their neighbors in the eighteenth century. Created by Bill Nelson.

Prologue: The Wars of the Iroquois League

This book presents a narrative history of Iroquois warfare from approximately 1600 through the end of the American Revolution, roughly covering the period of colonial American history. For the peoples of the Iroquois League—the Mohawks, Oneidas, Onondagas, Cayugas, Senecas, and eventually, Tuscaroras—warfare was an important institution. War represented a many-sided expression of their world view, a complex, vital component of Iroquois culture that was at times an almost daily part of their lives. Older histories asserted that Iroquois warfare was economically motivated, an attempt by the members of the Iroquois League to become European-style imperialists and monopolize the fur trade in northeastern North America. Economic competition and rivalry for trade were certainly important factors in Iroquois warfare, especially in the seventeenth century, but not its beginning or end. Modern scholarship has demonstrated that the Iroquois waged wars for a variety of reasons, many of which had little or nothing to do with economics. Indeed, Iroquois motivations for war originated within their culture as often as they came from external considerations. Powerful cultural traditions, such as the mourning war, a societal need to satisfy beliefs about the dead and allay the suffering and grief of the deceased's surviving kin, mixed with the eagerness of young men to pursue war, which served as a means of social and political advancement, combined to make warfare a necessary and desirable function of Iroquois society.

The presence of Europeans and their colonists provided another powerful motivation for Iroquois warfare. Europeans influenced and incited, both directly and indirectly, conflict with the Iroquois League, as well as conflicts between the Iroquois and other Indian nations. In the seventeenth century, for example, European diseases devastated Iroquois populations, leading to a massive expression of mourning war traditions. Competition for European trade influenced Mohawks to make war on Mahicans to open access to Dutch traders. And warriors from several Iroquois nations attacked Indian trading convoys along the upper St. Lawrence River in order to pilfer their furs and trade goods. In the eighteenth century, the French and British competition for empire in North America pulled the Iroquois into wars not of their own choosing and strained the bonds of their union, and the war of the American Revolution produced a civil war that ripped the Iroquois League apart. Without European colonization, these wars would not have occurred. The French, in particular, proved to be an implacable foe for much of the colonial era, and even when the Iroquois were at peace with their neighbors in Canada, they seldom hesitated to strike a blow at the French if they believed it was to their advantage. Ironically, after the French were gone, the Iroquois League faced its greatest setbacks in war.

The Iroquois League did not fight its wars as a united, monolithic entity. Indeed, the Iroquois League was seldom at war with anyone. Its individual member nations, and at times only portions of these, drove the warfare often attributed to the whole. At times two or more Iroquois nations were allied in war against a common enemy, but at other times various Iroquois nations waged wars against foes with whom their partners in the Iroquois League were at peace. The Mohawks, for example, raided Canada in the early 1660s while other members of the Iroquois League were concluding peace treaties with the French. Similarly, individual Iroquois nations occasionally waged simultaneous wars that were completely independent of each other. In the seventeenth century, the Senecas and Cayugas warred against the Susquehannocks in Pennsylvania at the same time that the Mohawks were fighting New England Algonquins, Mahicans, and the French. Neither conflict had much of anything to do with the other. The Iroquois League's pluralistic military activities were made possible by the loose union that characterized membership in the league. It was a sort of elastic association, in which each nation was free to pursue its own foreign policy independent of the others. As long as the

Iroquois nations kept peace with one another, unity was preserved and the league endured. To be certain, in times of crisis the Iroquois nations could function much like a united confederacy, at least after a fashion. Large armies made up of warriors from many Iroquois nations took the field against their enemies, but this was the exception, not the standard. At no time in the colonial period did all five Iroquois nations universally wage war against a common enemy: there were always factions and divisions that precluded 100 percent Iroquois participation in any conflict.

According to some still prevailing popular beliefs, the Iroquois won the vast majority of the wars they waged, and in the process they created a massive Indian empire through the subjugation of Indian nations from the St. Lawrence River to the Mississippi Valley, leading them to sometimes be referred to as the "Romans of the New World." In reality, the Iroquois created no expansive territorial empires, although they did establish far-reaching networks of trade, sometimes through war, and they did destroy and disperse a variety of Indian peoples along their borders. Nor were Iroquois warriors singularly unbeatable in battle. Far from it. Europeans, Americans, and many Indian nations turned back Iroquois invasions, defeated and killed Iroquois warriors in combat, and attacked and burned Iroquois villages almost as often as the Iroquois emerged victorious in these types of conflicts. Yet through all the disruption, damage, and destruction that they inflicted and sustained, the Iroquois League endured. The Iroquois tasted defeat, but they were never completely destroyed. Perhaps because they waged war as individual members of a loosely united, voluntary league, rather than as a unified political state, they were never conquered. Victory over one Iroquois nation did not convey victory over the others or the league as a whole, a deceptively simple distinction that does much to explain how and why the Iroquois League remained an influential and important entity in colonial America longer than any other Indian nation. Only when they fought each other, as occurred during the American Revolution, did the Iroquois come close to annihilation. Even then, however, they endured.

Lastly, it must be stressed that this a selective overview of Iroquois warfare in colonial America. It is not possible to trace every raid, battle, or conflict involving the Iroquois League during this period. The Iroquois left few records to offer insight into their wars, forcing historians to rely on the writings, reports, and observations of European colonists and soldiers to piece together the world of Iroquois warfare. Much of the fighting took place far from the eyes of Europeans, however, especially in the seventeenth century, which means that most European records of Iroquois warfare are second-hand accounts, retellings of what others saw, said, or heard. As such, there is often some confusion among the sources about the specifics of which Iroquois nation was involved in a battle, who was attacking whom, and whether or not the conflict was part of some larger Iroquois strategy or merely an isolated engagement. The lack of direct sources and the voluntary nature of association in the Iroquois League sometimes make it difficult to grasp with any certainty why and how the Iroquois waged their wars. These limitations have prevented some Iroquois conflicts from being included here, as there are very likely many Iroquois skirmishes, raids, and battles for which there are no surviving records. It does not mean that they did not occur, just that there is no specific knowledge of them. Similarly, if a conflict is not covered here, it does not mean that it was not important, but rather that the known sources to reconstruct it were too limited. Indeed, the Iroquois wars covered here are those for which there are the most abundant and complementary sources, which by default mark these episodes as fairly major conflicts. If there is perhaps an overemphasis on the Mohawks or Senecas at the expense of the other Iroquois nations, it is not an intentional construction but rather a product of existing sources and the tales they tell.

A fair amount of anxiousness has accompanied the writing of this book. Production of a narrative synthesis that attempts to tie together a vast array of Iroquois scholarship was a daunting proposition. Creating a book accessible to a general readership ranging from the high school to collegiate level, while also trying to provide something useful for scholars, specialists, and Iroquois enthusiasts was even more intimidating. At times, I wondered if I was equal to the task, and on at least one occasion, I seriously considered aborting the project. But with encouragement from friends, family, and colleagues, I soldiered on. A May 2005 trip through New York with a colleague provided the inspiration needed to finish the project. Visits to Howe's Cave Indian Museum and Ganondagan State Historic Site rekindled my deep appreciation for the peoples of the Iroquois League, their culture, and their history. I can only hope that this book does justice to their past experiences in war.

What follows then is a narrative history of the major wars involving the peoples of the Iroquois League. I have tried to tell the story from the Iroquois perspective, although at times the actions of other Indian nations, Europeans, or colonists take center stage as the conflicts unfold. In creating a work of synthesis, I have incurred a deep debt to numerous Iroquois scholars whose writings have informed and guided much of what is found in these pages. The works of Jose Antonio Brandao, William Fenton, Barbara Graymont,

Francis Jennings, Daniel Richter, and Dean Snow have been invaluable throughout the completion of this project. In addition, the work of countless other scholars has provided assistance on a wide array of specific and stubborn topics. All who have written previously about Iroquois warfare, either directly or indirectly, have helped to shape what is good in this book. Any errors, mistakes, or poor assumptions are entirely my responsibility.

1

•

Born from Blood

When the five Iroquoian-speaking people who inhabited modern New York state joined with one another to form the Iroquois League, variously known as the League of Five Nations, or the League of Six Nations after the adoption of the Tuscarawas in the eighteenth century, they called their political union the Great League of Peace and Power. They created a political system where power derived from the cooperation of their member peoples, a reciprocal union rooted in peaceful coexistence. But it had not always been so. For generations, the members of the Iroquois League warred against one another in a seemingly endless cycle of rage and revenge governed by a cultural tradition known as the "mourning war." To relieve the grief of a deceased person's relatives, the dead had to be avenged, creating a perpetual state of internal conflict in which there was very little peace or power, only suffering and war. The creation of the Iroquois League was a response to this endless violence, a confederation system where individual Iroquois nations could settle their differences via peaceful ceremonies rather than war. Although the league created peace for the Five Nations, the Iroquois continued to embrace warfare as a necessary component of their individual and social culture. External warfare against neighboring Indian nations replaced internal fighting, a change in orientation that transformed the Iroquois's Great League of Peace and

Power into the most formidable political and military confederation in colonial North America.

IROQUOIS ORIGINS

The five Iroquois nations who would eventually join together to form the Great League of Peace and Power were part of a much larger group of Iroquoian-speaking people surrounding Lake Ontario and nestled along the upper St. Lawrence River in the east and the Susquehanna River in the south. The five peoples of the Iroquois League were centrally located within this culture area, occupying modern New York state from the Mohawk River valley in the east to the Genesee River and the Finger Lakes in the west. Farthest east along the river valley that today bears their name dwelled the Mohawks, who called themselves *Ganienkeh,* or "people of the place of the flint." To their immediate west resided the Oneidas, "the people of the standing stone," followed by the Onondagas, meaning "people of the mountain." Next came the Cayugas, "the people at the landing," and farthest west dwelled the Senecas, "the people of the great hill." Collectively they called themselves the *Haudenosaunee,* or "People of the Long House." It was a literal analogy to their principal dwelling, but also a metaphor for the framework and function of their league, which operated in many regards like an extended household.[1]

Their homeland, generally referred to as Iroquoia, placed the five Iroquois nations in a strategically advantageous position in northeastern North America. The Iroquois sat astride several crucially important waterways, vital avenues of transportation that provided access to networks of trade. The landscape of Iroquoia sloped upwards moderately from east to west, aiding the formation of a vast river network that allowed the Iroquois to travel almost anywhere they desired by canoe. Near the Mohawks in northeastern Iroquoia, Lakes George and Champlain provided northern access to the Richelieu River, which drained into the St. Lawrence, and eventually the Atlantic Ocean. The Mohawk River cut through their territory, joining with the Hudson River to provide a southern passage to New York harbor. To the south of Iroquoia, the Susquehanna and Delaware river systems offered additional routes to the Atlantic Coast. In the west, along the edges of lands settled by the Seneca peoples, the Allegheny River flowed south to its confluence with the Ohio River, providing access to the interior of the continent, and the Niagara River allowed Iroquois hunters and travelers access to Lake Erie and western Great Lakes. And in the north, numerous streams and small rivers flowed into Lake Ontario, which facilitated east-west travel in its shallow waters near the shoreline. In addition, the rivers provided a measure of security, as they all flowed away from Iroquoia, forcing enemies to travel upriver against swift currents to attack the Iroquois in their homes. Similarly, the inland location of Iroquoia buffered the Iroquois from the initial effects of European invasion, protecting them from war and disease, although in time both would find their way to the Iroquois heartland.[2]

Exactly how and when the Iroquois came to occupy their advantageous homeland is subject to debate. Like peoples from around the world, the Iroquois have a creation myth, a supernatural story that explains where they came from and offers powerful insight into their culture and values. Iroquois traditions tell that before there were human beings, there were the sky people, who dwelled far above the earth in the heavens. Life on earth began when a being the Iroquois call the Sky Woman fell from the heavens, having been cast out of the sky by her husband. Jealous that Sky Woman had become pregnant even though she had not been intimate with him, the husband uprooted a great tree, leaving a hole in the sky and exposing the world below. When his wife bent low to peer through the opening, Sky Woman's husband pushed her into the hole. The earth at this time consisted only of endless waters, but the spirits of birds and sea animals dwelled within the watery realm. Seeing the plight of Sky Woman, ducks flew to her rescue, catching her on their wings and gently laying her on the back of the Turtle, who allowed Sky Woman to rest on his shell so that she would not drown. To give the celestial visitor a new home, Turtle consented to bear the weight of the earth on his back so that Sky Woman might walk freely where she would. Many sea animals dove to the bottom of the waters in an attempt to retrieve soil to put on Turtle's back. All failed until Muskrat swam into the watery depths and returned with a mouthful of dirt, which he deposited on Turtle's back. With Turtle's help, this meager bit of sod grew until it became the continent of North America, where Sky Woman made her new home.[3]

Sky Woman soon gave birth to a daughter, who in time also became miraculously pregnant and had twin sons. The firstborn son, Tharonhiawagon (Upholder of the Heavens), who entered the world in the normal manner, was fair, good natured, and kind. However, his brother, Tawiskaron, was ugly, cruel, and evil. Impatient to leave his mother's womb, he tore a hole in her side so that he might escape, killing her in the process. From the start, the twin brothers were polar opposites, and as they grew to adulthood, a great contention developed between them. The good twin, Tharonhiawagon, labored under the guidance of the Turtle to transform the world into a beautiful place. From his mother's body, he created the sun, mountains, rivers, and lakes. Last, he created human beings to live in his beautiful world and gave to them corn and the animals, whose spirits agreed to allow themselves to be hunted for food. But Tawiskaron was jealous of Tharonhiawagon's creations, and he worked tirelessly to twist and malign all that the good twin created. Tawiskaron made darkness to subdue the sun, pounded the mountains so that they became jagged and hard, filled the streams with rapids and shoals, made some plants poisonous to eat, and turned the animal spirits against mankind. Eventually the strife of the twins culminated in a great cosmic battle, in which Tharonhiawagon prevailed and struck down Tawiskaron, banishing his evil twin to a cave deep underground. Unable to undo all of the wrongs that Tawiskaron had inflicted on the world, Tharonhiawagon taught human beings to grow and harvest corn for themselves and instructed them to perform ceremonies of thanksgiving to appease the spirits of the animals they killed. Tharonhiawagon then withdrew from the world, leaving humankind to govern their own existence. These human beings were the ancestors of the Iroquois.[4]

As with any creation myth, science paints a different but not altogether contradictory picture of Iroquois origins. The human habitation of the Western Hemisphere began in the wake of the last Ice Age, approximately 12,000 to 15,000 years ago. By 4500 B.C., a general warming trend and the withdrawal of glaciation allowed for widespread human habitation of the North American continent. By 1600 B.C., groups of human beings had reached central New York, having migrated up the Susquehanna River corridor from the south. For these ancestors of the Iroquois, life in the northeastern woodlands evolved in measured steps. Human society passed through several developmental stages, gradually transforming from mobile hunter-gather groups to semi-sedentary communities that subsisted on a mix of agriculture and hunting and fishing. The invention and refinement of tools, techniques, and languages paralleled the shifting socioeconomic patterns. Most important of all developments was agriculture, specifically the domestication of corn, squash, and beans, which allowed for greater populations and denser settlement patterns, giving rise to large villages. In these settlements, Iroquois society divided power between men and women. Men held all political positions, both civil and military, but they owed their offices to the support of the women in the village. A gathering of the elder matrons of each village, sometimes referred to as "clan mothers," selected each male leader, and they also could remove chiefs who did not conduct themselves in the best interests of the people. Labor was similarly divided: men cleared away trees and rocks from agriculture fields, and women planted and harvested the crops. Men also hunted and fished to add to the agriculture yield and provide balance to the Iroquois diet.[5]

By the sixteenth century, a sizable population of Iroquoian-speaking people inhabited large, stockaded villages in forest clearings and on hill-tops overlooking waterways throughout what is now Pennsylvania and New York. The central component of their village world was the long-house, a large arched, rectangular structure that served as the living space for a number of related family groups or households. A French Jesuit priest once remarked that "their cabannes [cabins] are in the shape of ton-nelles [tunnels] or arbors, and are covered with the bark of trees."[6] His description was very close to current understandings about the construc-tion of Iroquois longhouses. The frame and roofing rafters were composed of saplings, lashed together and secured at the base by twisting them into the ground. Sheets of elmwood bark covered the frame, providing stabil-ity and insulation against the weather. There were no windows, but every longhouse had an entryway at either end of the structure and openings in the roof for natural lighting and the ventilation of smoke. The floor was dirt, packed down hard from the frequent passing of feet. Longhouses were approximately 25 feet wide and between 80 and 100 feet long. A central corridor, perhaps 10 or 12 feet wide, ran the entire length of the interior of the house. There were firepits and cooking hearths at regular intervals along the corridor, allowing enough space for two or three family groups to access the fire. Raised platforms ran along the walls on either side, subdivided into small apartment cubicles, in which lived families of three to five persons each. In the summer, the Iroquois generally slept in these elevated compartments to avoid damp conditions and fleas, but in the winter they tended to place mats on the ground so that they could sleep closer to the warmth of the fires. Large storage areas capped each end of the longhouse, and additional storage was located between apartment cubicles and in lofts that ran above the cubicles along the walls on either side. The number of residents depended on the size of the related family group, or clan, living in the house. The larger the clan, the bigger the longhouse. As Iroquois population increased, it was not uncommon for longhouses to be 200 feet long and for clans to inhabit multiple long-houses in the village.[7]

Inside Iroquois villages, longhouses were arranged in group or clan clus-ters, or set in parallel rows. A large Iroquois village could contain more than 100 longhouses and have a population of more than 2,000 people. Average village populations were somewhat smaller, although villages of

1,000 or more residents were not uncommon. By the early seventeenth century, there were between 10 and 13 major villages in Iroquoia: the Mohawks had three or four, the Oneidas established one village, the Onondagas had one or two, the Cayugas occupied two or three villages, and the Senecas had two. In addition to the villages, there were numerous smaller settlements, sometimes called hamlets, usually located within a few miles of the larger village. There were also a number of seasonal camps that served special purposes, ranging from hunting and fishing to war. All together, the total population of the five Iroquois nations was perhaps slightly more than 20,000 people.[8]

Aside from the longhouse, the dominant feature of Iroquoian villages were their defensive works. Early European explorers who encountered these villages called them "cantons," meaning "a place for soldiers," or "castles," as befitted their appearance and military purpose. Indeed, Iroquois villages were heavily fortified. They were situated atop hills or ridges away from navigable waters, such as rivers or lakes, that might allow easy access for an enemy attack, and the forest surrounding the village was cleared away so that attackers could not use the cover of trees to get close to the settlement. Two or three rows of palisades — pointed wooden stakes inserted vertically in the ground — enclosed the village, reaching upwards of twenty feet tall. Bark, brush, and other materials filled in the spaces between the stakes to offer protection against arrows or other projectiles passing through the palisades. Platforms, bastions, and towers commonly were located at intervals in the palisade, allowing the village's defenders an elevated vantage point from which to hurl rocks and shoot arrows at attackers. There were few opening in the palisades, all of which were small and easily blocked by logs or other obstacles during times of attack. The main gate was constructed of thick timbers, and often adorned with fierce carvings and images or, if the village's warriors had met with recent success, the heads and scalps of enemy combatants. Additional outer works could have included a ditch or earthwork ramparts, obstacles that would have further hindered any concerted push against the palisades. Obviously, with so many wooden structures, fire was a prominent concern, and some Iroquois villages had an elaborate system of wooden troughs that brought in water from nearby creeks or ponds to help fight fires.[9]

THE TIME OF TROUBLES

It was not coincidence that Iroquois villages were so heavily fortified. Before the arrival of the Europeans, the five Iroquois nations were surrounded by other Indian nations, most of whom were enemies. Other Iroquoian speakers occupied lands to the north and west, including the Wendats (Hurons), Eries, Wenros, Petuns, and Neutrals. In the east and southeast, along the lengths of the Hudson and Delaware Rivers, were the Algonquian-speaking Mahicans and Lenapes (Delawares). The Susquehannocks, another Iroquoian-speaking group, established villages south of the five Iroquois nations along the Susquehanna River; and the Shawnees, an Algonquin people, dwelled in regions of Pennsylvania lying southwest of the Iroquois. None maintained friendly relations with the Iroquois in central New York. Rivalries over hunting territories, trade, and other resources produced tension between the Iroquois and their neighbors, resulting in a state of almost perpetual warfare.

Simultaneously, the Iroquois engaged in a deadlier and far more detrimental conflict. According to Iroquois oral traditions, the five Iroquois nations violently battled one another in a repetitive cycle of raids, rage, and revenge, sometimes referred to as the "blood feud." So horrific was this internal warfare that the Iroquois named it "the time of troubles." It is a fitting description. The foundation of the ceaseless conflict lay in Iroquoian spiritual beliefs, which held that each individual had the capacity to do good or evil, traits that people inherited from the twin brothers borne by Sky Woman's daughter, the mother of all life. Human beings were inherently good, but when a person gave in to evil temptations, bad things, such as war, were more likely to occur. Moreover, the Iroquois held that no bad deed could go unpunished, and they could suffer no act of war to go unavenged. Iroquoian concepts of power would allow no other response. Spiritually, the death of a person was a traumatic event for the Iroquois, which caused the deceased's relative profound grief. They covered their faces and clothing with ashes and withdrew from daily village life, refusing to perform any tasks or even to feed themselves. This extreme response reflected Iroquoian spiritual beliefs about death, which meant not only the loss of a loved one, but also a reduction in the collective spiritual power of the entire nation. The deceased's family, clan, and village felt an even more acute loss of power. Moreover, Iroquois spiritual beliefs maintained that the spirits of the dead haunted their village, causing mischief and sickness. Only through loud and pronounced expressions of grief, usually by women, could the dead spirits be convinced to hasten down the path to the afterlife. But if a person's death was the result of violence or war, then the only way to appease the spirits and relieve the grief of the deceased's relatives was to exact revenge on the killers.[10]

Thus, the Iroquois waged wars of retaliation and revenge to appease the spirits of the dead, ease the grief of the living, and regain lost power. These conflicts have been termed mourning wars because their foundations lay in mourning the dead. The primary objective of mourning wars was the capture of enemies. A successful attack against the enemy was not one that eradicated his villages or added another nation's territory to that of the Iroquois, but rather one that resulted in captives. These captives were brought into Iroquois villages, where they were presented to families who had suffered losses. The eldest women in each family or clan decided the fate of the prisoners. Male captives, especially enemy combatants, generally faced death, but only after enduring a slow, painful torture process deeply rooted in Iroquoian concepts of spiritual power. Condemned captives were secured to poles in an open area of the village by a short length of rope, where Iroquois men and women taunted and assaulted them. The Iroquois beat prisoners with sticks, sliced open their bodies with knives and sharpened shells, and seared their flesh with flaming sticks or hot pokers. The process was slow and extremely painful, a ritualistic form of torture designed to make the victims beg for death. Conversely, captives waged their own battle against their tormentors by refusing to cry out in pain or beg for mercy. Indeed, the Iroquois expected captives to respond with insults and even encourage the executioners. It was a contest for power: if the Iroquois villagers broke the will of the victims, they absorbed their spiritual power. If the victims refused to yield, they maintained their dignity and power. Still, the end result was death. When the victims were near death, the Iroquois scalped them, poured hot sand onto their exposed skulls, and then finally ended the suffering with a knife to the chest or a hatchet stroke in the neck. Even then, the Iroquois believed they could absorb their captives' spiritual power. The women of the village carved the body of the deceased into pieces, boiled it, and then served it to the warriors, who ate it, literally consuming the captive's power.[11]

Ritual torture and cannibalism were designed to restore spiritual power lost when Iroquois people died. But another form of power, a physical notion of power that corresponded to the number of people in each Iroquois nation, was also replenished through captive-taking. Male captives most often faced torture and death, but captive women and children usually met with a different fate: adoption. Elder women in the village decided which captives would be adopted, and even these were treated roughly at first. Adoptees faced mild torture and ridicule, but then would be suddenly and dramatically rescued and treated with great tenderness and love. In what was known as a "Requickening" ceremony, the adopted person was given the name of a dead Iroquois person and forced to assume the identity and role of the deceased. This assured that the spiritual power of the dead would not leave the nation, but remain in the person of his or her replacement. Moreover, adopted captives ensured that the community would endure by keeping the nation's population stable and maintaining the nation's physical power. Those captives who embraced their new identities and assimilated into Iroquois society could expect to enjoy the same rights and privileges as any other Iroquois person, and they could even ascend to positions of civil or military authority. Conversely, captives who rejected adoption or refused to assimilate were executed, generally by a quick blow to the head.[12]

Through the torture and adoption of captives, the five Iroquois nations maintained the spiritual and physical power of their people. In practicing these arts on each other, however, the Iroquois planted the seeds of their own destruction. Mohawks, Oneidas, Onondagas, Cayugas, and Senecas became locked in a desperate struggle, where the death of every warrior demanded retaliation, which in turn created only more cries for vengeance. There could be no end to the mourning wars and no victory; only the extermination of one's enemy or one's self. As one historian has surmised: "A mourning war was a viscous cycle, for almost every war party suffered casualties, which demanded more captives and more torture. And every war party provoked a counter-raid from the enemy, carrying death into an Iroquois village and carrying away captives—which of course demanded a further escalation."[13] It was indeed a time of troubles, as the violence between the Five Nations threatened to destroy them all. Iroquois oral traditions sum it up best: "Everywhere there was peril and everywhere mourning. Feuds with outer nations, feuds with brother nations, feuds of sister villages, and feuds of families and of clans made every warrior a stealthy man who liked to kill."[14]

THE GREAT LEAGUE OF PEACE AND POWER

In this wilderness of war, Iroquois traditions tell of an Onondaga *sachem*, or chief, named Tadodaho, who was feared by all Iroquois for his cruelty and prowess in war. Tadodaho was the embodiment of evil, a deformed and warped man who loved to kill. Even his hair was possessed of an ill will, twisted and matted so that Tadodaho appeared to have a head full of writhing snakes. Although Tadodaho was thought to be insane, many Iroquois believed that he was a mighty sorcerer, and Onondaga warriors followed his lead, hoping for glory and success in war. Tadodaho gave them both, leading successful raids against the neighboring Cayugas and traveling farther west to strike at the Seneca peoples, but he was also feared by his own people. Onondagas who questioned Tadodaho's love of violence disappeared or died mysteriously, adding to the war leader's reputation as a powerful conjurer who could strike down his enemies with hidden magic.[15]

However, there was one Onondaga man, Hiawatha, who denounced Tadodaho. Rather than follow the deranged war leader, Hiawatha advocated peace with other Iroquois peoples. Tradition relates that from an early age Hiawatha loved peace more than war, a trait that befuddled his Onondaga kinsmen. As an adult, he frequently challenged Tadodaho's calls to war and attempted to influence the war leader to give up violence. Tadodaho refused, and the Onondaga people continued to follow his lead into war. Then, shortly after holding two councils to preach peace, Hiawatha lost his two oldest daughters to mysterious illnesses that resisted all known medical treatments. Many Onondagas whispered that Tadodaho had killed Hiawatha's children with evil magic, but Hiawatha persevered in his desire for peace. He called a third council, during which he kept his youngest daughter close to him. Still, a horrible accident befell her. During a melee in which Tadodaho's warriors squabbled and wrestled over possession of feathers from a large eagle they had shot down, Hiawatha's only remaining daughter was knocked to the ground and bludgeoned to death. Worse yet, the young woman had been pregnant with Hiawatha's grandchild.[16]

Stricken by grief, Hiawatha fled to the wilderness, where he became a lonesome wanderer. In time, Hiawatha came into the territory of the Mohawks, where he met a man from the Huron nation, Deganawidah, also known as The Peacemaker. A supernatural being who may have been the reincarnation of Tharonhiawagon, the good twin, Deganawidah eased Hiawatha's suffering and restored his spirit. Taking three strings of wampum, Deganawidah performed what the Iroquois call the condolence ceremony. Using a string of wampum for each blessing, Deganawidah first wiped the tears from Hiawatha's eyes so that he might see clearly. Next Deganawidah cleared his ears so that he might once more hear kinds words, and last, he unstopped his throat so that Hiawatha could speak and breathe easily. The condolence ceremony was the key element of Deganawidah's teachings, which he called The Good News of Peace and Power. "When men accept it," Deganawidah told Hiawatha, "they will stop killing and bloodshed will cease."[17] Hiawatha became The Peacemaker's disciple, and together they visited each of the five Iroquois nations, instructing them in the condolence ceremony and the art of peace. Oneidas, Cayugas, and Senecas joined the Mohawks in accepting The Good News of Peace and Power, but the evil Tadodaho would not allow the Onondagas to embrace the Peacemaker's message. Hiawatha would not be swayed, however, and after lengthy efforts, he won over Tadodaho. According to Iroquois tradition, Hiawatha combed the tangles and snakes from Tadodaho's hair, cured the deformities of Tadodaho's body by rubbing them with wampum, and set his mind at peace with the words of the condolence ceremony. Cured of his insanity and evil inclinations, Tadodaho embraced The Good News of Peace and Power, allowing at long last the blood feuds to end.[18]

Deganawidah's message of peace helped the Iroquois set aside their grievances and live together in peace. Traditionally, this marks the establishment of the Iroquois League, which they named The Great League of Peace and Power in honor of The Peacemaker's good news. The Iroquois conceived of their league as a great longhouse stretching across all of Iroquoia and sheltering all five Iroquois nations under its roof. As such, each nation had a duty to perform to keep the longhouse secure. The Mohawks were the guardians of the eastern door, the Senecas guarded the western door, and the Onondagas, the centrally located nation of the five, became the keepers of the central council fire. Above the whole stood the great Tree of Peace, atop of which perched the spirit of the eagle, who watched over the affairs of the league and protected their newfound peace. It was the duty of each representative to the council to uphold that peace, and they metaphorically were considered to be support poles for the great longhouse, literally holding up the tree of peace.[19]

To promote peace and prevent renewal of the blood feud, all five Iroquois nations agreed to send representatives to a central council at the main Onondaga village, where they could hold condolence ceremonies to right wrongs between their peoples and avoid extending the cycle of mourning war. Clan mothers from each village selected a number of representatives, sometimes called peace chiefs, who came together at the Onondaga's principal village to form the central council, a body of fifty civil leaders from the five Iroquois nations. Although the number of representatives from each Iroquois nation varied, they voted in unison for their nation, giving each of the five member nations a single vote. All decisions made by the council had to be unanimous; there was no majority rule. But in the early days of its existence, the central council primarily officiated condolence ceremonies where the relatives of an offending Iroquois person presented gifts to the relatives of an injured or deceased person. The ceremonies followed The Peacemaker's teachings, as the presents helped to wipe away tears, open ears, and restore lost voices, blunting the need for revenge to alleviate grief. They were remarkably successful at keeping the five Iroquois nations from feuding with each other.[20]

The Great League of Peace and Power, commonly referred to as the Iroquois League of Five Nations or the Iroquois League, also promoted unity of its member nations through its political structure. Although the league maintained a central council and selected representatives to attend the body, the council did not exercise total authority over the Five Nations. The Iroquois did not intend for their council to interfere in the internal affairs of their nations, and as such, the council had no power to enforce its rulings. Each Iroquois nation, from the Mohawks to the Senecas, maintained autonomy of action, and if they did not choose to follow the advice of the central council, there were no repercussions. This would seem to be a weak central government, but in actuality the system provided the Iroquois League with tremendous flexibility, as the member nations could pursue diverse and even conflicting agendas without disrupting the whole. It allowed the Five Nations to remain at peace with each other by keeping the local village the central political and social unit of the league. So long as they continued to practice the condolence ceremonies to keep peace between league members, the Five Nations remained loosely united, free to pursue actions independent of one another, and, as later events will show, militarily powerful. Thus, at the time of its creation, the Iroquois League was essentially a ceremonial institution designed to promote peaceful interaction between the Five Nations in place of the violence and war that had previously governed their relations.[21]

THE GREAT LEAGUE FOR WAR AND SURVIVAL

After the formation of their league, the Iroquois took pride in their devotion to peace. Yet other Indian nations continued to associate the Iroquois with war rather than peace. Indeed, with their league functioning as a sort of mutual nonaggression pact between league members, the Five Nations increasingly turned their violent attentions against external enemies, who came to view the Iroquois League as more of an enemy military alliance than a peaceful union. The Five Nations believed it was their duty to spread the Peacemaker's message to other Indians nations and to bring them into the Iroquois League. Only then could peace exist for everyone. Those Indian peoples who resisted were considered enemies, and the Five Nations warred against them to force their submission to the Iroquois League. Moreover, although formation of the league ended the internal blood feud between the Five Nations, it did not alter the Iroquois's cultural connection between war and mourning. Warfare continued to be a necessary function for a society that placed high values on appeasement of grief and the preservation of power through the taking of captives. Warfare also played an important role in helping the Iroquois deal with deaths on a personal and emotional level, as the Iroquois believed that failure to assuage grief could lead to evil consequences. As the mythical figure of Tadodaho demonstrates, the Iroquois believed that unchecked grief caused a person to lose all sense of reason and become a slave to rage, leading to actions that could be harmful for themselves and for their community. Generally, the family members of a deceased person intensely mourned the dead for 10 days by refusing to take part in any community activity or even take care of themselves. This was followed with approximately a year of lesser mourning, during which the family neglected their appearance but gradually worked themselves back into the normal rhythms of daily life. At all times, relatives and other members of the community performed condolence rituals, including that taught by the Peacemaker, to ease the pain felt by the deceased's family. At times, however, no amount of ceremony or goodwill could stem the suffering. On these occasions, women from the aggrieved family could call on the warriors of their village to lead an attack against an enemy people to provide the families of the dead with captives.[22]

Warfare served other important functions in Iroquois society as well. Combat allowed young men to prove themselves as warriors. Becoming a member of a war party was a rite of passage as boys became men, and there were powerful incentives for young men to seek out battle, as success in war elevated a man's prestige and status. Sometimes being a renowned warrior led to political influence, and a reputation as a victorious war captain could secure marriage into an influential clan or lineage. Moreover, young men who witnessed the torture of an enemy captive learned by example how to conduct themselves if ever they should fall into the hands of their enemies. War also functioned as a community institution by providing Iroquois society with an outlet to express group cohesion and community pride. All Iroquois who took part in the torturing of captives were able to physically participate in the Iroquois's triumph over their enemies and symbolically express their superiority over their foes.[23]

Naturally, as warfare served such an important function in Iroquois society, there was a process and protocol to coordinate military endeavors. The Iroquois formed war parties for two reasons: as part of a mourning war to exact revenge or adopt captives, or because the village governing council had called for an attack against an enemy. In the case of a mourning war, someone's grief over the loss of a relative was so severe that the elder women of a village decided that only revenge or the adoption of captives could ease their suffering. The clan mothers selected a warrior or group of warriors, presented them with war belts made from wampum, and asked them to avenge the deceased by raiding the enemy and obtaining captives. These warriors were often relatives of the deceased person, but not of the same household. The Iroquois feared that close male family members would become "drunk with the blood lately shed" and unable to function rationally or effectively in war.[24] The clan mothers thus chose from among the deceased's male relations living in different longhouses. The warriors chosen to receive the war belt could decide for themselves whether or not to accept the clan mothers' request, but the public accusations of cowardice that accompanied refusal made such a decision unlikely. If the warrior accepted the clan mothers' request, he then assumed the burden of organizing a war party, selecting a target, and exacting revenge.[25]

The scenario was not that much different when a village council made the decision to go to war. The decision-making process still involved the village's clan mothers, who met in council with the leading men of the village to discuss the need for war. Evidence was presented to justify the decision for war, which mainly involved a recounting of an enemy's transgressions against the Iroquois community. If war was declared, the council appointed respected warriors from the village to serve as captains, informed them of the grievance against the enemy, and "let them know the indispensable necessity they were under to avenge themselves against those that they believed had insulted them."[26] The war leaders then held their own council, during which they either accepted or declined the call to war. If they accepted, the war captains sang the war song and began to create war parties. On those occasions when a major effort was needed, civil chiefs and war captains together traveled to neighboring Iroquois villages and requested that they too accept the call to war.[27]

Although there was some distinction between mourning wars and wars called for by village governing councils, the two forms of Iroquoian warfare were not mutually exclusive. Revenge was a powerful motivation in either scenario, and the principal objective in both cases was the expansion of Iroquois power through the taking of captives. The measure of a warrior was calculated on the number of captives he brought home to the village for adoption or torture. Accordingly, the taking of captives accorded higher military honors than killing enemies or taking their scalps. Either through adoption or execution, the Iroquois obtained the power of a captured enemy and added it to their own. Killing an enemy demonstrated bravery and skill in combat, but it did not bring equivalent forms of power to the community. Iroquois understandings of war thus differed greatly from those of Europeans, as an Onondaga spokemen explained: "We are not like you Christians, for when you have taken prisoners of one another you send them home, [although] by such means you can never rout one another."[28]

Additionally, the selection of war parties for either form of conflict was similar: village leaders selected a war captain, who in turn invited other young men to join him in forming a war party. Volunteers were seldom in short supply, because young Iroquois men generally were eager to increase their public stature through war. Once the war party had been formed and a starting time determined for the campaign, the war captain held a feast for his warriors on the eve of their departure. A dog was butchered and cooked in the "war kettle," and all members of the war party ate of its flesh. The warriors painted their faces and bodies in grotesque patterns, sang war songs and danced around a war pole, and lastly, prayed to the sun for success in battle. In return for guidance to and from the enemy's village, Iroquois warriors promised to torture, kill, and eat those captives that they did not adopt. The following morning, the members of the war party, dressed in their finest clothes, paraded in a grand procession past the other members of the village. Once outside the village, the warriors proceeded to the edge of the forest, where they were greeted by the women of the village, who offered them their final farewell. The warriors removed their ceremonial dress, giving it to the women to take back to the village, and then clothed themselves in war attire, gathered their provisions and equipment, and departed. Their last action before leaving home was to carve a pictograph into a tree depicting the number of warriors in the party, the village or nation of the group, and the clan of the war leader. It was a public record of who they were and the exploits they were about the undertake.[29]

Before the arrival of the Europeans, large, multivillage campaigns often resulted in carefully orchestrated, large-scale battles, involving formations of warriors wearing wooden armor and elaborate headdresses. The outcomes of such battles, however, often were inconclusive, and loss of life was minimal. Generally, the Iroquois and their enemies formed into lines or massed groups facing one another across an open field, then hurled insults and fired arrows at each other. Occasionally, a few warriors from either side rushed forth to engage in duels with enemy combatants, but the killing and violence were limited. Mourning war campaigns, however, were personal and often more violent, generally taking the form of hit-and-run raids. On these campaigns, war parties traveled as quickly as possible, and sought out the easiest means of passage. Rivers and streams were the preferred avenues of transportation, as they allowed Iroquois warriors to cover great distances at speed. It was not uncommon for war parties to travel hundreds of miles to strike their enemies if waterways allowed for their passage. They traveled in canoes as far as the water could carry them toward their target, then filled their canoes with rocks and sunk them in shallow water. In this manner, they hid their transports but were still able to retrieve them for the journey home. Traveling by night and resting during the day, the Iroquois lived off the land as they went, hunting and fishing to provide food for the war party. Food was rationed to sustain the party over the length of the trip, and because they ceased all food-gathering activities the closer they got to their target, small depots of food and supplies were established along the way to be gathered up as they retreated. Similarly, Iroquois war parties often constructed small fortified positions along their path of advance, secure stations to which they could retreat if the attack went poorly or an enemy pursued them in wrath.[30]

On entering the vicinity of their target, the Iroquois war party approached as stealthily as possible. The war party traveled in single file behind the war captain, and the last man in the group covered their tracks to keep their presence hidden from any of the enemy who might happen on their trail. Secrecy was paramount, as the Iroquois preferred to surprise their enemy. In addition, maintaining secrecy allowed the war party to determine the strength of the enemy and evaluate his defenses. If the enemy appeared to be too strong, or if the war party was discovered, the war captain could abort the attack and withdraw. Such considerations were mandated by the premium that the Iroquois placed upon loss of life. Any raid or attack that resulted in multiple casualties would be considered a failure, as the intent of the attack was to weaken the enemy and increase Iroquois power through the taking of prisoners. Heavy casualties, especially deaths, were counterproductive to this goal, as it weakened, rather than strengthened, the Iroquois group sponsoring the attack. Thus, if the war party decided to attack, their strategy was to strike quickly, kill or capture as many of the enemy as possible, and withdraw before retaliation or pursuit could be organized. Iroquois warriors crept as close to the target village as possible, placing themselves in advantageous positions to launch a surprise attack. The assault began with loud war cries, followed by a volley of arrows into the unsuspecting enemy population. Iroquois warriors then burst from their places of concealment and rushed into the village to initiate hand-to-hand combat, take scalps from enemies wounded during the rain of arrows, and secure prisoners. The Iroquois pushed the attack as long as they held the advantage or until enemy resistance became organized, then immediately withdrew, taking any captives or other plunder with them. On rare occasions, an attack went so well that the Iroquois overwhelmed all resistance and controlled the village, but most often the Iroquois withdrew at the first sign of serious opposition or after the death of one of their warriors, even if they seemed close to victory.[31]

Regardless of how the raid ended, an Iroquois war party moved as rapidly as possible once the decision had been made to retreat, dragging their captives along the way. Any prisoners who slowed down the retreat, either deliberately or because of an inability to keep up, were quickly killed. Likewise, the war party eliminated any captive who tried to give away the location of the retreating war party by crying out or by leaving signs of their passage. Captives who did not resist had their hands bound behind their backs by ropes and were tied to stakes during the night so that they could not escape. Even then, they were at times mildly tortured by their captors. When the war party neared its home village, runners moved out ahead of the main group to inform the village that the war party was returning. If any Iroquois warriors had been killed during the raid, the relatives of the deceased were condoled so that they would not be overcome by grief when the war party entered the village. The villagers formed two lines, through the middle of which passed the war party and the captives. Sometimes referred to as the gauntlet, the Iroquois pummeled the captives as they passed with fists, feet, clubs, and other weapons. Captives were not usually killed in this process, as the captives' fate, either adoption or execution by torture, were determined by the clan mothers afterwards. However, the brutal beatings served as another form of communal expression as the Iroquois celebrated victory over their enemies. Additional expressions of superiority occurred shortly thereafter, when the war leader held a feast giving thanks for the victory, and the Iroquois raised the scalps or disembodied heads of their enemies on stakes above the palisades.[32]

The Iroquois experienced the other side of war when their enemies came to their door. Iroquoian defensive strategies were guided by the same principles that conditioned their raids, especially the desire to avoid sustaining heavy casualties. The most effective way of meeting this objective was to prevent enemy attackers from reaching Iroquois villages. The

Iroquois thus employed spies to watch the movements of their enemies, and scouts traversed the wilderness to watch for approaching enemy war parties. If alerted of an impending attack, Iroquois warriors tried to lay an ambush for their enemy, eliminating the threat before it could reach their villages, but the same cautious formula that induced Iroquois raiders to signal retreat when the fighting got fierce also mandated that the Iroquois call off an ambush if the enemy war party was too large or too wary. Instead, the Iroquois either retreated into their fortified villages and fought from behind their palisades, or if the enemy was considered very power-ful, burned their villages and fields to prevent them falling into enemy hands, and fled. Lost homes could be rebuilt and burned crops could be replanted, but the people had to survive for the spiritual and physical power of the nation to endure.[33]

Thus, even as they created peace among themselves, Iroquois culture assured that warfare would remain a central part of their existence. The creation of the Iroquois League brought peace to the Five Nations, but it also conditioned the Iroquois to turn their aggressions against surrounding Indian nations. Their culture needed enemies, and when the Iroquois could no longer find them among one another, they turned to external wars against other Indians. This consideration has led one historian to recast the Great League of Peace and Power as "the Great League for War and Survival," a wonderfully appropriate substitution, as the Iroquois did not fight wars for conquest or empire, but for survival.[34] Indeed, as European newcomers began to make their way toward Iroquoia in the early seven-teenth century, both war and survival would become increasingly more complex for the Iroquois League, and the Five Nations would find them-selves engaged in conflicts far and wide of their homeland as they strug-gled to survive and adapt in a rapidly changing world.

2

———————•———————

Guns and Furs

In the early 1600s, trade with European newcomers brought dynamic change to the Indian nations of northeastern North America. All Indian peoples within the reach of European commerce, including the Iroquois, faced new challenges. The eastern member nations of the Iroquois League, particularly the Mohawks, faced the greatest challenges and reaped the greatest rewards as they adapted to the arrival of the French and Dutch along the edges of Iroquoia. Yet this transition was marred by war. Europeans and the manufactured goods they brought with them complicated the Five Nations' relationships with their native neighbors, reordering the parameters of conflict and providing new sources of competition. The French alliance with the Hurons compelled the Iroquois to seek a similar arrangement with the Dutch, which in turn brought the Mohawks into conflict with the Mahican peoples who controlled access to trade at Fort Orange (modern Albany, New York). Competition for the fur trade fueled the conflict, spurring the Iroquois to reorient their military goals and practices in order to survive and thrive in a rapidly changing world.

THE FUR TRADE

When European explorers arrived along the fringes of Iroquoia during the early decades of the seventeenth century, the Five Nations already were at war. Few sources chronicle the Iroquois League's wars against the Indian nations of the northeast before 1600, but it is clear that the Iroquois fought against enemy "Adirondacks," a term that translates somewhat generically as Algonquians. The origins of the conflict are locked in the past, but the lengthy conflict spanned generations, pitting the Iroquois League against the Hurons above Lake Ontario, the Algonquins of the Ottawa River valley, the St. Lawrence Montagnais, and the Abenaki peoples of western New England. Much of this conflict centered on the upper St. Lawrence River valley. The lands around the lower Richelieu River, Lake Champlain, and Lake Ontario were a war zone, where Iroquois warriors conducted mourning war raids against their enemies. Huron, Algonquin, and Montagnais hunters traversed the region cautiously, and they hesitated to remain long near the Richelieu River, which came to be known as "the river of the Iroquois" because it was the favorite ambush locale of Mohawk warriors.[1]

Similarly, the reasons for Iroquois aggressiveness along the upper St. Lawrence at this time are unclear. The wars may have been born of necessity. What is known of Mohawk demographics suggests that the population of the eastern nations of the Iroquois League was expanding rapidly. Between 1580 and 1614, for example, the Mohawk population more than doubled, from an estimated 2,000 to at least 4,500. The increase likely was the result of migrations. Iroquoian people known to have inhabited the lower St. Lawrence River valley during the 1530s left the region by 1600, and they may have moved closer to Iroquoia and meshed into Mohawk or Oneida society. Simultaneously, during the mid-1500s, Mohawk peoples scattered to the west and east of the Mohawk River valley appear to have began congregating alongside their brethren in the central Mohawk heartland. Whatever the source of the population explosion, the Mohawks could sustain such demographic growth only through an expansion of their hunting territories, which likely brought them to the upper St. Lawrence, where they collided with Huron traders and Algonquin hunters. Not forgetting the fundamental importance of mourning war rituals to Iroquois society, it is very likely that warriors from the Five Nations also prowled the region in search of captives for torture and adoption. Indeed, not long after establishing Quebec, Samuel de Champlain resolved to build a fortified French post in the upper St. Lawrence country to "secure the freedom of some tribes who dare not come that way for fear of their enemies, the said Iroquois, who infest the bank all along the said river of Canada."[2]

Access to hunting grounds and the search for captives are the most plausible explanations for Iroquois aggression toward other Indians, but another factor—trade—soon added another impetus for the fighting. Iroquois warfare in the St. Lawrence River valley did not begin with the fur trade, but it did intensify after the first manufactured goods obtained in trade from Europeans began to trickle up the St. Lawrence into Iroquoia. In the 1500s, emerging nation-states in Europe sought to emulate the success of the Spanish and to create their own vast empires of wealth in the Americas. Yet for the most part, these dreams eluded those Europeans who most actively reached toward the New World. The French, Dutch, and English failed to duplicate Spanish discoveries of gold and mineral riches, nor could they discover a Northwest Passage to the valuable trade markets of the Pacific Rim. Yet each, in turn, stumbled on other forms of wealth—fish, furs, and land—that made colonization in North America not only possible, but eventually profitable as well.[3]

By the late sixteenth century, the Gulf of St. Lawrence and the Grand Banks of Newfoundland teemed with hundreds of European ships from several different nations, including France, England, Holland, and Portugal. These were fishing and whaling vessels, whose crews had braved the hazardous journey across the North Atlantic in pursuit of the immense bounty of fish, whales, and seals found in those waters. No single European nation exercised dominion over the region, which was dotted by small, make-shift camps along the coast where the Europeans obtained supplies and prepared their harvests for the return journey across the Atlantic Ocean. It was in these shore camps that some of the earliest interactions between Europeans and northeastern Indian peoples occurred. During what must have been confused and tense meetings, European mariners met native hunters, and through a process of trial and error, the two peoples developed an informal exchange in which Europeans traded kettles, knives, and beads for a variety of furs the Indians wore or displayed on their bodies. Among these, the pelts and skins of fur-bearing woodland animals, especially the North American beaver, were considered particularly valuable by the Europeans. Overhunting in Europe had rendered many desirable fur-bearing animals extinct, a factor that combined with prevailing European fashion trends to make furs an attractive and profitable commodity. Furs offered high value per volume, because the Indians obtained and cured the furs, providing European traders with an essentially finished product whose market value more than paid for the cost if its transportation to Europe.[4]

Thus, a sustained pattern of trade evolved as the European newcomers discovered a form of extractable wealth every bit as valuable as gold or silver. What began as a limited exchange between strangers in the fishing camps quickly spread inland along the river corridors used by European

explorers and colonists. The exchange intensified after 1600, correspond-
ing to two important developments. First, during the first decade of the
seventeenth century, the French, English, and Dutch all established settlements or trading stations along the Atlantic Coast, providing markets for
furs and sources of manufactured goods. Second, after 1600, the European
demand for animal pelts, particularly beaver, increased as fashion trends
among the nobility increasingly emphasized fur-lined or felt-laced clothing and hats. The exchange in furs with the European newcomers thus
quickly became an important component of native life in northeastern
North America. The fur trade bound Indian nations and European newcomers together in a mutually dependent and reciprocal relationship.
Indian peoples valued and in some regards became dependent on European
trade products, especially metal tools and weapons, firearms, cloth, and
alcohol; European traders depended on Indians to provide furs and purchase European manufactured goods. Moreover, because the Indians voluntarily performed all the labor involved in hunting, trapping, and
preparing the furs, European groups involved in the fur trade could dis-
pense with the cost, difficulty, and violence associated with conquering
and subjugating the Indian nations.[5]

Most Indian nations sought to manage trade in the manner they
thought most beneficial for themselves, although Europeans seldom
understood their motivations. Europeans laughed at Indians who traded
valuable furs for glass beads and shiny metal objects, seldom compre-
hending that native peoples held these items in high esteem for deeper
reasons than childlike fancy. For many northeastern Indian nations, bright
and vibrant objects contained powerful elements of spiritual power, called
manitou by Algonquian speakers. Displayed on an individual's body as
decorative jewelry or fabricated into ceremonial objects to commemorate
important events, items such as wampum, beads made from shells found
on Long Island Sound, and copper ingots from the Great Lakes were
highly prized commodities because of they possessed *manitou*, which
increased their possessor's access to the spiritual power that governed all
life. Indian peoples initially afforded the same significance to glass beads
and brass objects obtained in trade with Europeans, incorporating these
objects alongside wampum and copper in their ceremonial functions.[6]

Conversely, Indians marveled at the Europeans' attachment to furs, for
which the newcomers seemed willing to pay exorbitant prices. As one
Native trader once remarked, "the English have no sense; they give us
twenty knives like this for one beaver skin."[7] Indeed, Europeans valued
beaver pelts so greatly that they seemed willing to meet any demand to

obtain the furs. "The Beaver makes everything perfectly well," remarked a Montagnais, "it makes kettles, swords, knives, bread; in short, it makes everything."[8] Pressed on various fronts by eager European traders, Indian traders quickly learned to drive a hard bargain. They often refused to trade with the first trader or ship they encountered, and instead made Europeans compete with one another, in that way getting the best deal possible for their furs. As they became more experienced with European trade goods, Indian peoples came to value the items they obtained more for their usefulness than for their spiritual power. Native traders increasingly asked for metal tools, kettles, and eventually firearms, commodities that eased the rigors of their daily existence while also increasing their military power in relation to other Indian nations.[9]

That is not to say there was no strife associated with the fur trade, which drew Indian nations and Europeans into complex and competitive networks of exchange. Indeed, their relationship was often uneasy, as trade disputes resonated well beyond economic boundaries. As Indian nations increasingly embraced European products, trade became central to their existence. By the mid-seventeenth century, European manufactured goods had become so commonplace that some Indians had abandoned their traditional tools and weapons in favor of the superior quality of the trade goods. In so doing, however, they became dependent on European traders to provide these items, as they could not produce them themselves. As cloth, brass pots, and iron tools replaced native clothing made from animal skins, earthen cookware, and stone tools, the skills and techniques used in the production of traditional items were lost. Younger generations were not interested in learning to become craftsman, unless it was to create something useful for trade, and "as the last people passed away who came of age before the Europeans arrived, many native craft skills died with them."[10] Such considerations forced Indian nations to consider any disruption of trade, especially a deliberate cessation of trade resulting from strained negotiations, as an act of war.[11]

Conflict was inevitable, especially as Indian nations competed with each other for access to European trade. Indian peoples closest to European settlements were the first to obtain metal weapons and firearms, advantages they exploited against their rivals. In turn, Indians further removed from the coastal regions, including the Five Nations, fought to gain direct access to European trade goods and level the playing field with their enemies. Not surprisingly, Indian nations near the European trade centers tried to keep other native peoples away to perpetuate their own power and status. As a French Jesuit priest related in 1633, "these people [Algonquins or Montagnais along the lower St. Lawrence River], in order to monopolize the profit of the fur trade, prefer that the Hurons should not go down the river to trade their peltries with the French, desiring themselves to collect the ... merchandise of the neighboring tribes and carry it to the French."[12] In addition, Europeans encouraged Indian competition. More and more animals were killed, quickly eradicating the animal population of the coastal region and forcing Indian hunters to look inland to obtain furs for trade. The best trapping lands became contested ground, prompting rivalries and conflicts between Indian nations. Moreover, as Indians hunted and trapped fur-bearing animals in unprecedented quantities, a market transition took place in which Indian traders increasingly gave more furs in trade for fewer manufactured goods, shifting the economic advantage to the Europeans.[13]

ENTER THE FRENCH

European newcomers likewise sought to exclude other European nationals from cutting into their fur trade profits. In the late 1500s, the French established a trading post at Tadoussac near the mouth of the St. Lawrence River. In time, the French cultivated trade alliances with several Algonquian-speaking nations, including the Micmacs, Montagnais, and Algonquins. Under the able leadership of Samuel de Champlain, the French slowly moved up the St. Lawrence River, eventually establishing a permanent settlement on high ground overlooking the river during the summer of 1608. Located on the site of an abandoned Iroquois village, Champlain called his settlement Quebec. Almost immediately, the city became a staging area for the expansion of French commercial enterprises.[14]

As the fur trade grew, the French became involved with the Huron Confederacy, a loosely allied group of Iroquoian-speaking people. The Hurons, whose population of 20,000 to 30,000 rivaled that of the Five Nations, occupied the region between Lake Huron and the Ottawa River, a vital trade corridor between the St. Lawrence River valley and the western Great Lakes. Long before the arrival of the French, the Hurons' strategic location allowed them to become important middlemen in the vibrant native economy of the Great Lakes. A successful agricultural people, the Hurons traded surpluses of beans, corn, and squash to more migratory bands of Indian hunters to the north and west, receiving in exchange furs and copper. By reprising their traditional role as native middlemen, the Hurons stood to profit tremendously from the fur trade with their French partners. They tightened their control over the supply of furs moving east from Great Lakes, which they brought annually to the French at Quebec in great caravans of canoes laden with the wealth of the forest. In return, the Hurons obtained manufactured goods for their own use and as commodities that they could trade to the Indian nations of the west. Combining French trade goods with their agricultural surplus allowed the Hurons to quickly become an even more potent economic presence in the Great Lakes region. Indeed, by the 1620s, they provided nearly two thirds of all furs obtained by the French.[15]

Meanwhile, the Five Nations had no direct access to European trade goods, although this did not prevent the new commodities from finding their way into Iroquoia. Even though Iroquois relations with the Algonquins, Montagnais, Hurons, and other Indian nations who traded with the French was antagonistic, the Iroquois still managed to acquire a scattering of new and exotic items. These were primarily goods that were similar to items prized for their spiritual connotations: glass beads supplemented wampum and other shells in ceremonial functions, whereas fragments of brass or iron from broken kettles and pots joined copper ingots as valued raw materials used in fashioning personal jewelry and ornamentations. But Iroquois access to these items depended on the willingness of the Indians who inhabited the regions between the Five Nations and the Europeans to trade with them. Moreover, the nature of the river systems in and around Iroquoia, which flowed outward from the Iroquois heartland rather than inward, kept the Iroquois from participating equally in emerging trade networks with the Europeans. Most commerce remained downstream from the Iroquois, as few Frenchmen were inclined to move upriver from Quebec.[16]

To compete with their rivals, the Iroquois needed to obtain direct access to European trade goods. This necessity became more acute once metal weapons, or cooking pots that could be made into arrow points or club heads, became prevalent in the inventories of European traders. Without a firm trading relationship with either the French or their Huron partners, however, the Iroquois had to rely on warfare to obtain these highly desired products. Once the French and Hurons established their trade partnership, the potential for plunder governed where and when Iroquois war parties struck their enemies. Their preferred area of engagement was the largely uninhabited region surrounding the junction of the Richelieu and St. Lawrence Rivers, where Iroquois warriors could waylay Huron and Algonquin canoes laden with trade goods obtained down river from the French. The area was easily accessible, especially for the Mohawks, who paddled up Lake George and then down Lake Champlain to reach this new hunting ground. As their operations intensified, the Iroquois occasionally built fortified camps along the Richelieu corridor, bases from which they could launch their plundering raids. It proved to be a successful but dangerous strategy, as it did not take long for the Hurons and other Indian enemies of the Iroquois to seek revenge.[17]

Iroquois attacks on Huron trade convoys also upset the French, who had bound themselves to their Indian trading partners through political alliances to maximize profits and stabilize trade relationships. But these trade alliances brought the French into the complicated world of Indian relations in the northeast, in which the Hurons, Algonquins, and Montagnais maintained a long-standing enmity with peoples of the Iroquois League, and a side effect of the new alliance system compelled the French to support their allies in conflicts with other Indian nations. In 1609, Samuel de Champlain, commander of the French settlement at Quebec, agreed to assist the Hurons and Montagnais in an attack against the Mohawks, whose raids along the St. Lawrence River had become too much to bear. That May, Champlain and a detachment of nine French soldiers, armed with early versions of matchlock muskets called arquebuses, joined a mixed war party of more than 300 Hurons and Montagnais on a campaign into Mohawk country. The war party moved up the St. Lawrence River to its intersection with the Richelieu River, then turned south toward Lake Champlain. The endeavor faltered a bit on reaching the lake, and only 60 native warriors and three French, including Champlain, boarded canoes and continued the campaign. As they reached the eastern frontier of Iroquoia, the party moved only by night, erected small but effective barricades to protect their camps, and remained vigilant for any sign of their Mohawk enemies. On the evening of July 29, scouts reported that a party of several hundred Mohawks were constructing fortifications on the western shore near the southern tip of the lake. Messengers were dispatched to confirm that the Mohawks intended to fight, and after receiving confirmation, the Hurons, Montagnais, and French anchored their canoes together off the far shore and spent the night hurling insults and taunts at their adversaries, who responded in kind. In the morning, both sides made their final preparations, and the battle was joined.[18]

The Battle of Lake Champlain, as it is sometimes called, demonstrated the impact of European firearms on native warfare in North America. The Mohawks did not contest the landing of the Hurons, Montagnais, and French but instead remained behind their barricades until all of their enemy's warriors reached the shore. Concealing the French in their midst, the Hurons and Montagnais quickly advanced toward the Mohawk fortifications, and the Mohawks sallied forth, led by three war chiefs, to engage them in a traditional massed battle. Warriors on both sides were outfitted in wooden body armor and carried shields of wood and woven cotton that afforded good protection against arrows and war clubs. Before the battle could degenerate into a melee of individual fights, however, the Hurons and Montagnais parted ranks, allowing Champlain and the two other French musketeers a clear shot at the unsuspecting Mohawks. "I marched on until I was within some thirty yards of the enemy," recalled Champlain, "when I saw them make a move to draw their bows upon us, I took aim with my arquebus and shot straight at one of their three chiefs."[19] Champlain's shot, either by luck or boastful exaggeration, killed two of the Mohawk war chiefs and badly injured the third. A second French soldier fired immediately thereafter, and the stunned Mohawks fled the field. They were unaccustomed to sustaining such heavy losses at the outset of an engagement, especially when it involved their leaders, and in the fever of the moment they decided to quit the fight rather than risk additional losses. The Hurons and Montagnais immediately took up the pursuit, and by the time the rout was complete, as many as 50 Mohawks lay dead and at least a dozen had been taken prisoner.[20]

The next year, Champlain and the French participated in another attack against the Mohawks. In all, 200 Algonquin and Huron warriors, with Champlain and three French soldiers in tow, traveled up the Richelieu River to dislodge a group of Mohawks that had been discovered building a fortified outpost along the lower portion of the river. This time the Mohawks were better prepared, having erected a sturdy circular fortification to protect themselves. The French fired into the fortification with some effect, and a passing party of French fur traders added the firepower of their arquebuses to the assault, but the Mohawks held out. Eventually, Champlain led a charge against the walls, which were pulled down, although the Frenchman was wounded by an arrow "tipped with a very sharp bit of stone."[21] Only 15 Mohawks survived the final assault, all of whom were captured by the Algonquins and Hurons.[22]

In the face of this new enemy and their powerful arms, the Mohawks temporarily withdrew from the Richelieu region and suspended their raids along the upper St. Lawrence River. Yet other Iroquois from the Five Nations continued to harass and attack the Hurons, who, in 1615, again recruited Champlain for another assault on Iroquoia. This time the target was the Onondagas and Oneidas, who had been hijacking Huron trading convoys on the Ottawa River. The results of the campaign, however, were far different from the two earlier forays. After crossing Lake Ontario, the

Hurons and their French allies came on a heavily fortified Onondaga or Oneida village, which they proceeded to besiege. Attacking the town proved difficult. Four concentric rings of 30-foot high palisades defended the perimeter, and numerous platforms atop the ramparts allowed Iroquois warriors to fire arrows and hurl stones at the besiegers from relative security. Faced with such formidable obstacles, Champlain and the Huron war leaders quickly fell to arguing. The Frenchman wanted to make a direct assault against the walls, but the Hurons balked at the loss of life such an attack would incur, and instead proposed to taunt the honor of the Iroquois warriors until they sallied forth to engage in individual duels. Champlain eventually convinced the Hurons to make an attack using mantelets, mobile wooden screens that protected advancing attackers from arrows and stones, and a cavalier, a large wooden tower that allowed Champlain's musketeers to sweep the platforms atop the palisades with gunfire. Still, the attack was futile. Iroquois archers felled two Huron war leaders early in the assault, and, as had happened to the Mohawks six years prior, the Hurons called off the assault to avoid greater loss of life. A sortie by the Iroquois was repelled by French musket fire, and once the Iroquois were safely reentrenched behind their walls, the Hurons abandoned the campaign and departed for home.[23]

Despite the Onondagas' or Oneidas' successful resistance to the Huron-French attack, the introduction of firearms and metal tipped weapons into native warfare forced the Iroquois to reconsider the way they approached combat. They discarded their wooden body armor and shields, which were only marginally effective against metal weapons and afforded no protection whatsoever against French guns. Moreover, continued use of wooden armor became impractical as Iroquois warriors learned to adapt their fighting style to the new weaponry. Shortly after the stunning debut of French firearms in the 1609 rout of the Mohawks, Champlain recorded that the Iroquois had already learned to "throw themselves on the ground when they hear the report" of the guns being fired.[24] Wooden armor was too cumbersome for use in evolving Iroquois tactics, which also included hiding behind trees for protection until after the guns had fired. Armor and shields remained present in Iroquois society as teaching and protective tools in the education of young warriors, but they no longer found a place in Iroquois wars. The massed formations used for traditional intertribal battles were similarly dropped in favor of the hit-and-run raids characteristic of mourning war campaigns. Continued massed confrontations between warriors now armed with European weapons, mostly iron and brass tipped arrows and axes with a small scattering of guns, promised to result in a large number of casualties, an outcome Iroquoian concepts of war could not tolerate.[25]

The impact of Champlain's gun battles on the outlook of the Iroquois toward their native enemies is less clear. The Iroquois learned to respect and perhaps even fear French firearms, and they certainly came to count the French among their many enemies. Mohawk raids against Huron trade convoys moving along the St. Lawrence River were curtailed for at least a short period, but within a decade they appear to have resumed in full force, making any movements of trade goods along the contested Richelieu-St. Lawrence region dangerous. In 1622, Champlain recorded that French-allied Indians "who go in quest of beavers, do not dare go into certain parts [the lower Richelieu River] where these abound, because they are afraid of their enemies [the Mohawks]."[26] The resumption of raiding corresponded to the arrival of a new group of Europeans, the Dutch, who established a trade post along the upper Hudson River, offering the Iroquois a new source of European products. Determined to secure their own access to European trade goods, especially guns, the Mohawks gravitated toward the Dutch and resumed their war against the French-allied Indian nations.[27]

GUNS ALONG THE HUDSON

While the Hurons and their French allies were defeating the Mohawks in 1609, an English explorer named Henry Hudson sailed up the river that now bears his name and made contact with various Indian peoples along the way. Though he was an Englishman, Hudson sailed for the Dutch, who sought the fabled Northwest Passage, an all water route through or around North America to the riches of the Orient. Like many other explorers before and after him, Hudson did not find what he sought. Instead he found furs, the same commodity that fueled French commerce and colonization along the St. Lawrence. Hudson's explorations marked the Dutch entrance into the North American fur trade, and Dutch traders returned to the region to continue the trade every year until 1614, when the Dutch established a trading post on the upper Hudson River. A decade later, the Dutch erected a larger post, Fort Orange (modern Albany, New York), which became the center of a brisk trade. As Europe's premier manufacturers and paramount garment producers, the Dutch had an almost insatiable appetite for furs. Moreover, they had a plethora of manufactured items to offer in exchange, which included firearms. As Dutch products generally were of a better quality than French goods, and also considerably cheaper, Indian peoples from far and wide made their way to Fort Orange to trade with the Dutch.[28]

The Mohawks were among the most frequent customers who called on the Dutch at Fort Orange. The establishment of Fort Orange was a major event for the Five Nations, as the Dutch trade center opened a new and potentially beneficial outlet for acquiring European manufactured goods. The Mohawks' close proximity to Fort Orange allowed them to travel to the post regularly, where they traded furs, often taken from other Indians in raids, for tools, axes, and kettles, which they often broke apart and made into arrowheads. What the Mohawks really wanted, however, were guns. Unlike the French, who initially refused to trade guns for furs, the Dutch made firearms available for purchase to Indians. Champlain and other French officials feared that their Indian allies, whose population easily surpassed that of the French colonists in Canada, could eventually turn against them, and the French did not want their own firearms used against them. The Dutch government had similar reservations, but unscrupulous Dutch traders nonetheless peddled their guns to any Indian nations that could meet their asking price.[29]

The Mohawks were willing to meet that price, but their access to Dutch trade was limited and conditional, as the Mohawks had to cross through Mahican territory on the west side of the Hudson River to reach the fort, then re-cross Mahican lands to bring Dutch trade goods to their confederates in the Iroquois League. The relationship was tense from the start. Sporadic fighting between the two groups occurred after the establishment of Fort Nassau, but open war was averted. By the early 1620s, however, Mohawk-Mahican relations began to deteriorate quickly.

Although no singular cause can be identified for the increased tension, several possible explanations exist. Political concerns may have played a role, as reports speak of a Dutch-sponsored effort to create a Mahican-Algonquin-Huron trade alliance. Economic unification of these Indian nations would provide many advantages to the Dutch, including access to vast quantities of furs from the Great Lakes and Canada; but it would pose a serious threat to the Mohawks, who would be confronted by enemies on multiple fronts and perhaps muscled out of the fur trade at Fort Orange. To keep this alliance from taking shape, the Mohawks may have decided to attack the closest member of the proposed alliance, the Mahicans. But more immediate concerns sparked conflict. The Mohawks, who could not remain permanently in the Mahican-controlled territory around Fort Orange, may have sought direct access to the Dutch, who only seldom journeyed to Mohawk villages to trade. If the Mohawks had tired of conducting their commerce with the Dutch in accordance with parameters set by the Mahicans, they could have sought to eliminate the Mahicans as middlemen between themselves and the Dutch. Yet another cause of tension may have been diplomatic. In 1626, Champlain recorded that the cause of the war had been the refusal of the Mahicans to grant Mohawk warriors "free passage to go and make war on a nation called the Loups [wolves], with whom the Iroquois were at enmity."[30] This violation of native diplomatic protocol, in which nations at peace with one another customarily allowed passage through their territory, may also have been a source of malcontent between the Mohawks and the Mahicans.[31]

The cause of the conflict is uncertain, but it is clear that by 1624, the Mohawks had resolved to go to war against their Mahican neighbors in an effort to drive them away from Fort Orange. To keep their northern flank secure, the Mohawks first arranged a tentative peace—more of a cease-fire—with the French-allied Indian nation to the north. The process began in 1622, when two Mohawks negotiators met with French-allied Indians at Trois Rivieres, an important trade depot upriver from Quebec. During the negotiations, both sides obtained "a pledge from their enemies not to injure them, nor to prevent them from hunting anywhere in their territory."[32] Champlain, eager to bring closure to the disruptions that Mohawk raids caused the French fur trade, lent his support to the accord. Still, because of mutual distrust and animosity, the peace was not finalized until 1624, almost two years after the initial agreement had been reached. Although peace between the Mohawks and the French-allied Indians would last only three years, it was for the moment a mutually beneficial pact, as it kept the Mohawks' northern frontier safe, while it allowed the Hurons, Algonquins, and the French to pilot their trade convoys along the St. Lawrence River without fear of Mohawk raids.[33]

The Mohawks then turned their full attention to the Mahicans. Little is known of the progress of the four-year long war, other than that the Mohawks emerged victorious. The Mahicans received assistance from allied-Indians east of the Hudson River, probably the Pocumtucs and Sokokis, but it was not enough to halt the Mohawk onslaught. By 1628, the Mohawks had driven the Mahicans east into the Connecticut River valley. There the Mahicans surrendered, agreeing to pay the Mohawks a yearly tribute in wampum, or at least to include the Mohawks as partners in the Mahican-controlled wampum trade with the Indians on Long Island. It is very likely that some Mahicans remained near the upper Hudson River, while other small bands continued to move about the region for many years, but the majority of their people were forced east as a result of the war.[34]

For the most part, the Dutch stayed out of the conflict, although they supplied the Mahicans and encouraged them to keep up the fight. Dutch traders understood that a Mohawk victory would not necessarily be in their best interests, as they stood to profit most from the fur trade if they were able to carry out a free and open trade with as many Indians as possible, who could compete with one another for Dutch trade goods. If the Mohawks defeated the Mahicans, however, the Iroquois might try to control native access to Fort Orange, potentially restricting other Indian nations from trading at the post. But Dutch efforts to assist the Mahicans came too late and were too limited to be successful. In July 1626, a veteran trader named Daniel van Krieckenbeeck led six other Dutchmen from Fort Orange in support of a Mahican war party moving against the Mohawks. Van Krieckenbeeck and his associates were armed with arquebuses, but they apparently took few protective measures, such as wearing breastplates or other armor. This proved disastrous, as Mohawk warriors armed with bows and arrows ambushed van Krieckenbeeck and his party. The Dutchman, three of his companions, and an unknown number of Mahicans were killed. The victorious Mohawks then "well roasted" one of the deceased Dutchmen, and "carried a leg and an arm home to be divided among their families, as a sign that they had conquered their enemies."[35]

Van Krieckenbeeck's defeat, and the unfortunate fate of one of his comrades, prompted the Dutch at Fort Orange to stay out of the rest of the fighting. The battle may also have influenced Dutch behavior after the war. When the Mohawks emerged victorious, the Dutch faced a decision: either accept the Mohawks as their new primary trading partners, or refuse and risk war with the Moahwks and a disruption of the fur trade at Fort Orange. Naturally, the pragmatic Dutch acquiesced to the new arrangement along the Upper Hudson. Indeed, even before the Mohawk-Mahican War had ended, the Dutch sent a trader, Pieter Barentsz, who had good relations with the Iroquois, to assure the Mohawks that the Dutch desired only peace. To his satisfaction, Barentsz learned that Mohawks "wised to excuse their act [the killing of van Krieckenbeeck], on the plea that they had never set themselves against the whites."[36] Apparently the Mohawks also wanted peace, which the Dutch had little choice but to accept. The Dutch continued to have misgivings about the situation, and their relationship with the Mohawks was tense, but war with the Iroquois was not considered an option. As the influential Dutch landowner Kiliaen van Rensselaer speculated, "the savages [Mohawks], who are now stronger than us, will not allow others who are hostile and live further away and have many furs to pass through their territory," but there was little they could do to alter the situation.[37]

Van Rensselaer's fears about Mohawk designs became reality. During the next 15 years, Fort Orange essentially became a private enclave of the Iroquois League. The Mohawks guarded all routes of passage to the post and allowed only select Indian nations to trade with the Dutch. The Mohawks allowed some Mahicans to return in exchange for annual tribute payments, but primarily only nations of the Iroquois League obtained access to Fort Orange. The Dutch opposed the Mohawks' policy, and relations between the two deteriorated quickly. Dutch traders beat and occasionally kidnaped Mohawk leaders, and during one particularly violent encounter, Hans Jorisz Hontom, commandant at Fort Orange, kidnaped a Mohawk headman, accepted a ransom for his release, and then killed the chief in a gruesome manner, purposefully going out his way to "emasculate the chief, hang the severed member on the stay and so killed the *sakima* [sachem]."[38] Mohawk warriors responded to Dutch transgressions by killing cattle, vandalizing homes and other property on the estates of wealthy Dutch landowners around Fort Orange, and threatening to kill certain Dutchmen whom they held in low esteem, including Hontom. On one occasion, Mohawks set fire to a Dutch ship as it lay at anchor near Fort Orange, then watched it burn as the helpless Dutch looked on from the fort.[39]

In 1641, the relationship between the Mohawks and the Dutch grew so tenuous that the Mohawks approached the French with an offer of peace. During negotiations, the Mohawks asked the French to build a trading station in their territory and in return promised to end all ties with the Dutch, even if it meant war. But the governor-general of New France, Charles Huault de Montmagny, did not trust the Iroquois to keep their word, nor did he believe an alliance with the Mohawks would prove more beneficial than the current arrangement with the Hurons. A trading agreement with the Mohawks almost certainly would have caused friction between the French and their existing Indian allies, as the Iroquois obtained many of their furs by raiding the Algonquins, Montagnais, and Hurons. Montmagny saw little to gain, so he haughtily rebuffed the Mohawks, providing the foundation for renewal of war between the Iroquois League and the colony of New France in the 1640s.[40]

Despite their strained relationship, trade between the Mohawks and the Dutch was far too lucrative for either side to risk a war against the other. In 1643, the Dutch recorded what is believed to be the first formalized treaty with the Mohawks. Although the Dutch feared that the Mohawks' refusal to allow most other Indian nations to trade at Fort Orange would prove financially disastrous, Iroquois demands for European manufactured goods, especially firearms, ensured that the Dutch would reap a bountiful harvest of furs. And thanks to their monopolistic association with the Dutch, the Five Nations soon became better supplied and better armed than the French-allied Indians to the north. Before the 1643 treaty, profit-minded traders, such as Arent van Curler, had flouted restrictions against trading firearms to the Indians, secretly arranging the transfer of guns to the Mohawks and other Iroquois. Now, however, the Dutch government eased restrictions against selling guns to Indians, and, during the 1640s, the Dutch traded hundreds of muskets to the Five Nations. In 1643, a French estimate placed the number of firearms in the hands of the Mohawks at nearly three hundred. A year later, the Dutch signed a deal to send "firearms to the Mohawks for a full 400 men, with powder and lead."[41] Moreover, the Mohawks and the other Five Nations Iroquois quickly learned how best to use firearms in warfare, adapting the weapons to native concepts of combat. Their preferred tactic was to fire in volley from an ambush site, inflicting as many casualties as possible and disorienting their enemy so as to render retaliation or resistance difficult.[42]

To keep guns flowing into Iroquoia, the Five Nations needed to present the Dutch with a steady stream of furs. Hunting for furs provided few problems for the Iroquois, as the Dutch generally entertained trade only from May to November, allowing hunters from villages throughout the Iroquois League to continue their traditional practice of hunting through-out the winter months. According to one observer, Iroquois hunters "go in large parties, and remain out from one to two months," returning "with from forty to eighty beaver skins, and with some otter, fishers, and other skins also."[43] By 1640, however, there apparently were few fur-bearing animals in Iroquoia, so the Five Nations were forced to look elsewhere for the vital trade resource. Furs could be obtained in great quantity from the French-allied Indians to the north, but the question remained whether the Mohawks would obtain the pelts as fruits of peaceful exchange or as the spoils of war.[44]

The answer had already been given in the from of actions taken by French-allied Indians in the wake of the fragile 1624 peace accord with the Mohawks. While the Mohawks made war on the Mahicans, the Hurons, Algonquins, and other French-allied Indians moved south into the Richelieu and Champlain valleys, regions the Mohawks claimed as their own hunting grounds. The migrations were an attempt to open trade lines with the Dutch at Fort Orange, who could supply the northern Indians with wampum, a commodity that the French were unable to offer in trade. Initial Mohawk reactions are unclear, as they were focused on their war with the Mahicans, but events quickly transpired that the Mohawks could not ignore. The Mahicans, perhaps with Dutch assistance, attempted to forge a military alliance with the French-allied Indians against the Mohawks. At least some form of agreement was reached, as in June 1627, French-allied Indians attacked a group of Mohawks near Lake Champlain, taking three prisoners, two of whom were tortured to death. On learning of these events, a nervous Samuel de Champlain urged his Indian trading partners to restrain their warriors, reminding them if they renewed the war with the Mohawks, "the whole river [the St. Lawrence] would be closed to them, and they would neither be able to hunt nor to fish without incurring great danger, and being in constant fear and anxiety [of Mohawk attacks]."[45] Of course, Champlain cared primarily about the effect renewed war with the Mohawks might have on French trading interests, but his appeals came too late. The French-allied Indians did send diplomats to the Mohawks to offer compensation for the prior attacks, but the Iroquois greeted them coldy. "While you come here to arrange peace," they declared, "your companions kill and massacre our people."[46] The Iroquois punctuated their displeasure by killing the entire delegation. The peace with the northern Indians was over.[47]

The Mohawk response was likely motivated as much by economics as by diplomatic or political concerns. Lacking the requisite raw materials required to continue purchasing Dutch guns, first the Mohawks, and later the other nations of the Iroquois League, intensified their raids against Huron, Algonquin, and Montagnais trade convoys along the St. Lawrence and Ottawa Rivers. Iroquois warriors ambushed eastward-moving canoes laden with rich furs, which the Mohawks took to the Dutch at Fort Orange, and the raiders also plundered westward bound canoes carrying French trade goods, which they used to complement what they received in trade from the Dutch. Mourning war considerations also motivated raiding, as Iroquois warriors took captives or scalps as well as furs and trade goods, but from an economic viewpoint, the Iroquois campaigns came to constitute a constant blockade against French and Indian commerce along the Upper St. Lawrence River. In the early 1640s, a French Jesuit described the scene: "In former years the Iroquois came in rather large bands at certain times in the summer, and afterward left the river free; but this present year, they have changed their plan, and have separated themselves into small bands of twenty, thirty, or a hundred at the most, along all the passages and places of the river, and when one goes away, another succeeds it."[48]

The French moved to protect their Indian allies and their own economic interests, but there was little the French could do to stem the Iroquois onslaught, as the comments of a French priest reveal:

> It is almost impossible to make either peace or war with these barbarians [the Iroquois]; not peace because war is their life, their amusement, and their source of profit all in one; not war because they make themselves invisible to those who seek them and show themselves only when they have heavy odds in their favor. Go and hunt them in their villages and they fade into the forest. Short of leveling all the forests in the country, it is impossible to trap them or halt the destruction of these thieves ... It is not that these thieves are always all around us, but that one is never sure either that they are there, or that they are not, hence we have to beware of them all the time. Were it not that we hope God will eventually deliver us, the country would have to be abandoned, for we are well aware that human strength and wisdom alone cannot save us.[49]

The priest's assessment illustrates how Iroquois warfare had evolved in response to the arrival of the French, Dutch, and other European groups. Small-scale raids that primarily were limited contests for plunder and captives, with relatively few casualties or fatalities, gradually expanded into large-scale wars fueled by economic considerations and made more deadly by the incorporation of European firearms and metal weapons. These were trade wars, during which the Iroquois targeted anyone they saw as obstacles to their economic advancement, whether they be French-allied Indians to their north or Mahicans along the Hudson. As the middle decades of the seventeenth century dawned, however, mourning war beliefs would again dominate Iroquois warfare, as a deadly combination of social, political, and economic factors compelled the Iroquois to escalate their campaigns to near genocidal levels of hostility and aggressiveness, imperiling and threatening the survival of Indian nations along the borders of Iroquoia and beyond. The human and political landscape of native North America was about to change forever.

3

•

The Great Mourning War

During the mid-seventeenth century, the Five Nations waged a series of aggressive wars against an ever-widening group of enemies. Indeed, during this era the peoples of the Iroquois League were at war with virtually everyone else in northeastern North America. The conflicts, which in scale were unlike anything before associated with Iroquois warfare, combined economic factors with a resurgence, or perhaps an intensification, of mourning war principles. The "Beaver Wars," as a generation of historians dubbed these conflicts, may have had economic undercurrents, but they were the product of a fierce struggle for survival. The arrival of European infectious diseases in Iroquoia resulted in an almost cataclysmic loss of life, depopulating villages throughout the Five Nations and threatening the very survival of the Iroquois League. In response, Iroquois warriors answered the calls of their clan matrons for unprecedented levels of mourning wars. Well armed by their Dutch trade partners, the Five Nations endured, although not unscathed, through the turbulent period by imposing death, destruction, and captivity on neighboring Indian nations.

DISEASE

Disease accompanied the first Europeans who crossed the Atlantic Ocean. European explorers, soldiers, and colonists brought with them a host of microscopic pathogens destined to decimate the native population of North America. In the islands of the Caribbean, where disease became the greatest ally of the Spanish conquistadores, Indian peoples died at an unbelievable rate. On the island of Hispaniola, for example, the Taino Indian population suffered a 90 percent population loss in less than two decades. Nor was mainland North America spared the scourge of disease. Everywhere Europeans came, invisible assassins followed. During the 1620s, New England colonist Thomas Morton recorded that Indians sick with disease "Died on heaps, as they lay in their houses; and the living, those that were able to shift for themselves, would run away and let them die, and let their carcasses lie above ground without burial ... the bones and skulls upon their several places of their habitations made such a spectacle."[1]

North America was fertile ground for epidemic diseases transplanted from Europe, Asia, and Africa. Viral diseases such as influenza, smallpox, measles, and typhus had ravaged European populations for centuries, but in North America they found new victims whose bodies had not built up the natural defenses that came from years of exposure. Thus, these diseases invaded native communities with an almost 100 percent infection rate. The results were correspondingly catastrophic. Estimates place the mortality rate from initial exposure at between 50 and 55 percent within a decade of the first outbreak, with recurrences or new infections escalating the death toll to 90 or 95 percent within half a century, after which populations figures generally stabilized. Yet recovery from an initial infection often weakened victims so badly that they succumbed to a secondary illness. Respiratory infections, such as whooping couch and pneumonia, may have been responsible for many of the deaths attributed to the viral diseases, while even relatively benign childhood illnesses, such as chickenpox, became a dangerous killer among native peoples of all ages.[2]

Epidemics worsened after 1600 when large numbers of European families reached the new world. Among these colonists were thousands of children, who were more likely to carry infectious viruses than their parents, most of whom had developed some immunity during their own childhoods. The role of European children in the spreading of disease to North America proved tragically ironic for Indian peoples, however, as the majority of the viruses these children carried afflicted not other children but rather adults seemingly in the prime of life, those between ages 15 and 50. It is during these mature adult years that the human immune system produces the most violent reactions to infection, which rendered the suffering from the severe symptoms associated with these diseases—fever, pustules, vomiting, and swelling—all the more painful and pronounced. To make matters worse, with the most able-bodied adults in a native community among the sickest of all, much of the daily work was not done. Without hunting, gathering, and harvesting to provide fresh food and water, native society ground to a halt, making recovery from disease all that much more difficult. And without regular care from adults, who were themselves too sick to perform their normal tasks, many children and older people who might have otherwise recovered from their ailments instead died.[3]

Among the deadliest killers transplanted to North America was small-pox. Extremely communicable and contagious, smallpox is an airborne virus that rapidly spreads through contaminated dust particles or moisture droplets to enter the respiratory system and settle in the lungs. Infected persons show few symptoms during an incubation period of 10 to 14 days, after which they develop a high fever, vomiting, and general flulike mal-aise. Several days later, small, erupting pustules—the pox for which the disease is named—begin to appear all over the body. Most afflicted persons die shortly thereafter, but for those who do not succumb to the disease, the pustules dry and fall off in a week to 10 days, leaving survivors scarred by pockmarks for the rest of their lives. Some victims are left blinded if the disease migrates into their eyes. Painful and debilitating, the entire infec-tion process generally takes less than a month, resulting either in death or disfigurement.[4]

William Bradley, governor of the English colony at Plymouth, pro-vided a graphic description of the suffering imposed on native peoples by smallpox. Anyone stricken by the disease, Bradford recorded,

died most miserably, for a sorer disease cannot befall them ... usually they that have this disease have them [pustules] in abundance, and for want of bedding and linen and other helps they fall into a lamentable condition as they lie on their hard mats, the pox breaking and matting and running one into another, there skin cleaving by reason thereof to the mats they lie on. When they turn them, a whole side will flay off at once as it were, and they will be all of a gore blood, most fearful to behold. And then being very sore, what with cold and other distempers, they die like rotten sheep.[5]

Unfortunately for the Five Nations, smallpox was the first recorded European infectious virus to reach Iroquoia. In December 1634, Harmen Meyndertsz van den Bogaert, a Dutch surgeon traveling among the Iroquois, made note of a severe smallpox outbreak among the Mohawks, who likely contracted the disease from Dutch traders or visitors. Bogaert's notes about the effect of the disease, which included a large number of recently dug graves and separation of political leaders from the village

population, indicates that he arrived after smallpox had already commenced its assault on the Mohawks. It is impossible to trace the precise
route that smallpox followed through Iroquoia, but by the winter of
1640–1641, the Senecas were battling the disease. The results were devastating. By the early 1640s, roughly half the peoples of the Iroquois League
were dead, reducing the total population of the Five Nations to about
10,000. The Mohawks were not only the first to be stricken, but also the
hardest hit. Their mortality rate may have been as high as 75 percent.
Over the next 30 years, recurrences of smallpox, along with the infiltra-
tion of other European killer diseases, continued to plague the Five
Nations. In the early 1660s, a particularly nasty strain of smallpox killed
1,000 people as it cut through the Oneidas, Onondagas, Cayugas, and
Senecas, including more than 120 Onondaga children. There was nothing the Iroquois could do to stop the onslaught, and native medical treatments, many of which involved sweating, purging, and fasting to purify
the body, only made the situation worse, as smallpox, in particular, is best
treated by keeping infected persons dry, warm, and well nourished.[6]

In the midst of their suffering, the Iroquois turned to the rituals of the
mourning war to expel their grief and ease the pain of so much death.
Political and religious leaders were powerless to save their people from
disease, failures that reinforced traditional Iroquoian beliefs that untimely
deaths had to be the work of some malevolent force. As such, the dead
had to be avenged, and the spiritual and political power of the clan, village,
and nation had to be preserved and replenished. As smallpox and other
diseases battered their villages, clan matrons called on all able-bodied
men to strike back at their enemies—real or imagined—who had brought
this suffering on the Five Nations, and to obtain captives whose ritual
torture and adoption would preserve the power of the Iroquois people.
In the process, they initiated an open-ended pattern of conflict, a great
mourning war to preserve the Iroquois League.[7]

THE GREAT MOURNING WAR

The so-called Beaver Wars were once thought to have been driven
strictly by economic concerns, but the massive death toll caused by
European diseases was the real motivator behind Iroquois warfare during
the mid-seventeenth century. Iroquois raids during this period increased
in number and intensity in years immediately after an outbreak of disease,
demonstrating a definitive link between disease and increased warfare. In
addition, available statistics reveal that the number of captives taken by

the Iroquois during the Beaver Wars was on average two to three times greater than the number of enemies they killed. Both scenarios illustrate that the acquisition of enemy captives to replace Iroquois population losses was the primary factor in the Beaver Wars, which were not a series of conflicts designed to impose Iroquois control over the fur trade, but rather an Iroquois fight for survival, one vast, prolonged mourning war.[8]

The first documented case of this pattern occurred in 1634, the same year that the Dutchman van der Bogaert reported that smallpox had broken out among the Five Nations. That spring Iroquois war parties launched attacks against their linguistic cousins and traditional enemies, the Hurons. The first raids against the Hurons seem to have been carried out by the western Iroquois, particularly the Senecas, suggesting that disease had already reached their villages. Economic desires remained important during the early Beaver Wars, particularly among the Senecas, whose access to European trade goods was the poorest of all the Five Nations. Raiding the Hurons, who were well supplied with cloth and metal trade goods from the French, would have helped alleviate possible shortages of such items in Seneca country. Yet the acquisition of captives remained the primary objective, as illustrated by the aftermath of a major battle between the Senecas and the Hurons. The Hurons, having learned of an impending Seneca attack, resolved to lay a trap but instead were themselves ambushed in the forest as they moved south to intercept the invaders. The Senecas outnumbered their opponents by three to one, numbers that allowed them to overcome a force of 500 Hurons. The Senecas killed perhaps 100 Hurons during the battle and its aftermath, but they returned to Iroquoia with more than 100 captives, a large body of prisoners who could fill the mourning war needs of the smallpox ravaged nation.[9]

The great mourning war intensified as disease took an ever increasing number of lives. To counter such staggering losses, Iroquois military strategy evolved from small-scale raiding to massive, coordinated attacks. The campaigns of the 1640s secured huge numbers of captives and systematically eliminated the Hurons as a functional, autonomous Indian nation. In the summer of 1642, Senecas and other western Iroquois warriors descended on an isolated village inhabited by Huron peoples belonging to the Arendaronon nation. According to French Jesuits, who recorded an account of the attack, the Iroquois "spared neither sex, not even the children, and destroyed all by fire."[10] It is unlikely that the Iroquois killed all the Hurons in the village, but rather that they killed or drove away enemy combatants, secured the remaining Huron population as captives, pillaged the village of furs and trade goods, and then burned or destroyed the buildings and fields. The attack reflected a new strategy, in which the need to replace dying Iroquois became so paramount that the Five Nations adopted an entire Huron village. In the process, those Hurons who refused to be assimilated, along with captured Huron warriors, may have been ritually tortured on the spot as mourning war traditions reached fanatical heights as a result of the ravages of disease.[11]

Firearms fueled the success of the Iroquois. Thanks to their Dutch trading partners, Iroquois warriors had a far greater number of firearms than did the Hurons, who were unable to obtain firearms from the French in quantities to match the number of guns in Iroquois hands. Initially, most Five Nations' warriors preferred to use their firearms in ambushes. They would fire a volley from a concealed location to surprise and disorient their opponents, then rush forth to finish the attack with axes, clubs, and knives. As the Beaver Wars progressed, however, Iroquois warriors quickly became skilled marksmen, able to hit individual targets in battle despite the limited accuracy of arquebuses and other cumbersome smooth-bore muskets. With accuracy came an increased capacity to kill or seriously wound their opponents, who were far less likely to dodge or deflect musket balls than arrows, and less able to continue fighting or escape from battle after suffering a gunshot wound. Hand-to-hand combat remained a near constant feature of every Iroquois-Huron engagement, but the Five Nations' skill with firearms, along with the fact that they had more guns than their enemies, were important factors in determining the outcomes of battles both large and small.[12]

Moreover, disease and internal divisions with the Huron Confederacy weakened their ability to resist the Iroquois onslaught. Jesuit missionaries and French traders brought smallpox and other diseases to the Hurons in the 1630s, resulting in population losses similar to that of the Five Nations. In addition, the Jesuits exercised considerable influence over the Hurons whom they converted, becoming a polarizing influence within Huron society. "With the growth of the Jesuit mission, the formerly prosperous Huron Confederation was wracked by intensified factionalism," one historian has surmised, "the missionaries sowed discord by demanding that their converts reject and denounce the traditional religious rituals biding the people in unity."[13] French policies allowing the sale of firearms only to Christian converts worsened the factionalism, making it difficult for Huron leaders to unify their people for defense. Through it all, zealous Jesuits saw the hand of God in traumatic events that led Hurons to accept baptism, even if they did so as they lay dying or in a desperate attempt to find a solution to their problems.[14]

Throughout the 1640s, the Five Nations raided Huron settlements, ambushed Huron trade flotillas, and captured as many Huron people as possible. Jesuit priest Gabriel Lalemont, reporting to colleagues on the extent of the destruction, noted that the Iroquois "have everywhere and at almost all seasons committed massacres."[15] The Hurons responded in kind, whenever possible. In late summer 1636, Hurons warriors ambushed a party of approximately 30 Onondagas who were fishing along the southern shore of Lake Ontario, killing one and capturing seven. Two years later, a large war party of 300 Hurons and Algonquins invaded Iroquoia, possibly to strike at the Oneidas. Iroquois warriors captured a few Huron scouts, whose lies about the size of the war party led the Iroquois to make a foolish attack. Outnumbered three to one, the Iroquois were easily defeated. The Hurons killed 17 or 18 Iroquois and took 80 prisoners with them north, where at least three Iroquois were tortured to death in Huron villages. There were other successful Huron attacks, but despite these few success, the stress and strain of near constant Iroquois attacks made effective Huron resistance difficult. In the summer of 1642, numerous Huron raids against the Iroquois faltered because of poor organization, disunity, and faulty leadership, leaving an exasperated Jesuit priest to confess that "nearly all ... have ended only in disaster."[16]

The Iroquois onslaught was too focused and too intense for the Hurons to resist. Within five years of the Senecas' assault on the Arendaronon village, the remainder of that Huron nation had abandoned their other towns, which lay too close to Senecas. It was only the beginning. By the end of the 1640s, the great mourning war against the Hurons reached its height, as massive war parties, featuring warriors from all Iroquois nations, invaded Huron lands and systematically began to destroy their villages. In July 1648, an Iroquois army composed mostly of Mohawks and Senecas attacked two Huron villages, including the village of Teanaustaye, which was inhabited by some 400 families belonging to the Attigneenongnahac nation. A Jesuit missionary in the town encouraged Huron resistance, baptizing warriors even as the battle raged, but it was not enough. By the time the assault ended, the villages were in ruins, as many as 700 Hurons were dead or captured, and more than a 1,000 other Hurons had been driven away. The vast majority of those taken prisoner were women and children, precisely the type of captives preferred for adoption. The Senecas gunned down the Jesuit missionary, who remained to face the Iroquois after helping Huron survivors flee, cut him to pieces, and burned his dismembered body in the village mission.[17]

The Iroquois returned in March 1649, when more than 1,000 Iroquois warriors attacked three major Huron towns, known to history by their Jesuit-given names of St. Ignace (Teanhatentaron), St. Louis, and St. Marie, that lay in the heart of Huron territory between Lake Simcoe and Georgian Bay. During an intense three-day battle, the Hurons fought hard to protect their homeland, costing the Five Nations invaders nearly 200 killed or captured warriors. Still, the Iroquois overran St. Ignace in a daring attack after dark, where only three Hurons were reported to have escaped death or capture, then went on to overwhelm St. Louis as well. Much of the Iroquois success can be attributed to the timing of their attack, which caught the Hurons off guard. The Iroquois army had spent the winter months concealed in forests north of Lake Ontario, allowing them to reach the Huron villages in early spring, long before the Hurons would have normally expected such a massive attack. Still, once the initial shock wore off, the Hurons' resistance stiffened. The Iroquois attack on the third Huron village, a fortified Jesuit mission town of St. Marie, faltered, and the Hurons surged back on the offensive, retaking St. Louis. The Huron's determined resistance influenced the Iroquois to end the campaign, although it seems the Iroquois lost some of their focus even before the attack on St. Marie, as many Iroquois warriors had fallen back to the two conquered Huron villages to torture and kill captives. When it was all over, the Hurons had temporarily beat back the Iroquois, but at a tremendous cost. At least 230 Hurons warriors died in the fighting, along with two captured Jesuit priests at St. Louis, whom the Iroquois tortured to death. Perhaps 400 others were taken as prisoners.[18]

The campaigns of 1648 and 1649 effectively destroyed the Hurons as an independent Indian nation. Demoralized and defeated, thousands of Huron survivors fled their homeland in many directions, some seeking asylum within the French settlements, others questing west for shelter among other the Indian nations of the Great Lakes, and still others wandering as refugees along the fringes of their former homeland. The French missionary Paul Ragueneau chronicled the exodus. "In consequence of the losses incurred," he recorded, "fifteen villages have been abandoned, the people of each scattering where they could—in the woods and forests, on the lakes and rivers, and among the islands most unknown to the enemy. Others have taken refuge in the neighboring nations."[19] But dispersal did not save the Hurons from continued harassment and war. Iroquois warriors hunted down every remaining Huron they could find, allowing refugees little security or shelter. After the destruction of St. Ignace and St. Louis, a large portion of the surviving

Hurons, estimated at close to 6,000 people, congregated on Christian Island in the southeastern quadrant of Georgian Bay. Iroquois warriors followed them, establishing a blockade on the mainland, and launching a series of attacks throughout the year. Food on the island became scarce, and when Hurons came ashore to hunt or forage, Iroquois warriors ambushed them. Entire parties of Huron hunters left Christian Island never to return, including more than 150 Hurons who came ashore in small groups, perhaps hoping that some might escape Iroquois detection and return with food. The plan failed, and as the situation on the island became more desperate, Iroquois warriors crossed the waters and assailed the island itself. During the summer of 1650, a war party of 30 Iroquois attempted to besiege the Huron settlement on the island, which had been fortified against such an attack. The Hurons managed to drive the Iroquois off, but many Hurons were killed in the process. A party of 100 Onondagas tried again in the fall, but were deceived by the Hurons, who allowed the Iroquois to enter their village and then ambushed them. The Onondagas lost 30 warriors as they fought their way out of the settlement. Yet even though Christian Island provided a defensible refuge for the Hurons, Iroquois hostilities and the blockade on the mainland soon forced the Hurons to flee. Unable to hunt and forage on the mainland, the Hurons on Christian Island slowly starved to death. After several hundred people died of hunger, the Hurons abandoned their refuge. Many followed their Jesuit missionaries to Quebec, but the majority scattered to the west.[20]

The Five Nations' stubborn insistence on attacking the Huron refugees on Christian Island demonstrates the extent to which the Iroquois would go to obtain captives. Throughout the 1650s, Iroquois warriors continued the hunt, canvassing the vast expanse of land above Lake Ontario from Lake Huron in the west to the St. Lawrence River in the east. Refugee Huron groups were assailed, as were mixed parties of Hurons, French, and other French-allied Indians who tried to bring relief to the few remaining, beleaguered Hurons. Five Nations warriors were quite audacious in their attacks, and seemingly worried little about numbers or even their own losses. In June 1650, for example, a small Iroquois party at night snuck into the camp of 60 French and Indians and systematically killed 7 Hurons while they slept, despite losing 8 of the 10 warriors in their party in the process.[21]

Iroquois aggression forced the remaining Hurons into closer alignment with the French. Many settled around the French fortified settlements at Trois Rivieres and Montreal, while another, larger contingent took up residence at the town of Lorette outside Quebec. Yet even the French could not offer complete protection to their Huron allies. Iroquois warriors haunted the approaches to and from the French settlements, waylaying any Hurons who moved along the St. Lawrence River or who dared to travel out into the surrounding countryside. Still, the need to hunt, fish, and trade brought Hurons out into open places, where Iroquois warriors were waiting. Although the raids here were smaller in scale than those the Iroquois had launched against the Huron homeland, the objectives were the same. Iroquois warriors often killed Huron men, but they seem to have exerted special efforts to capture Huron women and children alive. At Trois Rivieres in May 1651, a Huron man left the safety of the fort to tend to crops in a nearby field. Four Iroquois warriors, who had been lay- ing in wait, killed him. Two months later, six Huron men crossed the river from Trois Rivieres to gather hay and tend to livestock when they were attacked by Iroquois, who killed one Huron, took another prisoner, and killed a good number of cattle to deny food to their enemies. Yet outside Montreal in May 1652, Iroquois warriors in two separate attacks took pris- oner three Huron women and three Huron children whom they could have easily killed in the fields and forests outside the town. A month later at Trois Rivieres, Iroquois warriors discovered two Huron men outside the fort, killed and scalped them, then fled when assistance arrived from the settlement.[22]

Huron refugees tried to fight back against their Iroquois tormentors, but they achieved little lasting success. Instead, it seems that the battered remnants of the Huron people could not muster enough manpower or willpower to seriously threaten the Five Nations. Near Montreal in November 1650, a small war party of Mohawks ambushed a flotilla of 10 Huron canoes moving upriver from Quebec to launch a campaign against the Five Nations. The Iroquois attack dispersed the flotilla—most of the Hurons fled—while taking at least seven Hurons prisoner. In early 1652, a Huron war party left Trois Rivieres seeking revenge against the Iroquois. Their focus or organization was poor, however, for the Hurons walked into an ambush shortly after leading the fort, during which time their war leader was slain and the remainder of the party captured, save a single Huron warrior who escaped.[23]

These raids were not random, but rather a product of continued mourn- ing war needs. Women and children, who made good captives and offered the most utility in offsetting Iroquois population decline from disease, were spared; men, who were less desirable as captives, and who were a source of power and military strength, were killed. But the attacks also reflected a grander strategy. The Jesuit priest Isaac Jogues, a captive of the

Mohawks during the Beaver Wars, was convinced that "the design of the Iroquois, as far as I can see, is to take, if they can, all the Hurons; and, having put to death the most considerable ones and good part of the other, to make of them but one people and only one land."[24] Father Jogues had ample reason to reach such a conclusion. Between 1631 and 1663, the Iroquois attacked the Hurons at least 73 times. More than 500 Huron people are recorded as having been killed during these raids, with an astonishing 2,000 — one-fifth of their postepidemic population — captured and deported to Iroquoia. These numbers are likely low-end estimates, as the reports and accounts, mostly from Jesuits, used to compile such figures are incomplete, while at the same time bearing witness to only a fraction of Iroquois raids against the Hurons. Within the context of the mourning war traditions that directed Iroquois warfare against the Hurons, the Iroquois had decided to force all the Hurons to assimilate into the Five Nations.[25]

The Iroquois did not hide their intentions. According to one historian, "The original conception of the Mohawks [and other Iroquois] was the melting pot ... they would not *create* an empire but rather *become* one by incorporating conquered peoples in themselves and literally remolding them into Mohawks [and other Iroquois] through adoption into families and thus 'naturalizing' them as full 'citizens' of the tribe."[26] Accordingly, after the effective destruction of the Huron Confederacy in 1648–1649, Iroquois warriors sometimes offered their Huron enemies the opportunity to join them willingly as captives rather than fight. At Christian Island, the Onondagas who assailed the Huron refugees encouraged their embattled enemies to lay down their arms and "seek refuge" among the Onondagas in Iroquoia, where "in [the] future they might be but one people."[27] It is true that the Iroquois recognized a cultural and linguistic bond to the Hurons, as conveyed in 1756 by Oneidas who informed the French that the two peoples in ages past had "comprised one cabin and one country," but there was a simple logic behind recruiting the remaining Hurons to assimilate into the Iroquois League rather than compelling them into union by force.[28] If the Hurons joined willingly, the Five Nations were likely to gain more people, as there would be no casualties of war, and the Iroquois would also avoid losing any of their own warriors in combat. Moreover, Hurons who voluntarily subjugated themselves to the Five Nations might prove less likely to resist assimilation, a process that was crucial to successfully completing mourning war and requickening ceremonies. Because captives who resisted acculturation ultimately were executed, resulting in no net gain for the Iroquois, it was far better to secure willing prisoners who might reasonably be expected to accept their new situation without much resistance.[29]

Not surprisingly, some Hurons, who shared the mourning war tradition with the Iroquois enemies, decided to offer themselves willingly as captives rather than suffer severe casualties by resisting. In 1651, Jesuit priests reported that the entire Huron population of two towns, St. Michael and St. Jean-Baptiste, had voluntarily surrendered themselves to the Senecas. They were re-formed into the village of Gandougarae, where an estimated 900 to 1,200 Huron refugees resumed their lives as Senecas. Similarities existed throughout Iroquoia. Yet not all Hurons accepted unification with the Five Nations; some resisted from the moment of their capture. The Iroquois almost always killed and scalped such troublesome captives, whether male or female, adult or child. Those Hurons who did not resist being taken captive still faced the harrowing march to Iroquoia. Women and children generally were spared physical abuse during the journey, so long as they did not resist or slow the pace of the war party. Male captives, however, suffered greatly, as the Iroquois tormented enemy combatants almost as soon as they gained possession of them. They stripped them of their clothes, pummeled them with clubs, pulled out fingernails, and cut off fingers. Most of the torments were intended to provide physical pain to the captives without killing them, although cutting off fingers also reflected practical considerations in that it made it difficult for a captive to effectively wield a weapon against his captors, should the opportunity arise. Once the war party reached a Five Nations village with its prizes, Huron captives faced the traditional Iroquois mourning war rituals. Captive men were forced to run the gauntlet and then often endured the slow process of execution by ritualistic torture. Women and children often escaped the gauntlet and the more extreme forms of torture, although adult women could expect to be deprived of their clothing and secured to a scaffold, where all members of the Iroquois community could prod them with sticks and cast insults at them. At some point, all prisoners were given rest, fed, and then forced to dance and sing for the amusement of their captors.[30]

In every case, the process ended when the clan matrons or village civil chief decided the fate of the captives. Those marked for death were tortured, but those chosen for adoption quickly found their circumstances changed, as the Iroquois suddenly treated them with great affection. Requickening ceremonies brought them into a family or clan lineage, but the process of assimilation into Iroquois society had only begun. Adoptees essentially were placed on probation and watched closely by their new Iroquois relatives. Those who showed a willingness to engage in their new life could expect all the same rights and privileges as any other member of the community. Those who resisted accommodation, either passively or aggressively, were punished. It seems that the Iroquois made a conscious effort to help captives assimilate, as killing every captive who resisted would be counterproductive to the mourning war principles that had resulted in captive taking in the first place. Still, adopted Hurons who would not conform or accept their new role, despite various Iroquois incentives to do so, were executed. According to Jesuit missionary Paul le Jeune, the Iroquois likened the killing of problematic captives to the eradication of a troublesome beast. "They say: It is a dead dog," he recorded, "there is nothing to be done but to cast it upon the dung hill."[31]

Whether or not the captives came willingly, accepted assimilation or resisted, there was a massive influx of Hurons into Iroquoia, a demographic and social phenomenon that changed the composition of the Five Nations forever. As a noted historian of the Hurons commented, "the Iroquois must have killed, either directly or indirectly, several thousand Huron, although not nearly so many as died of disease. Ironically, however, they also provided homes and an acceptable life for more Huron than were to survive anywhere else.... Conquerors and conquered were to share a single destiny."[32] Indeed, in some Iroquois villages, there were more adopted Hurons than there were people of the Five Nations. In the 1650s, Jesuit observers asserted that Iroquoia was composed of "more foreigners than natives of the country," estimating that non-Iroquois, mainly Hurons, accounted for as much as two-thirds of the population of some Iroquois villages.[33] Estimates made by Jesuits and other outside observers may be of questionable accuracy, but they demonstrate an emerging demographic shift in which the racial composition of the Five Nations was becoming increasingly more cosmopolitan. Indeed, in 1650, the Jesuit Paul Ragueneau recorded the speech of a Huron man captured by the Iroquois as he wandered near the borders of Iroquoia. His words testify to the evolution underway among the people of the Iroquois League. "I have been seeking you," the Huron told his captors, "I am going to my country to seek out my relatives and friends. The country of the Hurons is no longer where it was, you have transported it to your own: it is there that I was going, to join my relatives and friends, who are now but one people with yourselves: I have escaped the phantoms of a people who are no more."[34]

Although thousands of Huron captives were assimilated into the Five Nations, it was not enough to completely compensate for the death toll left by European diseases. Moreover, the Iroquois were continually losing additional numbers of their own people in war. Many Iroquois warriors died in the raids they launched on the Hurons, while retaliatory attacks brought additional death and suffering to Iroquois villages. After the destruction of the Huron Confederacy in 1648–1649, these factors led the Five Nations to attack groups of Iroquoian-speaking peoples inhabiting regions west of the Five Nations. During the 1650s, the Senecas, Cayugas, and Onondagas expanded their war against the Hurons to include the Petuns, Neutrals, and Eries, in part because these Indian nations offered asylum to refugee bands of Hurons, but also because their similar language and culture made them tempting targets for obtaining captives to replace the dead and dying in Iroquoia. An added impetus may have been the military vulnerability of the western Iroquoians, most of whom were poorly armed in comparison with the warriors of the Five Nations.[35]

It did not take long after the crucial blow fell against the Hurons for the Five Nations to expand their great mourning war to the Iroquois-speaking nations west of Iroquoia. Late in 1649, a large Iroquois war party composed of Senecas, Onondagas, and perhaps Mohawks began a campaign against the Petun, or Tobacco, peoples, neighbors of the Hurons who inhabited lands south of Georgian Bay. The Iroquois initially may have attacked the Petuns as part of their determined efforts to hunt down Huron survivors, many of whom had obtained refuge among the Petuns. In December, the Petuns discovered that a large body of Iroquois had entered their territory, and they organized an ambush near a village the Jesuits called St. Jean. The Iroquois, however, learned of the ambush when they captured two Petun scouts and came to the village by an alternate route, bypassing the Petun trap. On December 7, the Iroquois destroyed St. Jean, which was essentially devoid of defenders. Although their warriors had not been defeated or killed by the Iroquois, the destruction of St. Jean, a major Petun settlement that may have housed more than 500 families, proved too much for the Petuns to overcome. In the spring of 1650, Petun survivors began a mass exodus of their territory. Some joined the Huron refugees on Christian Island, but the bulk of the Petuns obtained sanctuary among the Ottawa peoples on Manitoulin Island in northern Lake Huron. Their flight eventually took them all the way to the southern shores of Lake Superior, where a mixed group of perhaps 500 Petuns and Hurons reconstituted themselves as the Wyandot nation. After nearly 50 years of wandering the Great Lakes region, in 1701 the Wyandots eventually found a new homeland on lands bordering the southwestern end of Lake Erie.[36]

The destruction of the Petuns had a disastrous effect on other Indian nations inhabiting the eastern Great Lakes region. It demonstrated to the

Five Nations that they could successfully expand their great mourning war to other Iroquoian peoples, while still chasing down the remnants of the Hurons. The lesson was not lost on Indian peoples in the region, some of whom decided to leave their lands rather than face an Iroquois attack. Among those who fled were the Allumette peoples, who inhabited lands along the Ottawa River. Their population was too small to withstand both disease and an Iroquois invasion, so they chose to relocate rather than risk elimination or incorporation into the Five Nations. The Nipissing peoples were another nation that chose to leave the region before they became a focus of Iroquois attention. A former trading partner of the Huron Confederacy, the Nipissings endured sporadic Iroquois attacks in the early 1650s, but quickly opted to retreat rather than fight. The Nipissings' removal took them far north and west of the Five Nations, where they eventually settled along Lake Nipigon on the northern side of Lake Superior.[37]

Those western Iroquoian peoples who chose to remain endured determined attacks from the Five Nations throughout the 1650s. A confederacy of Iroquoian-speaking peoples known as the Neutrals were the next to face Iroquois warriors. Inhabiting lands east and west of the Niagara River, and controlling the hunting territories and rich natural resources found through the lower Ontario Peninsula, the Neutrals had previously clashed with the Five Nations. In 1637, Iroquois warriors attacked the Wenros, native peoples affiliated with the Neutral confederacy, who lived to the east of the Niagara River, and forced 600 Wenros to abandon their lands and seek refuge northwest of Lake Ontario. In 1647, Senecas crossed the Niagara River and attacked the Neutral Confederacy proper, raiding a Neutral village between the northern end of the Grand River and the bottom of Lake Simcoe that may have housed many Wenro refugees. Economic considerations may have triggered these attacks, with the Senecas moving to block the formation of a trading alliance between the Neutrals, Eries, and Susquehannocks that would have diverted furs and other trade around the southern perimeter of Iroquoia to reach English outlets in the Chesapeake region.[38]

That danger became even greater after the Five Nations defeated the Hurons, leaving a number of native peoples, the Neutrals included, to assume the Hurons' former position as middlemen in the fur traffic flowing east from the Great Lakes. In addition, large numbers of Huron refugees settled among the Neutrals, almost ensuring that the Iroquois would turn their attention to the west. During the summer of 1650, the Five Nations initiated a sustained war against the Neutrals. In August, 600 Senecas attacked a village situated on the eastern frontier of Neutral territory.

Many Neutrals were reported captured, but the Seneca campaign ended in failure when a large party of Neutrals and refugee Hurons ambushed the Senecas as they withdrew. Two hundred Senecas were killed or captured, providing powerful motivation for an intensified assault the next year. In the spring of 1651, more than 1,000 Iroquois warriors, mostly Senecas but also many Mohawks, destroyed the Neutral village of Teoto'ntdiaton, killing all the young and old men they could find, while rounding up the women and children as captives. The Neutral Confederacy, unable to survive the devastation, broke apart, leaving smaller groups to disperse and cope as best they could. One entire village of Neutrals relocated to Seneca territory, where they joined the Huron refugees as voluntary captives, but the majority of the Neutrals fled to the west and were absorbed into other Indian nations, losing their identity in the process.[39]

The Five Nations completed the destruction of the western Iroquoians by launching a series of attacks in the mid-1650s against the formidable Erie Nation. The Eries, called the Cat people by the Hurons, occupied lands along southern Lake Erie stretching from southwestern New York to the northwestern corner of Pennsylvania. Perhaps aware of their precarious position, or perhaps as a result of previously established animosities with the Iroquois, Erie warriors repeatedly attacked the Senecas and Onondagas between the winter of 1652 and spring of 1654. The Eries burned a Seneca village, ambushed and killed 80 Onondaga warriors returning from a raid along Lake Huron, and captured and murdered a prestigious Onondaga war leader near his village. The attacks were enough of an affront that the Onondagas organized an army of perhaps 1,200 warriors and recruited 700 Mohawks for an invasion of Erie territory. Beginning in the fall of 1654 and carrying over into the spring of 1655, the Onondagas and Mohawks attacked Erie villages, culminating in a great battle for an Erie village in which the Iroquois overran the town after scaling the palisades using upturned canoes as ladders. The Iroquois suffered heavy losses during the campaign, but imposed a great massacre of Erie warriors and took many captives. The war lasted for two years beyond 1654, but the later campaigns consisted mainly of Iroquois war parties hunting down the remnants of the Eries. By 1656, the Eries, too, had been dispersed and dissolved by the Five Nations.[40]

The Five Nations' victory over the Eries left the Susquehannocks as the only remaining major Iroquoian-speaking people not to have been dispersed by the Iroquois. The Five Nations would not find the Susquehannocks an easy target. By 1650, the Dutch were worried about the Susquehannocks' growing fur trade with New Sweden, a small colony along the lower Delaware River, and they recruited their Mohawk trading partners to punish the Susquehannocks. The war, however, turned out to be difficult for the Mohawks. Initially, the Mohawks met with success, taking more than 500 captives after assailing the main Susquehannock village in 1752; but their advantage quickly dissolved, and the Mohawks found themselves in a fierce fight. The Susquehannocks had obtained an ample supply of firearms from the Swedes, and their firepower rivaled even that of the Mohawks. Well armed and numerous, the Susquehannocks withstood subsequent Mohawk attacks and even began to strike back. A temporary peace with the Mohawks ensued after the Dutch absorbed the colony of New Sweden in 1655, although the Susquehannocks sought to press their advantage and continued sporadic attacks against other Five Nations Iroquois. Both sides managed to avoid open war for the time being, but it was only a temporary truce in what would become a generation-long war between the Five Nations and the Susquehannocks. By the time the 25-year conflict had ended, the Susquehannas would share in the fate of their Iroquois-speaking brethren, but not before putting up a spirited resistance.[41]

WAR WITH NEW FRANCE

Since its inception in the early 1600s, the colony of New France had posed a threat to the security and prosperity of the Five Nations. In the years after Samuel de Champlain's intervention in Huron-Iroquois affairs, however, the French in Canada were at worst an indirect threat, viable as an enemy only in that they supplied arms to Indian nations hostile to the Iroquois. The Iroquois, particularly the Mohawks, were in reality the aggressors. Their raids against trade convoys along the upper St. Lawrence posed serious problems for the security and prosperity of New France, so much of which was rooted in the fur trade. In the early 1640s, the Mohawks continued their blockade of the upper St. Lawrence, attacking the trade convoys of French-allied Indians and pillaging large numbers of furs, which were then traded to the Dutch for firearms and other European supplies. The French had to take action. In 1642, French missionaries established the settlement of Villa Marie on Montreal Island, ostensibly in an effort to further the conversion of Canadian Indians to Catholicism. Yet the location of the settlement, which quickly became known as Montreal, ensured that it would become a focal point of trade. Montreal Island is located at the junction point where the Ottawa River intersects with the St. Lawrence, 150 miles upriver from Quebec. Montreal's attractive location allowed Huron and Algonquin traders to save time and effort by reducing the distance they had to travel to reach the French, plus its location at the mouth of the Ottawa River afforded New France's Indian allies an easy avenue of access to the settlement. Moreover, the French could potentially use Montreal as a military base from which to provide security against Iroquois attacks on the fur convoys moving along the rivers. After all, the Richelieu River, the primary path to and from Mohawk country, drains into the St. Lawrence only a few miles downstream, a fact not lost on the French, who began construction of a military post, Fort Richelieu, at the junction the same year they established Montreal.[42]

To the Five Nations, the new French outposts were signs of aggression, coming so soon after Governor Montmagny had rebuked Iroquois peace overtures, and they quickly let their displeasure be known. In August 1642, a war party of several hundred Mohawks attacked Fort Richelieu, killing one French soldier and wounding a handful of others. Whether the Mohawks attacked because they believed the fort lay within their territory, or because they feared the installation would curtail their movements up and down the Richelieu corridor, is unclear. It is obvious, however, that the Mohawks perceived the establishment of Fort Richelieu and Montreal as a threat to their welfare. The Iroquois understood that the French were now supplying firearms to any of their Indian allies who converted to Catholicism, a practice that in time might counter the firepower advantage the Five Nations. Accordingly, Iroquois warriors made the new French settlements a focal point of their activities over the next several decades.[43]

The war with New France was not directly part of the great mourning war, but it was a political by-product of it. The French were not ignorant of the escalating Iroquois attacks on the Hurons, and on at least some level, the French felt compelled to aid their most important trading partner. The Mohawks recognized this as well, and for the remainder of the 1740s, they made sporadic attacks against the French, usually carried out by smaller war parties intent on plunder or killing their enemies. During the fall of 1644, the Mohawks attacked several times in the vicinity of Fort Richelieu, and in each case their objective appears to have been to kill French soldiers or colonists rather than obtain captives. Indeed, figures indicate that Iroquois warriors killed two to three times more French than they captured, marking the conflict with New France as something different from the great mourning war going on in the west.[44]

The French responded to Iroquois attacks indirectly, encouraging their Algonquin allies to make raids into Mohawk territory, hoping to break the Iroquois blockade of the upper St. Lawrence. In 1643, Algonquin warriors struck down the Richelieu River and ambushed an Iroquois war party near Montreal, but if the objective was to break the Iroquois stranglehold on the upper St. Lawrence, the attacks failed. Indeed, the Iroquois tightened their cordon around the new French settlements and continued to waylay fur-laden canoes coming out of the west with little fear of retaliation. In June 1643, for example, a war party of 40 Mohawks ambushed a Huron flotilla only a league outside Montreal, captured 23 Hurons, 13 of whom were tortured to death, and appropriated all the furs. The same war party then broke into smaller groups, one of which attacked Montreal itself while another killed three French colonists working in fields outside the settlement. Indeed, in March 1644, Jesuit Charles Lalemont wrote from Montreal that the Iroquois had cut off the passages between the new French settlements and the west, killing or defeating those Indians who tried to push through in either direction.[45]

The Iroquois raids proved damaging to New France. The economy of the colony was so strongly linked to the fur trade that any disruption of the fur supply prompted a crisis. Lacking the offensive capability to strike back at the Iroquois, Governor Montmagny reversed his earlier policies and offered to make peace with the Mohawks. But in return for peace, which the Mohawks accepted, Montmagny promised French protection only for those Indians who had converted to Catholicism, leaving nonconverts to fight off the Mohawks without aid. Surprisingly, however, the Mohawks also invited French-allied Indians, particularly the Hurons, to seek separate accommodations for peace. The Hurons, already hardpressed by the Senecas, accepted, sealing the agreement with a promise to trade a portion of their furs with the Mohawks, who in turn could take them to the Dutch. Exactly what the Mohawks were trying to engineer with these agreements is unclear, but at the least they created a situation where they could focus future hostilities on either New France or the Hurons, while hoping to keep the other out of the conflict.[46]

In any case, it was a fragile peace that was short lived. In 1646, the Hurons violated their agreement with the Mohawks by trading their entire fur harvest to the French. Two years later, Mohawk warriors joined Senecas in destroying the Huron Confederacy. Peace with New France did not last much longer. In 1646, tensions between the Mohawks and French increased when the Mohawks killed Isaac Jogues, a Jesuit priest who had once been an Iroquois captive and now sought to establish a mission among the Mohawks. While Jogues was away on a trip to New France, crop failures and illness plagued the Mohawks, leading many Mohawks to conclude that the Jesuit was an evil sorcerer sent by the French to curse their people. When Jogues returned to the Mohawks in 1646, they executed him. The Mohawks then sent embassies to the other members of the Iroquois League seeking an alliance against the French, but with the great mourning war against the Hurons ramping up, their response was cool.[47]

For the time being, the Mohawks would have to fight the French alone. And they did. In 1648, the Mohawks launched a series of attacks around Trois Rivieres to retaliate for Mohawks being held prisoner by the French. For the next two years, there was little fighting because many Mohawk warriors had joined the Senecas in the major campaigns against the Hurons, in part because the Mohawks hoped the Senecas would attack the French once the Hurons were no more. In 1650, after Mohawk warriors had returned from the destruction of the Huron Confederacy, the Mohawks stepped up their assault on New France. During 1651 and 1652, in particular, the Mohawks launched a series of attacks against Montreal, Trois Rivieres, and even Quebec. Canadian colonists seem to have been a special target of the raids, as the Iroquois made a point of terrorizing and intimidating French colonials by attacking them in and around their homes. In May 1650, a war party invaded a French home near Quebec, killed two servants, ransacked the home, and then set fire to a neighboring house. A similar episode occurred in May 1651 at Montreal, where the Iroquois broke into a house, beheaded one man, butchered his wife, and scalped another man, who somehow survived the ordeal. During the summer of 1651, an Iroquois war party caught a Frenchman alone outside Trois Rivieres, shot him twice, and split apart his skull with a hatchet, leaving the weapon in place for other French colonists to discover. In a futile effort to retaliate for these types of attacks, the governor of Trois Rivieres led a detachment of 40 settlers and 10 Indians in pursuit of a Mohawk war party. The Mohawks ambushed the group, killing 11 men, including the governor, and taking 8 others prisoner.[48]

In 1653, the Iroquois unexpectedly approached the French at Montreal with an offer to restore peace. The petition was the work of the western Iroquois nations, especially the Senecas and Onondagas, who sought to keep New France neutral in their ongoing war against the Eries and perhaps even forge a trading relationship with the French. The Onondagas took the lead in the peace process by agreeing to allow Jesuit missionaries to establish a base in their country in return for French promises to supply firearms and remain neutral in Iroquois conflicts with other Indian nations. The Mohawks, realizing that the other Iroquois nations would not join their war against the French, reluctantly followed the Onondagas' lead, although they may have participated only to secure trade goods or other material benefits from the peace agreement. Indeed, friction quickly developed between the Onondagas and Mohawks as each nation sought to assert control over the creation of peace. The Onondagas reached an agreement with the French mandating that all trade and diplomacy between the Five Nations and New France would take place in the central Onondaga village, completely bypassing Mohawk country, even though the Mohawks traditionally were thought of as the eastern door of the confederacy. Infuriated Mohawks rebuffed the French, asking "will you not enter the cabin by the door ... by beginning with the Onnonta-chronnons [Onondagas], [you] try to enter by the roof and through the chimney. Have you no fear that the smoke may blind you, our fire not being extinguished, and that you may fall from the top to the bottom?"[49] The Mohawks sought to redirect the location of the Jesuit mission to their territory, perhaps hoping in this way to keep their monopoly of access to European trade. Additional strife surfaced between the two nations over refugee Hurons in the French settlements, whom both the Onondagas and Mohawks sought to obtain as a concession of peace. According to the Jesuits, the tension eventually erupted into violence a few year later, as "the two sides [Mohawks and Onondagas] fought with each other until the ground was stained with blood and murder."[50]

Like other peace agreements before it, the peace of 1653 between the Five Nations and New France proved quite fragile. The peace was not the product of a united initiative by the Iroquois League, but rather the work of individual Iroquois nations each seeking to advance their own interests. Political uniformity within the league had yet to manifest itself, as evidenced by the Mohawks. From 1654 to 1657, while the rest of the Iroquois League observed its peace agreement with the French, the Mohawks attacked the French and their Indian allies on at least 10 occasions. Some of the raids involved large numbers of Mohawk warriors, as occurred in May 1656, when the Mohawks sent either one or two armies of more than 300 warriors to attack Christian Hurons near Montreal and Quebec. In the process, the Mohawks gained nearly 80 Huron captives and also attacked a Jesuit convey en route to Onondaga territory. Moreover, the Mohawks' defiant stance resulted in more violence between themselves and other members of the Iroquois League. In 1654, the Mohawks killed an Onondaga chief. In 1655, they were accused of killing two Senecas, and a year later they shot a Seneca diplomat, although the Mohawks claimed it was an accident. Clearly, the Iroquois League was divided, with at least one member nation—the Mohawks—determined to strike their own course, regardless of the consequences.[51]

It is difficult to gauge the depths of the rift between the Mohawks and the rest of the Five Nations, especially after the Mohawks' continuing attacks on the French grew into a larger conflict. Late in 1656, a new administration took over governance of New France, removed restraints from the colony's Indian allies, encouraged them to attack the Iroquois, and imprisoned Mohawks captured near the French settlements. Such actions may have been intended to force the Mohawks into fuller compliance with the 1653 peace agreement, but instead they escalated the conflict. Determined to break the Onondaga-French alliance, a Mohawk party marched to Onondaga country to expel the Jesuits from the mission there, but surprisingly found them already gone after having been forced out by the Onondagas. The Jesuits had proved unpopular among the Onondagas, who quickly tired of the missionaries' intolerance of native rituals and polarizing politics. The removal of the Jesuits eased tensions between the Onondagas and Mohawks, and by the summer of 1658, Onondagas and Oneidas joined Mohawks in renewing war against the French.[52]

By 1660, however, the Iroquois League had perhaps reached the zenith of its military might. Iroquois warriors had destroyed the Huron Confederacy, absorbed or dispersed a wide range of Iroquoian-speaking peoples beyond their western borders, and paralyzed New France both militarily and economically. Indeed, some French colonists feared that "if we do not go to humiliate these barbarians [the Iroquois], they will destroy the country and drive us all away by their warlike and carnivorous nature."[53] Yet despite their victories and the fears of their enemies, the Five Nations did not emerge significantly stronger from the great mourning war. Although the Five Nations adopted thousands of Indian peoples, their population barely remained stable thanks to the continued ravages of disease and the tremendous loss of life they endured in their military campaigns. That the Iroquois League had not succumbed to disease, warfare, or internal strife was perhaps the Five Nations' greatest accomplishment during this turbulent era, but the peoples of the Iroquois League remained vulnerable, a condition that would soon be brought home to Iroquoia with devastating clarity. Indeed, events were already in motion in France and to the east and south of the Five Nations that would soon confront the Iroquois with challenges greater than anything they had yet endured in the era of European colonization.

4

•

The Longhouse in Peril

As the 1660s began, Iroquois warriors continued to experience military victories, even as they took their raids into the heart of New France; but emboldened by their success, the Iroquois pushed too wide and too far. Well-armed Indian nations to the east and south blunted Iroquois offensives, and the French struck back the Mohawks with a show of overwhelming force. Overmatched and alone, the Five Nations fell victim to internal divisions. Pro-French leaders steered their people toward accommodation with New France, while anti-French factions, undermined by the collapse of New Netherland, found few adherents. As their doom approached, four of the five Iroquois nations avoided destruction by willingly embracing the French. Only the Mohawks resisted, and for that they paid a heavy price. Yet from the ashes arose new opportunities and new allies. The English replaced the Dutch on the Hudson, and from Albany emerged the foundations of a new and fruitful alliance, the Covenant Chain.

THE LONGHOUSE IN PERIL

During the first half of the 1660s, the Five Nations continued to escalate their conflict with New France. Mohawk, Onondaga, and Oneida warriors raided the upper St. Lawrence and stalked the outskirts of French settlements, seeking opportunities to attack exposed or vulnerable groups of French colonists or their Indian allies. At the same time, Seneca, Cayuga, and Onondaga warriors intensified the conflict with the Susquehannocks to the south, sending war parties against their enemy's main village. And just for good measure, the Mohawks rekindled fires of dispute with their old rivals, the Mahicans, and started new conflicts with a host of New England Algonquins. Indeed, during the first half the 1660s, the Iroquois League seemingly was at war with everyone else in the northeast.

In the spring of 1660, the Iroquois pressed their advantage against the French by moving an army of 500 Mohawks into the region between the St. Lawrence and Ottawa Rivers. They were soon joined by Onondaga and Oneida war parties, containing perhaps 200 or 300 warriors combined. As they Iroquois moved through the region, some Onondagas broke off from the main army to hunt and were discovered by a party of Huron refugees, who alerted the nearby settlements. Dollard des Ormeaux, the commander of Montreal, hastily organized an attack force of 17 French volunteers and 44 Hurons and Algonquins to ambush the Iroquois. The party quickly traveled to a makeshift fortification the Algonquins had constructed near Chaudiere Falls along the Ottawa River, where they soon found themselves surrounded by the much larger Iroquois army. The Huron war leader, Annaotaha, secured a parley, which resulted in 24 Hurons defecting to the Iroquois after recognizing adopted Huron relatives and friends among the attackers. Disgusted by this perceived treachery, the French opened fire in violation of the truce, which prompted a determined Iroquois response. When the battle was over, 12 of the 17 French volunteers and most of the Hurons and Algonquins who remained loyal to the French were dead. Only five French and five of their Indian allies survived, all of whom the Iroquois later tortured to death in retaliation for the French sneak attack. Still, the Iroquois had suffered heavy casualties—40 of their warriors were killed or wounded—that forced the army to withdraw, sparing Montreal and the outlying French settlements for the moment.[1]

The losses may have prompted some in the Five Nations to think of peace with the French, although the Mohawks continued to raid New France regularly, along with sporadic attacks by Oneidas and Onondagas. In the fall of 1660, large Iroquois war parties returned to waylay fur shipments moving along the Ottawa River, and the next year proved even more disastrous for New France. In February 1661, 160 Iroquois warriors attacked Montreal, capturing 13 French colonists. In March, an even larger war party, estimated to exceed 250 warriors, returned to Montreal, killing or capturing at least 10 French residents. The raids continued throughout the summer and fall of 1661, with the Iroquois launching at least 10 documented attacks against the French settlements. By year's end, an estimated 39 French colonists had died and another 61 were captured as a result of Iroquois raids. Even far away Quebec was not secure, as 27 people were reported killed or captured in the fighting. At that time, it was the worst casualty total for a single year in the colony's history.[2]

Not all Iroquois attacks against the French and their Indians allies resulted in victory. An Iroquois war party composed of 100 Oneidas and Mohawks was wiped out during the spring of 1662 near Lake Huron by a large party of Ottawas and Ojibwas on their way to trade with the French. These Great Lakes Indian nations had replaced the Hurons as New France's principal trading partners and, in an effort to provide security to their new allies, the French had supplied them with firearms. The well-armed trading convoy discovered the Iroquois as they hunted in the forest, fell on them from an ambush site, and very nearly killed or captured the entire group. Enemies of the Five Nations occasionally carried their attacks into Iroquois territory as well. In May 1663, a group of Algonquins from the Sillery settlement near Quebec moved down the Richelieu River intending to strike into eastern Iroquoia. On reaching Lake Champlain, however, they came across a war party of 40 Mohawks and Oneidas returning from a raid against Montreal. The Algonquins ambushed the Iroquois, killed and scalped 10 Mohawks, captured 3 others, and rescued a captured French colonist. Neither defeat proved crippling to the Five Nations, but such episodes illustrate that the war was not entirely one sided.[3]

While the Mohawks, Oneidas, and Onondagas pressured Canada, conflict again flared up between the western members of the Five Nations—particularly the Senecas, Cayugas, and Onondagas—and the Susquehannocks, the only remaining Iroquoian-speaking people in the northeast not yet consumed by the Five Nations. Again, the Iroquois found the Susquehannocks to be a well-armed, determined, and aggressive enemy. The Susquehannocks had enjoyed a brisk trade with the colony of New Sweden until its absorption by the Dutch in the 1650s, a prosperous relationship that sated the Swedes' hunger for furs and brought guns to the Susquehannocks in return. After New Sweden came under Dutch management, a smoldering conflict between the English and Dutch led to closer relations between the Susquehannocks and the English colony of Maryland. That relationship solidified into an alliance after the Oneidas attacked the Piscataway Indians, a nation the government of Maryland considered to be within their protective custody. Interpreting the attack against the Piscataways as the start of an Iroquois war against Maryland, and bulwarked by orders from colony proprietor Lord Baltimore to initiate hostilities with the Dutch, Maryland supplied the Susquehannocks with muskets and ammunition, sent a squad of 50 Maryland soldiers to help defend the Susquehannocks' heavily fortified major settlement, and encouraged their new Indian allies to make war on the Iroquois.[4]

The alliance with Maryland, and the guns it provided, allowed the Susquehannocks to take the offensive against the Iroquois during the summer of 1661, when a Susquehannock war party killed three Cayugas outside one of their villages. The Iroquois retaliated, first sending a war party against the Delawares, rumored to be allied with the Susquehannocks, then in 1663 outfitting an army of 800 Senecas, Cayugas, and Onondagas for an assault on the Susquehannock's main village. When the Iroquois reached the Susquehannocks' principal village, often referred to as the Susquehannock fort, they found their prospects for success poor. The village was protected on one side by the Susquehanna River and by thick tree trunks on the other, and at either flank European-style bastions had been erected in which were mounted several cannon that the Susquehannocks had obtained from the Swedes. A few well-timed blasts from the guns convinced the Iroquois that they could not take the fort by siege, so they instead tried a ruse to gain access through the gates. A party of 25 Iroquois warriors asked to be conducted inside the fort to discuss peace and purchase provisions for their return home, a request that was granted. The Iroquois may have intended that this group then try to force open the gates from the inside, but the Susquehannocks quickly subdued the delegation, for whom they had their own plans. The captured Iroquois were lashed to scaffolds on top of the bastions, and in clear sight of their brethren, systematically burned to death by the Susquehannocks. The main body of Iroquois warriors decided to retreat, and although they were hounded for two days by pursuing Susquehannocks, the army escaped back to Iroquoia. Afterward both sides continued to launch small-scale raids against the other for several years, during which time the western Iroquois were hard-pressed by the Susquehannocks.[5]

As war raged on the northern and southern frontiers of Iroquoia, the Mohawks were busy fighting enemies on their eastern flank as well. Throughout the 1650s, the Mohawks had maintained mostly peaceful relations with the various Algonquian tribes inhabiting the lands from the upper Hudson River to the Connecticut River Valley, including the Mahicans, Pocumtucs, and Sokokis (part of the western Abenaki confederation). By 1660, however, a sharp dip in the New England fur trade combined with a decline in the demand for wampum to leave the New England Algonquians in serious economic distress. To gain access to furs and to find outlets for their wampum, the New England Algonquians cultivated closer relationships with Algonquian peoples to their north, including eastern Abenakis and the Montagnais, both of whom were tied by trade and alliance to New France. Fearing that the French would try to build an Algonquian coalition against them—indeed, the Jesuit priest Gabriel Druillette had labored unsuccessfully to form exactly such a union a decade earlier—the Mohawks expanded their war against the French to include the New England Algonquians.[6]

In 1660, the Iroquois raided an Abenaki village, also engaging Sokokis who came to the assistance of their fellow New England Algonquians. In 1662, more than 200 Mohawks besieged a Penobscot (eastern Abenaki) village, which the Sokokis retaliated for by attacking a Mohawk village. The war was on. It escalated further in early December 1663, when a large Mohawk war party sacked the Sokoki's southern village on the Connecticut River, killing between 30 and 40 Sokokis and destroying the Sokokis' food stores. The Sokokis abandoned what was left of the village and sought safety elsewhere. A particularly intense conflict developed between the Mohawks and the Pocumtucs, who inhabited the middle Connecticut Valley. The Dutch, whose trade was disrupted by the war, pressured the Mohawks to make peace with the New England Algonquians. The Mohawks agreed, but a peace delegation of 30 Iroquois, including the Onondaga leader Garakontie, was ambushed in May 1664 by Montagnais and Algonquins, who cut several captured Iroquois to pieces and hijacked the delegations' possessions. A month later, a Mohawk delegation led by a headman named Saheda reached the Pocumtuc village, where they were duped into entering the fort by the Pocumtucs' false pledges of peace. The Pocumtucs killed the Mohawk ambassadors, mandating a revenge attack by the Mohawks. That assault came in the winter of 1664–1665, when the Mohawks destroyed the central village of the Pocumtucs. Details are incomplete, but tradition holds that the Pocumtucs held off a direct Mohawk assault on their town, only to fall victim to a well-planned ambush when they tried to pursue the retreating Mohawks. The Pocumtucs abandoned most of their village along the Connecticut River shortly afterward.[7]

The dispersal of the Sokokis and Pocumtucs did not necessarily mean that the Mohawks were winning the war against their eastern neighbors. The Mohawks soon discovered that the New England Algonquians, like the Susquehannocks, were numerous, well armed, and ready for a fight.

These Indian nations had traded extensively with three different groups of Europeans—English, French, and Dutch—in the process securing an ample supply of firearms, ammunition, and metal weapons. In 1666, the Mohawks and Mahicans agreed to lay aside their animosities and embrace peace; but the New England Algonquians continued to fight for another decade, highlighted by occasional raids into Mohawk country, including the 1669 siege of the Mohawks' central village by more than 600 Algonquians. The situation was distressing enough that the Mohawks asked the Dutch to mediate peace with the eastern Indians, but the Dutch, beset by serious problems of their own, refused. In 1664, the English started what would be the second of three wars against the Dutch in the seventeenth century, a conflict that featured the conquest of New Netherland by Colonel Richard Nichols with just 300 English soldiers. The Dutch, who were taken completely by surprise, offered no resistance. Moreover, it would have been unlikely that they could have put up much of a fight if they had tried, owing to an ammunition and powder shortage in the colony. The deficiency, caused by disrupted trade on the Atlantic as a result of the war with England, may have also contributed to the difficulties of the Iroquois in their wars against the Susquehannocks and New England Algonquians.[8]

Although the establishment of a new European regime on the upper Hudson must have been disconcerting to the Five Nations, it was only one of many challenges facing the Iroquois League by the mid-1660s. By trying to wage three simultaneous wars, the Iroquois League had overextended itself, seriously straining its military capacity. Despite the successes of the great mourning war against other Iroquoian peoples, the population of the Five Nations had not regenerated to pre-epidemic levels. In fact, during the 1660s, the number of Iroquois warriors remained well below that of previous generations, and the warrior population appears to have been declining rather than expanding. Moreover, unlike the Hurons and western Iroquoians defeated by the Iroquois League over the previous two decades, the Susquehannocks, Mahicans, and western Abenakis were more than holding their own against the the Iroquois. These Indian nations had few internal divisions, perhaps because missionaries had not yet infiltrated their societies in a meaningful fashion, and they all had easy access to European trade, leaving them well armed and capable of waging successful warfare against the Five Nations. In addition, the French were becoming more assertive, smallpox returned to Iroquoia, and the Dutch failed to provide adequate firearms and ammunition because of the English campaign against New Netherland. In short, the Five Nations were in serious trouble.[9]

The peoples of the Iroquois League were not insensitive to their vulnerability. Many Iroquois leaders realized that the only way out of their current dilemma was to make peace with one or more of their enemies, but significant disagreement existed between league members over which enemy they should approach about a cessation of hostilities. The western Iroquois advocated peace with the French, which would allow the Iroquois to focus their collective attention on the Susquehannocks. Pro-French factions had been steadily gaining influence among the Onondagas, whereas the Senecas and Cayugas had been so busy with the Susquehannocks that they had not participated in Iroquois attacks against Cananda. At the other end of Iroquoia, however, the Mohawks preferred to continue fighting the French while calling off the war with the Mahicans and New England Algonquians. For the Mohawks, the French were the greater enemy, whose list of transgressions, which included arming northern Indians hostile to the Five Nations, was too great to allow for peace. With the Iroquois League still lacking a centralized political structure, which allowed member nations to make war and peace on an individual basis as they saw fit, there was little chance a general peace involving all of the Five Nations could be concluded with any of the peoples the Iroquois were fighting. Indeed, during a 1661 council involving most, if not all, of the Five Nations, a general resolution was passed favoring peace with New France, but it was not binding on the members of the league. The Mohawks, along with some Onondagas and Oneidas, ignored the call for peace and continued to attack the French.[10]

The Mohawks' decision to follow their own agenda illustrates the voluntary nature of association in the Iroquois League, but the participation of some Oneidas and Onondagas in continued raiding against New France suggests that efforts to make peace factionalized Iroquois communities within the same nation. In 1661, for example, an Onondaga headman named Garankontie, a strong advocate of peace with the French, led an embassy to Montreal to discuss peace with the French. At the same time, another Onondaga leader, Otreouti, known to the French as "La Grande Gueule" (big mouth), recruited a war party of 30 Onondagas and set out to attack Montreal. Otreouti, who had been one of several Iroquois who escaped from a Montreal prison in 1658, wanted revenge against the French for his captivity. Otreouti and his warriors surprised a small group of French colonists in a field outside Montreal, killing two, taking another prisoner, and beheading a French priest. Otreouti donned the dead priest's cassock and paraded about the field, which lay within sight of the Montreal inhabitants. A few days later, as Otreouti led his warriors back to their Onondaga village, he came across Garakontie's peace embassy. The Onondaga diplomats feigned illness to prevent Otreouti's warriors from attacking them, and Garakontie labored for hours to convince Otreouti to release his entourage. In the end, Otreouti and his warriors allowed Garakontie and his party to continue their voyage unmolested, but the episode illuminates the divided nature of the Onondagas.[11]

Regardless of which members of the Iroquois League wanted peace with New France, their furtive efforts for reconciliation with the French came too late to stave off serious reprisal. For years military leaders, Jesuits, and colonists in Canada had beseeched their home government to humble the Five Nations, whom they considered to be their greatest enemy in war and entirely untrustworthy in peace. In the early 1660s, the Jesuit Gabriel Lalemont explained to the home government that where the Iroquois were concerned, "One cannot assume any other standard than that of their own self-interests. . . . Nothing but the terror and fear of our arms, or the hope of some considerable profit in their trading, or the aid to be obtained from us against their enemies, can hold them in check; and even that will not prevent some from separating from the rest and coming by stealth to slay us."[12]

These dramatic expositions on Iroquois duplicity eventually had their intended effect. While Mohawk warriors continued to maraud French settlements in the early 1660s, the new king of France, Louis XIV, decided to heed the call of his subjects in Canada and crush the Iroquois League. Shortly after ascending to the throne in 1661, the young monarch placed New France under direct royal control and ordered his minister of finance, Jean Baptiste Colbert, to develop a plan to secure effective governance and profitable trade in Canada. Colbert reorganized New France along military lines, installing Daniel de Remy de Courcelle as governor-general, a position that combined military and civil authority into one person. Protection of French colonists and the fur trade were paramount issues for Colbert, so he supported his new governor by dispatching nearly 1,200 French soldiers from the famous Carignan-Salieres regiment to New France, almost all of whom were equipped with new, state-of-the-art flintlock muskets. There was little doubt in the mind of their commander, Lieutenant General Alexandre de Pruoville, Marquis de Tracy, that his soldiers and their guns would soon "plant lilies over the ashes of the Iroquois."[13]

Of all the Five Nations, the Mohawks were the most problematic for the French. It was logical, then, that Courcelle and Tracy designed their campaign against the Iroquois League primarily as an attack on the Mohawks. After arriving in Trois Rivieres in July 1665, Tracy's army constructed several forts along the Richelieu River, extending as far south as Lake Champlain. French fortifications along the Five Nations' favorite invasion route did not altogether halt Mohawk raids—the Mohawks conducted small-scale raids near Montreal and outside the new French forts at least three times the next year—but they did put French troops in a better position to respond to Mohawk aggression or strike back at Iroquois villages. They also served as an imposing bargaining chip for pro-French Iroquois leaders trying to convince their peoples that peace with the French was preferable to war. Concerned by the threat of impending French military action, all of the Five Nations except the Mohawks finalized a peace agreement with New France by the end of 1665.[14]

Hoping to catch Mohawk warriors off guard in their villages, Courcelle decided on a winter expedition, despite sound advice against such a campaign. The governor-general ordered 300 bateaux constructed to ferry his army up Lake Champlain and outfitted his men with provisions and supplies, including snow shoes, for the winter campaign. The campaign got off to an inauspicious start in January 1666, when Courcelle made the mistake of sending a 600-man expeditionary force forward without waiting for his Algonquin guides, who were also expected to hunt during the march and supply the French army with meat. For three weeks, the French struggled to make their way south through several feet of snow, fighting a losing battle against subfreezing temperatures and raging blizzards. On several occasions, the troops got lost after following false trails. Dozens of French soldiers died in the clutches of the northern winter before the army launched an attack on what they thought was a Mohawk village. The French soon discovered that they were advancing on the recently established (1661) Dutch settlement of Schenectady, but once the citizens of the town learned that the French were only there to attack the Mohawks, they provided supplies and assistance to the ravaged army. The Algonquin guides finally caught up with the French a short time later, bringing in meat for the soldiers and guiding the army back to Canada. A party of 30 Mohawks, who came to trade with the Dutch, arrived as the French were leaving, leading to a brief firefight during which each side suffered about 10 casualties. The French continued their withdrawal without further incident, and by the time Courcelle's army reached the Richelieu forts, he had lost more than 60 men, one-tenth of his army, and he had fought no major engagements. The campaign to chastise the Mohawks had failed miserably.[15]

Yet the presence of a French army so close to Iroquoia convinced many Mohawks that the French were serious about bringing the war to their doorsteps. That summer, a Mohawk delegation led by a chief the English called Smiths John, conversely known by the French as "the Flemish Bastard," negotiated with Courcelle to include the Mohawks in the newly established peace between New France and the other Iroquois nations. But Courcelle refused, citing Mohawk treachery in the past, and instead ordered General Tracy to prepare for a full-scale invasion of Mohawk country. For the expedition, Tracy put together an army of more than 1,300 men, composed of 600 French regulars, 600 Canadian militia, and 100 Christian Hurons and Algonquins. The campaign began in October 1666, and this time the army moved quickly and efficiently, reaching the first Mohawk village in just two weeks. Nonetheless, the village was deserted, as were three others the French approached, the Mohawks having retreated to safe locations deep inside the forest. The French responded by looting and destroying the villages and the Mohawks' stored food supply, which according to the French was so vast that it could have fed every man, woman, and child in New France for two years. The French returned by route of Schenectady, where they were again treated kindly. Yet all was not a total loss for the Mohawks. Their four major villages lay in ruins, but these had already been close to abandonment as a result of the natural process of decay and infestation that forced eastern woodland peoples to relocate approximately every 20 to 25 years. Moreover, although the French assault certainly disrupted the lives of the Mohawks and challenged their economic viability, the fighting capacity of the nation had not been affected. No Mohawk warriors died in the campaign, an important consideration for a nation still entangled in a difficult war against its Indian neighbors to the east. Nonetheless, the magnitude of the blow should not be underappreciated. It sent a powerful message, and the Five Nations—the Mohawks especially—would not attempt attacks of any consequence on New France for the better part of two decades.[16]

Although Tracy's campaign did not directly defeat the Mohawks in battle, it did bring them to the bargaining table. All of the Five Nations except the Mohawks had chosen accommodation with the French by 1665, and the Mohawks reluctantly accepted French terms for peace after the destruction of their villages. Even then, it was not an easy choice for the Mohawks, who had a longer and deeper history of conflict with the French and their Indian allies than the other peoples of the Iroquois League. Experience left the Mohawks wary of peace and suspicious of French intentions. Moreover, the Mohawks had long enjoyed special influence and status among the Five Nations, owing to their close proximity to the Dutch. Controlling access to trade on the Hudson had made the Mohawks important and strong, both in terms of their internal relations with the other Iroquois nations, and in external conflicts with the French and other Indian nations. Peace with the French threatened to destroy all of this. The rising pro-French faction of Iroquois leaders was centered among the Onondagas, who stood to become the new version of the Mohawks if the Five Nations shifted their commercial and political allegiance from the Dutch to the French. Although the pro-French faction won some converts among Mohawk leaders, in 1666 the Mohawks accepted peace not because they agreed with the Onondagas, but rather because they had no other viable option.[17]

The terms of peace with New France were not onerous for the Five Nations. The Iroquois were expected to cease warring against the French and their Indian allies, and all legitimate trade in furs was to be routed through Montreal. In addition, the Five Nations were required to once again accept Jesuit missionaries into their villages. Pro-French Iroquois welcomed the return of the priests, as did Christian Hurons living among the Five Nations. Conversions of the Iroquois were brisk at first, perhaps owing to the influence of pro-French leaders or the general desire of the Iroquois people to avoid future wars with the French. The Jesuits converted an estimated 4,000 Iroquois in the decade after 1668, although a good many of these involved the baptisms of Iroquois people close to death. Still, many of their converts were important leaders, including the Onondaga headmen Garakontie, and an estimate that the Jesuits converted approximately 20 percent of the people in the Five Nations to Christianity testifies to their influence. In addition, the Jesuits played important roles in Iroquois religious and social customs that they likely did not even understand. Missionaries were viewed as potential sources of new spiritual power, a form of adopted captive who could transfer their power, and that of the French, to the Five Nations. This perhaps helps to explain the surprisingly high conversion rate among the Mohawks. Demoralized and perhaps even desperate, prominent Mohawk leaders such as Assendasse and Kryn embraced Jesuit teachings as a new means of reacquiring lost prestige and power. Many of their people followed their example. "God employed the arms of France to give their conversion a beginning," concluded missionary Francois Le Mercier, "Their courage weakened after their defeat; and they are now, of all the Iroquois tribes, the ones that gives the greatest hopes of its conversion to the Christian faith."[18]

Although they achieved success in converting peoples of the Iroquois League to Christianity, the Jesuits refused to moderate their strict requirements that converts reject native customs and live in segregation from traditional peoples in their villages. This was not an easy requirement for the Christian Iroquois to keep or for the Jesuit fathers to enforce. In the late 1660s, the Jesuits changed their strategy. Segregation was replaced by separation, as the missionaries began urging their converts to leave the villages of the Five Nations and migrate to New France. Two important settlements of Christian Iroquois were founded near Montreal, isolated both from traditional Iroquois and French colonists, who did not always provide the best examples of what Christian life supposedly entailed. Kanawake was peopled primarily by Mohawks, including Kryn, with a smaller population of Oneidas and Onondagas. By 1682, more than 100 Iroquois families, an estimated 600 people, were living there. Christian Iroquois also migrated to at least three other settlements, Lac des Deux Montagnes, or Oka, on Montreal Island; the Huron mission refuge of Lorette near Quebec; and the small community at Cataraqui at the eastern end of Lake Ontario. The establishment of the mission towns was an important development in Iroquois culture. Hundreds and eventually thousands of Christian Iroquois left for the new settlements, but many others did not migrate, resulting in divided family and clan lineages between the mission towns and Iroquoia that would have profound effects on trade, politics, and war over the course of the next century.[19]

THE COVENANT CHAIN

French missionary activity helped spur another important development in Iroquoia: the growth of a pro-English, anti-French political faction. The divisions wrought by the Jesuits did not sit well with traditional elements of Iroquois society, many of whom favored improved relations with the English at Albany, who for the moment appeared to be less intrusive than the French in their relationship with the Iroquois. This reaction was especially prevalent among the Mohawks, where the majority of pro-French people converted to Christianity and migrated to Kanawake, leaving a strong core of traditionalists who gravitated toward Albany. Perhaps seeking to reestablish their preeminence within the Iroquois League, the pro-English Mohawks labored to convince the other Iroquois of the advantages of trading and politicking on the Hudson. During the 1670s, the pro-English faction gained adherents and influence among the Five Nations, spreading from the Mohawks to the other four nations and establishing the foundation for a complex and at times confusing Iroquois-English alliance that would come to be known as the Covenant Chain.[20]

The pro-English Iroquois found an able and willing partner in Major Edmund Andros, who became governor of New York in 1674. Andros arrived in North America with instructions to assert the Duke of York's colonial land claims over those of other English colonies, especially the New England colonies and Virginia; expand the political boundaries of New York; and make the province the dominant force in the fractious world of colonial American politics. Opportunities to press New York's authority abounded in the mid-1670s, but Andros needed manpower to realize his ambitions, and he quickly grasped that a partnership with the Five Nations could prove mutually beneficial. The colony's relationship with the Iroquois had been mostly amicable, but the Iroquois had developed some hard feelings toward the English since they took control of New Netherland. Shortly after their arrival, the English had reached a deal with the Mohawks to replace the Dutch in Iroquois trade networks, but during the late 1660s and early 1670s, continued warfare with the Dutch disrupted the flow of trade goods to Albany and inflated the prices of the commodities that were available. Iroquois leaders had little patience for English explanations about global wars of commerce, especially after the English refused to help the Mohawks defend their villages against the French in 1666. Indeed, by the time Andros arrived on the scene, the English had earned a well-deserved reputation among the Five Nations as fickle friends and unreliable business partners.[21]

After 1674, the Dutch and English reached a lasting peace that allowed the resumption of normal business activities at Albany. Renewed trading opportunities brought the Iroquois, especially the Mohawks, back to Albany in large numbers. English products, like their Dutch predecessors, were generally cheaper and of higher quality that those offered by the French, and Governor Andros used trade relations to make overtures to the Mohawks for a grand alliance. As he labored to restore relations with the Five Nations, Andros carefully cultivated a special alliance with the Mohawks, artfully seizing on Iroquois stories of past military conquests to forward the notion that the Five Nations were the rightful masters of a vast empire of lands encompassing the Great Lakes, Ohio Valley, and the western Carolinas. The Iroquois themselves believed that their past military exploits afforded them the right to determine the usage of these lands, but the English would eventually build on that concept to imply that the Five Nations were the rulers of much of the interior of the continent. Key to the arrangement was an English promise to help the Five Nations maintain their control over their alleged empire by providing arms, ammunition, and military assistance. Naturally there was a catch. English officials such as Andros and his immediate successor in New York, Thomas Dongan, offered to help the Five Nations assert their sovereignty over Indian country because they intended to assert English sovereignty over the Five Nations. In exchange for trade and assistance, the English expected the Five Nations to become English subjects, a status that would allow England to claim dominion by proxy over the vast imaginary empire of the Five Nations, in the process making this illusionary empire real. This arrangement, which the French and other Indian nations did not recognize, and which the Five Nations did not entirely agree with, came to be known as the Covenant Chain.[22]

The Covenant Chain alliance took time to cultivate and would not reach its full maturity until the mid-eighteenth century. During Andros's tenure, the Covenant Chain consisted of little more than a military alliance between New York and the Mohawks that grew out of Andros's need to quell border wars in the English colonies and the Mohawks' need to revitalize themselves after the disastrous war with New France. In this arrangement, Andros provided guns and ammunition, and the Mohawks provided muscle to back Andros's agenda in several ongoing colonial conflicts. It was a mutually beneficial partnership. The Mohawks found the means for their resurgence, becoming the favored Indian nation of New York and netting the attending benefits of trade and association. Andros got the military backing he needed to impose settlements on defiant colonies, Indian nations, or both. In 1675, Andros and the Mohawks put their new alliance to the test, as the New York governor and Mohawk warriors exercised their combined wills to bring resolution to three ongoing conflicts: a bloody uprising of New England Algonquians against the English known as King Philip's War; Bacon's Rebellion, a frontier revolt in Virginia that had morphed into a war between the Susquehannocks and the English colonies of Virginia and Maryland; and the continuing war between Mahicans and Mohawks in the upper Hudson Valley. In each case, Andros grabbed an opportunity to expand the power and prestige of New York while suppressing individual conflicts that threatened to coalesce into a general Indian uprising against the English, and the Mohawks got to exact revenge and retribution against Indian enemies who had successfully warred against the Five Nations for more than a decade.[23]

The process began in 1675, when Andros recruited Mohawk warriors to deal a decisive blow against the New England Algonquian military alliance headed by the Wampanoag leader Metacom, known to the English as King Philip. In the fall of 1675, Metacom's war against Massachusetts raged in the Connecticut Valley, and the Algonquian warriors in his alliance came to Albany to trade for ammunition. A large portion of them established a winter camp along the Hoosick River, 40 miles east of Albany, where they believed themselves to be out of reach of enemy retaliation. Andros saw an opportunity and asked the Mohawks to attack Metacom's camp. New England authorities disapproved of the plan, recognizing the New York governor's action as a thinly veiled thrust for power, but they could do little to prevent the stroke. Andros housed Mohawk families at Albany, providing them with food, clothing, and shelter, while their warriors descended on the unsuspecting Algonquians. In February 1676, 300 Mohawks attacked the 500 Algonquins in Metacom's camp, routing the camp, killing perhaps as many as 70 Algonquians, and driving the remainder away. Metacom escaped, but subsequent Mohawk attacks throughout the spring and summer of 1676 helped end his rebellion. In March, the Mohawks intercepted a detachment of Algonquians heading for Canada to seek desperately needed supplies, and a June attack against a camp of mostly women and children disheartened the Algonquian warriors. Metacom moved his forces east to escape Mohawk pressure, a move that eventually backfired as New Englanders mounted increasingly effective attacks in the summer of 1676. By autumn the uprising had been defeated.[24]

As Mohawk warriors were dealing crucial blows to the New England Algonquians' hopes, Andros also encouraged them to push their longstanding war against the Mahcians and western Abenakis toward a conclusion. By 1680, Andros used diplomatic leverage to convince the Mahicans, western Abenakis, and other New England Algonquins give up the fight. Andros offered the defeated Indian nations asylum at Schaghticoke along the Hoosic River, about 20 miles east of Albany. There they would be placed under the protection of the New York government and watched over by the Mohawks, who came to refer to the refugees as their "children."[25]

Intervening in the Susquehannock war proved slightly more complicated. For the Five Nations, the war with the Susquehannocks had not improved much since the setbacks of the early 1660s. Indeed, the Susquehannocks continued to launch attacks into Iroquoia, much to the detriment of the Senecas, Cayuags, and Onondagas. To escape the pressure of mounting Susquehannock attacks, many Senecas, Cayugas, and Oneidas took advantage of a tentative peace with the Wyandots and Great Lakes Algonquians to move north of Iroquoia and establish six new villages on the far side of Lake Ontario during the decade from 1665 to 1675. These lands were formerly used by the Hurons and other Iroquoian peoples as hunting grounds, but the Five Nations considered themselves to be masters of the region by right of conquest. Here they were insulated against the Susquehannocks, but in exchange for security they accepted closer relations with the French. The villages had begun as base camps for hunters, and even as they evolved, the fur trade remained central to their existence. These Iroquois traded primarily with the French, traveling east along the northern shore of Lake Ontario and then down the St. Lawrence River to Montreal. Still, French officials feared the Iroquois were settling in the north country as a means to expand the trading empire of the English at Albany, and they resolved to keep a close eye on the *Iroquois du Nord*, as the French came to call the migrants.[26]

In 1675, the Susquehannocks became embroiled in a larger war with Maryland and Virginia, when a dispute over stolen hogs escalated into a full-scale war. A group of Doeg Indians was killed while trying to confiscate a Virginia frontier farmer's hogs as payment for goods the Indians had sold him. The killings set off a series of raids and counter-raids, quickly expanding to involve both Maryland and Virginia. Early in the conflict Susquehannock leaders sought to negotiate a peaceful resolution, but nearly 1,000 Virginians and Marylanders led by John Washington (great-grandfather of George) surrounded a principal Susquehannock town and murdered several Susquehannock headmen. Outnumbered by the Virginian settlers, the enraged Susquehannocks nonetheless wrought devastation across the Potomac frontier region, raiding and pillaging the settlers' isolated farms. Hard-pressed by the Indians, the frontier populace sought aid from the Virginia government; but colonial officials, fearful of potential disruptions in the profitable Indian trade, responded only with a bland and ineffective defensive strategy that did little to relieve the distress. Incensed, frontier settlers under the leadership of a Nathaniel Bacon, a young and out-of-favor Virginia aristocrat, began indiscriminately killing Indians, both hostile Susquehannocks and friendly Algonquian-speaking groups such as the Pamunkeys and Appomatoxes. Bacon's attacks greatly troubled Virginia lawmakers, who wanted to avoid a general war with the Indians. Virginia Governor William Berkeley declared Bacon an outlaw in early 1676, touching off a brief but violent frontier rebellion in which disaffected and disenfranchised frontier residents chased Governor Berkeley out of Jamestown and then burned the town. Bacon died of dysentery only a month later and the rebellion quickly collapsed.[27]

Within this vortex of confusion and chaos, Andros saw yet another opportunity to expand the power and prestige of New York and the Five

Nations. Andros used the threat of Iroquois force to end the war and compel the Susquehannocks to remove from the Potomac River region, promising to protect them from their enemies if they settled within the jurisdiction of New York. Andros' hoped to fuse the Susquehannocks with the Mohawks, the only Iroquois nation with whom they had not actively been at war, in order to bolster the population and fighting strength of his Mohawk allies. Reluctantly, the Susquehannocks agreed, although they did not merge with the Mohawks as Andros intended. Some joined the Delawares in southeastern Pennsylvania, others assimilated into the western Iroquois nations, and yet another group returned to their old home in the Susquehanna River Valley, where they became known as the Conestogas. Although they were not exterminated by the Iroquois in a literal sense, by 1680 the Susquehannocks in essence had ceased to exist, reduced to a constituency in other tribes or reconfigured as only a shadow of their former selves.[28]

For the Five Nations, the conclusion of the Susquehannock war was the most important of Andros's initiatives. Indeed, the results were equivalent to an incredibly successful mourning war. Hundreds of Susquehannocks found new homes among the Senecas, Cayugas, and Onondagas. Once among the Iroquois, the Susquehannocks influenced their new families and friends to wage wars against former Susquehannock enemies in the south, including the English provinces of Maryland and Virginia, which the Iroquois sporadically raided throughout the 1780s. Moreover, with the absorption of the Susquehannocks, the Five Nations gained legitimate claim to lands in what would become central and western Pennsylvania, territory once inhabited and controlled by the Susquehannocks. It was the beginning of a process by which the Covenant Chain alliance helped transform the Five Nations' imaginary empire from fantasy into reality. Yet no Iroquois nation benefitted more in the early years from the Covenant Chain alliance than the Mohawks, whose resurgence was directly tied to their alliance with Andros. Lastly, the successful resolution of these conflicts, along with the new English alliance, freed the Iroquois to explore new conflicts against the French and their Indian allies in the north and west. Indeed, shortly after the Susquehannock war had ended, Jesuit missionaries noted the Senecas and the other Iroquois were becoming increasing belligerent, as "they talk about nothing but renewing the war ... against the French."[29]

Emboldened by the Covenant Chain and the end of three difficult wars, the Five Nations looked forward to a future full of glory and power. Pro-English leaders were poised to overthrow the pro-French faction in village and league politics, all but ensuring a renewal of war with New France. Yet even as the Mohawks and other pro-English Iroquois reveled in their new found status, the seeds of disappointment were germinating all around them. They would soon discover that their new English allies were hesitant to support any military objectives other than their own, leaving the Five Nations once again overextended, alone, and surrounded by enemies.

5

•

The Longhouse under Siege

The Five Nations began the last decades of the seventeenth century with great prospects for the future. Armed with the Covenant Chain alliance with the English, the Iroquois looked to cast aside the French and gain control over the vast and profitable territories of the Midwest. Those hopes were quickly dashed, however, as the Five Nations' military endeavors came crashing down around them. In the chaos of war, the English proved to be unreliable allies, who were either unable or unwilling to live up to the promises inherent in the Covenant Chain. But it was the Iroquois who suffered the consequences, as the French and their Indian allies brought death and destruction into Iroquoia. The metaphorical longhouse of the Iroquois League was under siege, and by the dawn of the eighteenth century, four of its five fires were on the verge of being snuffed out. Humbled and humiliated, the Iroquois League survived, but only after learning hard lessons about power and alliances in an increasingly European-dominated colonial world.

WAR IN THE MIDWEST

The creation of the Covenant Chain brought the Five Nations, especially the Mohawks, closer to the English, which almost by definition implied that the Iroquois were distancing themselves from the French. Indeed, in the years after Andros and the Mohawks fashioned the Covenant Chain alliance, the Five Nations became increasingly hostile toward New France and its Indian allies. Yet the amorphous political nature of the Iroquois League allowed each Iroquois nation to make war or peace as they saw fit, regardless of what course the rest of the Five Nations pursued. Why then, did all five Iroquois nations turn against the French, rather than just the Mohawks, whose allegiance to the English was strongest? The answer can be found in a series of French transgressions, both real and imagined, that convinced the Iroquois that the French sought political and economic domination over the Five Nations, a threat that prompted a politically unified response and laid the groundwork for the a more centralized political union that many term the Iroquois Confederacy.

"French actions and policy [after the peace of 1667] conflicted with and threatened the security and survival of the Iroquois," historians have concluded; "in the long run, Iroquois hostility was the product of the threats they felt were posed by New France's expansionist policy."[1] Specifically, the French threatened Iroquois security in two important ways during the 1670s. First, the French expanded their trading networks and alliance system into the Midwest, in the process acquiring a host of new Indian trading partners and threatening both the economic and political security of the Five Nations. Second, the physical expansion of New France, represented by the construction of a series of military fortifications and trading posts along the borders of Iroquoia, implied that French intended to cut the Iroquois out of the fur trade and to impose direct military control over the Five Nations. Both actions were part of the rapid growth of New France between 1650 and 1680. In these decades, the population of Canada more than tripled to almost 11,000, the colony became almost completely agriculturally self-sufficient, and French officials and businessmen expanded their fur trading empire and secured new sources of furs. That process began in the 1650s with New France's tentative extension of alliances westward to refugee Hurons (Wyandots) and Ottawas, but expanded by the 1680s into a vast trading network largely centered in the lower Great Lakes region, or what the French came to term the *pays den haut* (upper country).[2]

One aspect of these new alliances that particularly angered the Iroquois was French insistence that the Five Nations cease all warlike activities against the Indian Nations of the Great Lakes and the Midwest, although many of these tribes were hostile to the Iroquois and often attacked the Five Nations. As early as 1670, a Seneca spokesman chastised the French for this apparent double standard:

> For whom does Onnontio [ceremonial name for the French governor] takes us? . . . He is vexed because we go to war, and wishes us to lower out hatchets and leave his allies undisturbed. Who are his allies? How would he have us recognize them when he claims to take under his protection all the peoples discovered by the bearers of God's word [Jesuits] through all these regions; and when everyday, as we learn from our people who escape the cruelty of the stake, they make new discoveries and enter nations that have ever been hostile to us—which, even while receiving notification of peace from Onnontio, set out from their own country to make war upon us, and to come and slay us under our very palisades.[3]

Moreover, the French had been trading arms to their new friends in the *pays den haut* to cement trade alliances. The discovery that the French were actively arming the Ottawas, Ojibwas, Illinois, and other Indian nations greatly troubled the Iroquois, as they were certain these nations would eventually use those guns to kill Iroquois peoples.[4]

An even more significant source of Iroquois resentment toward the French was the construction of several forts along the frontiers of Iroquoia, often situated on lands the Five Nations claimed as hunting territories. These forts were built as part of a generalized French strategy to protect their fur trade, Jesuit missionaries, and future territorial ambitions against competition or encroachment by rival European powers. Indeed, long before the French constructed forts down the Allegheny River to keep English colonists out of the Ohio Country, they built a network of forts to block England's access to the interior of North America. Beginning with the Richelieu River forts erected by Courcelle and Tracy in the mid-1660s, the French eventually built more than 25 forts and fortified trading posts along the upper St. Lawrence watershed and throughout the Great Lakes region. Of these, seven were situated around the easternmost Great Lakes, Erie and Ontario, in close proximity to Iroquoia and on lands the Five Nations believed they held dominion over.[5]

The Five Nations feared that the French were trying to pen them up and deny Iroquois warriors and hunters liberty to go where they pleased. In the 1690s, the French thought about building a new series of forts that would prevent the Iroquois from traveling west or north of Lake Ontario, but this was a by-product of renewed war between the Five Nations and New France. In the 1660s and 1670s, the French were trying to protect their significant investments in the fur trade and prevent their new Indian allies from suffering a fate similar to that of the Hurons. Neither consideration mattered to the Five Nations, who felt threatened by enemy Indians who traveled through Iroquois hunting refuges to trade at the new French posts. Indeed, control over the land where the French built their posts was a central factor in Iroquois discontent. When confronted by Five Nations diplomats, the French let it be known that they had the right to build the posts by virtue of their conquest of the Iroquois in 1666 and their alliances with the remnants of the Hurons, whom the French considered the true stewards of the region. Moreover, the French were displeased that Iroquois hunters traded most of the furs they obtained in the rich lands above Lake Ontario to the English. The Iroquois "do all their hunting, at present, on our allies' lands, which belong in some sort to the French," remarked Governor-General Courcelle in 1671, "The Iroquois, however, trade scarcely with any of us, but carry all their peltries to New Netherland [New York], depriving us thereby of the fruits of our land."[6] The Iroquois angrily denied that the land belonged to the French, reminding Courcelle that the French had fought only the Mohawks in 1666, had in reality conquered no one, and that the Five Nations controlled the lands above Lake Ontario because in the past they had "subdued whole nations of Indians that lived there, and demolished their castles [villages] in so much, that now great oak trees grow where they were built."[7] Neither side saw the other as the legitimate custodian of the lands in question, making the likelihood of a negotiated settlement improbable.[8]

Of the French forts, Fort Frontenac, at the eastern end of Lake Ontario, provoked the greatest concern and reaction among the Five Nations. In 1671, Courcelle scouted out the eastern end of Lake Ontario for a location to erect a fort, but he was recalled to France before he could complete his designs. Two years later, Courcelle's successor, Louis de Baude de Frontenac, selected a location at the eastern tip of Lake Ontario as the site for the fort that would bear his name. Although an Iroquois delegation is reported to have welcomed the construction of the post, the presence of 400 armed Frenchman may have influenced the response of the Iroquois, who had brought their wives and children with them. In addition, other difficulties weighed on the minds of the Five Nations, whose leaders were still divided between those who favored friendship with the French and those who sought accommodation with the English. The Iroquois' wars against the Susquehannocks and Mahicans continued in 1673, and they had been made all the more difficult by the outbreak of war between the English and Dutch. After the Dutch briefly recaptured New York, trade at Albany was again disrupted, leaving the Iroquois, especially the Mohawks, dependent on trade with the French to supply the arms they needed to continue fighting their native enemies. Thus, from a pragmatic standpoint, the Five Nations needed peace with the French in 1673, and thus they did not stand in the way of the establishment of Fort Frontenac, which they called Cataraqui.[9]

As many as 800 Iroquois traded at Fort Frontenac in 1674, demonstrating the Five Nations' dire need for trade goods. Within just a few years, however, the situation changed dramatically. By 1676, the wars against the Susquehannocks and Mahicans essentially were over, the English were firmly in control of New York, and Governor Andros was hinting at promises of aid should the Iroquois decide to strike the French. His words found eager ears among a growing faction of anti-French Iroquois, a group who steadily eroded control of clan, village, and national policies away from the pro-French faction during the 1670s. Moreover, the construction of Fort Niagara in 1676, which dominated the western end of Lake Ontario and sat astride the western door of the Iroquois League, greatly alarmed the Senecas and seemed to verify Iroquois fears that the French meant to surround and destroy the Five Nations. That very year Frontenac was forced to hold a conference with Iroquois leaders where he labored to convince them that the French forts were not a menace, and he urged the Five Nations not to make the mistake of attacking the posts. In the interim, the two French forts on either side of Lake Ontario served as launching points for French expansion into the Midwest, where four more forts were constructed over the next six years.[10]

Despite Frontenac's efforts, many Iroquois were growing hostile to New France. War was coming, if it had not already begun. The cessation of hostilities with the Susquehannocks and Mahicans, as well the Covenant Chain alliance with Andros, afforded the Five Nations an opportunity to focus their attention elsewhere. Although relations with the French in Canada were deteriorating in the late 1670s, the majority of the Iroquois were not ready to strike the French. War with New France's Indian allies in the *pays den haut*, however, was entirely another matter. Of growing concern to the Five Nations were the Illinois peoples, a confederation of a dozen Indian nations with a population of nearly 10,000. The Illinois were rapidly becoming one of the most important new trading partners of the French, and their principal village of Kaskaskias in present-day Illinois grew rapidly in size and importance during the 1670s. Moreover, the Illinois had increasingly sent their hunters farther and farther east after beaver and other furs, eventually extending their reach into territory in the upper Ohio Valley that the Five Nations claimed as their exclusive hunting grounds. At last, the Iroquois could stand no more. In 1680, jealousy of the Midwestern Indians' trade with the French, the desire to protect Iroquois hunting grounds, and fresh calls for mourning war campaigns after new outbreaks of disease combined to start a war.[11]

The exact beginning of the Five Nations' war against the Illinois is unclear, although it likely began in 1676. In June, Onondaga warriors returned with 50 captives from a campaign several hundred miles to the southwest, stopping for a time among the Senecas to torture and kill 13 of their prisoners. Two years later, the Jesuits recorded that an Iroquois war party had been defeated in Illinois country, although few details were given. The war escalated, or perhaps began in earnest, in 1680, when an army of between 500 and 600 Senecas and Onondagas set out to besiege Kaskaskias. Among them were numerous adopted Susquehannocks, eager to prove their worth to the Five Nations in battle. They chose an opportune time to attack. The absence of Iroquois raids for nearly a decade in the Great Lakes region had resulted in increased warfare among the various Algonquian nations, a scenario that worked in the favor of the Senecas and Onondagas, as the majority of Illinois warriors, including those who possessed French flintlock muskets, were away fighting or hunting when the Iroquois attacked Kaskaskias. Several hundred warriors remained, and although they were armed only with bows and arrows, their presence was enough to make the Iroquois wary of an outright attack against the large village. Instead, the Senecas and Onondagas remained on the opposite side of the Illinois River from the town, and the Illinois eventually attacked their camp as a diversion to allow the women and children of the village to retreat during the night. After a brief skirmish, during which a French official was wounded, captured, and subsequently released, the Senecas and Onondagas destroyed the abandoned town, then took up the trail of the departed Illinois. Several miles upriver, the Iroquois came across approximately 700 Illinois who had split off from the main body. The Senecas and Onondagas attacked, killing 30 Illinois and capturing 300 women and children, before heading for home. Not entirely satisfied, the Iroquois made a somewhat dastardly attack on an encampment of Miamis, an Indian nation hostile to the Illinois and friendly to the Five Nations, as they marched through the Ohio Country. They secured few captives, but gained another Algonquian enemy.[12]

The Illinois and other Algonquian nations in the Midwest immediately turned to the French for help, pleading with their trading partners to come to their assistance. Otherwise, in the words of the Ottawas, they were all dead. The French dispatched reinforcements to garrison their forts in the

Great Lakes and sent Rene-Robert, Chevalier de La Salle, to erect Fort St. Louis on a high bluff near the remains of Kaskaskias, which was rebuilt and quickly became a center for coordinating Algonquian strength and a place of safety for refugees. The Miamis took advantage of this haven and quickly relocated to the fort, as did more than 1,000 Shawnees who had been forced out of the Ohio Valley by the Iroquois. The French then settled on a plan to create a grand Algonquian alliance among all the peoples of the *pays den haut*, who together would hold back and perhaps even destroy the Five Nations.[13]

Fortifying the Illinois country and forging a pan-Algonquian alliance took time, and in the interim, the Iroquois again attacked the Illinois. In the early 1680s, Iroquois warriors swept through the Midwest, taking some 700 Illinois people prisoners. According to Jean de Lamberville, a Jesuit missionary among the Onondagas, the Iroquois army killed and ate another 600 Illinois, an episode that if even marginally true indicates that something seriously traumatic must have occurred to trigger such a fanatical action. Sporadic outbreaks of disease among the Five Nations during the 1670s, punctuated by the massive smallpox epidemic of 1679, would seem to indicate that the Five Nations still had a pressing need to replace their dead, making Lamberville's assertion either gross exaggeration or an audacious lie perhaps intended to spur French forces into more concerted action. Moreover, the Iroquois were simultaneously raiding Indian nations in Virginia and Maryland, from whom they took captives, indicating that gathering captives was as important to their military agenda as punishing the Indian allies of New France. Indeed, in 1682, Lamberville himself noted that Five Nations "have strengthened themselves, in this and preceding years, with more than nine hundred men."[14]

Nonetheless, the tide was turning. After 1682, Iroquois warriors raiding French-allied Indians in the Midwest found their enemies well armed, strongly provisioned, and ready for war. In 1683, a large Iroquois army was reported to have suffered several hundred casualties in a battle against warriors from the Ojibwa and Fox nations. Undeterred, an army of 200 Senecas and Cayugas set out to again attack Kaskaskias in early 1684. As they neared the town, the Iroquois waylaid a convoy of French traders headed for the post, taking 14 traders prisoner and confiscating seven canoes full of trade goods, which included a sizeable cache of muskets. The Iroquois released the traders, and despite learning that Kaskaskias was now protected by a fort garrisoned by French soldiers, the Iroquois continued with their attack. Despite being held by a force less than half its number, Fort St. Louis proved too strong for the Senecas and Cayugas, who were driven off after a six-day siege. Word of the attack, but not the outcome, reached Canada in 1684, where the new governor-general, Joseph Antoine Le Febvre de La Barre, quickly organized a combined French and Indian army to punish the Senecas.[15]

La Barre's planned invasion of Seneca country marked a shift in the war between the Five Nations and the Midwestern Indians, as the center of military activity now moved east to Iroquoia itself. Over the next 17 years, the Five Nations would find themselves heavily besieged in their own homeland, although La Barre's invasion never reached the Seneca villages. Determined to punish the Senecas, and perhaps other Iroquois, for their attacks against the Midwestern Indian nations, La Barre pieced together French soldiers, Canadian volunteers, and various allied Indian peoples into an army of more than 1,000 men. When the Iroquois learned of La Barre's invasion, they were duly concerned, and a delegation of Onondagas, Oneidas, and Cayugas under the Onondaga spokesman Otreouti immediately set forth to intercept the French army and seek a peaceful resolution. They probably expected the worst, but fortunately for the Five Nations, La Barre's invasion had quickly turned into a disaster. His troops were wracked by an outbreak of influenza and, owing to poor organization and lengthy supply lines, nearly out of provisions despite having only made it to the southern shore of Lake Ontario. Given these difficulties, La Barre had little choice other than to halt his advance and establish a camp at La Famine, near the eventual location of the English trading post at Oswego, which happened to be in the middle of a swamp.[16]

When Otreouti and his delegation arrived in September, they found not a mighty French military force come to punish them for their wars against the Midwestern Indians, but a sick, weak, and vulnerable force. Not surprisingly, it was the Iroquois, not the French, who dictated terms for peace. La Barre began to chastise the Iroquois for their war against the Illinois, but Otreouti quickly silenced the French governor-general. "I perceive that the Onnontio [La Barre] rages in a camp of sick people," Otreouti pointed out, then quickly warmed to the point. The Onondaga headman declared that "we [the Five Nations] have a power to go where we please, to conduct who we will to the places we resort to, and to buy and sell where we think fit. If your allies are your slaves or children, you may even treat them as such, and rob them of the liberty of entertaining any nation but your own," but the Five Nations would not be treated as such.[17] Otreouti then scolded La Barre for bringing an army to Iroquoia, arguing that the Senecas' actions were not just cause for war between New France and the Five Nations. The French would be allowed to go in peace, the Onondaga leader decided, if they would promise to keep the peace with the Five Nations and to prevent French missionaries from promoting the migration of Catholic Iroquois to the mission towns around Montreal. Given the dismal condition of his army, La Barre had little choice other than to accede to Otreouti's demands. He had recently learned from a Jesuit informant that the Senecas were preparing to ambush his army, almost gleefully looking forward to attacking the French, who they said "have a great desire to be striped, roasted, and eaten."[18] Fearing that his beleagured army would almost certainly be attacked if he refused Otreouti's terms, La Barre agreed to peace, vowed to withdraw French support from the Midwestern Indians, and limped back to Montreal a humbled and defeated man.[19]

Although Otreouti triumphed in his confrontation with La Barre, the Five Nations continued to prepare for war with the French. Jesuits, who pro-English Iroquois considered little more than French spies, were evicted from all nations other than the Onondagas, and even here the fathers would not remain much longer. The Iroquois then met with New York governor Thomas Dongan, who had replaced Andros in 1683, and Lord Francis Howard, lieutenant-governor of Virginia, to make peace with enemies on their southern flank and solicit English assistance against the French. Through the mediation of the Mohawk headman Odianne, the Virginians forgave Iroquois transgressions without demanding reparations, freeing the Five Nations to focus on the impending French invasion. But Dongan promised no direct aid, and instead he manipulated the Covenant Chain to assert English sovereignty over the Five Nations. He declared that the Iroquois could not to trade or negotiate with the French without New York's approval, a provision Odianne and other Mohawk headmen had agreed to previously; but now the Onondagas, Senecas, and Cayugas rejected his assertions and declared their independence to pursue any course of action they chose. If the English would not help fight the French, the western Iroquois nations refused to be bound by English objectives during the coming conflict. In addition, war leaders from four of the Iroquois nations—the Senecas, Cayugas, Onondagas, and Oneidas— met throughout the summer of 1684 at Onondaga to lay the groundwork for united military action against the French. It was the beginning of a process by which war with New France would galvanize the Five Nations into a more centralized political entity, the Iroquois Confederacy. Indeed, in 1686 the English noted that "all the [Five] Nations have been assembled in Onondaga and have kept council" regarding the crisis with the French, which had taken on added importance after Jesuit missionary

Jean de Lamberville informed the Iroquois that the French would attack them that summer.[20] It represented the maturation of Iroquois confederation, a process that had begun in the 1650s and 1660s when Iroquois leaders met an Onondaga not only to console one another but to discuss important issues and develop policies that would guide the entire Iroquois League.[21]

That process culminated in the 1680s, as village leaders from all the Five Nations met more frequently at Onondaga and reached consensus on common concerns that allowed the Iroquois to speak with one voice. During these councils, members of all three major political factions—pro-French, pro-English, and neutralists—reached out to like-minded leaders from other villages and nations, forging cross-national political alliances and laboring to bring the Five Nations under unified policies. But the architects of Iroquois centralization proved to be the neutralists, yet a third political division within the Five Nations, who would become increasingly influential as war with New France became a reality and the English at Albany proved themselves to be erstwhile allies at best. In addition, a new generation of leaders emerged who thought and spoke in more unified terms than their predecessors, pushing forward the process of confederation. As the decade of the 1680s came to a close, these Iroquois leaders continued to meet regularly at Onondaga, struggling for control over an increasingly centralized government as they discussed Iroquois policy toward the French and English. By the 1690s, these confederacy councils were meeting several times a year and were quite contentious, but the work of creating the Iroquois Confederacy was well underway. In 1687, however, the French took actions that ensured they would be the primary topic under consideration.[22]

THE LONGHOUSE UNDER SIEGE

When word of La Barre's conduct at La Famine reached French officials in Europe, the governor-general was quickly recalled. His replacement, Jacques Rene de Brisay de Denonville, arrived in Canada in 1685 with instructions to subjugate the Five Nations. "To secure the quiet of Canada by a firm and solid peace," his instructions read, "the pride of the Iroquois must be humbled, the Illinois and other Indian allies who have been abandoned by Sieur de la Barre must be sustained, and the Iroquois must from the outset be given, by a firm and vigorous policy, to understand that they will have everything to dread if they do not submit."[23] Denonville also was charged with protection of the fur trade, which faced challenges not only from the Five Nations, but also from a new English venture on Hudson Bay. Denonville quickly moved to crush the English outpost in the north and then turned his full attention to the Five Nations. Angered by Iroquois attacks on French traders in the *pays den haut*, concerned by reports that fur traders from Albany were establishing direct trading contacts with Great Lakes Indians, and fearful that the Midwestern Indian nations might agree to a peace deal with the Five Nations independently of New France, Denonville decided to go on the offensive. In his estimation, most, if not all, of his problems could be alleviated by laying waste to the Senecas. The Iroquois would be chastised, Albany traders would be made to respect and fear the threat of French arms, and the Midwestern Indian nations would be awed into obedience by the display of French military power.[24]

In June 1687, Dennonville departed Montreal at the head of more than 2,000 men, including 832 French regular soldiers, more than 1,000 Canadian militia, and 300 Indians, including a large contingent of Christian Iroquois from the mission towns near Montreal. During the march to Iroquoia, the army rendezvoused with 160 French backwoods traders, known as *coureurs de bois* (runners of the woods) and nearly 400 Ottawas, bringing Denonville's total troop strength to more than 2,700 men. The massive army proceeded in good order, with the *coureurs de bois* and Indians leading the way. Near Fort Frontenac, Denonville's troops took prisoner 200 *Iroquois du Nord* and destroyed the villages of Quinte and Ganneious on the northern shore of Lake Ontario. The governor-general then imprisoned a party of Onondagas and Oneidas, who had come to the fort with the Jesuit priest Jacques de Lamberville to treat for peace. Denonville was not yet done. When his troops brought in a Cayuga war party, which had been scouting movements of the French army, Denonville ordered the 36 captives, including their leader Ourehouare, sent to Europe to serve as a slaves on the king's galleys in the Mediterranean Sea.[25]

The first major challenge to Denonville's advance came as the army entered Seneca country, where the lead elements were ambushed by more than 700 Senecas divided into two flanking parties. Approximately 40 French and Indians were killed or wounded, although the Senecas lost as many as 50 men, with a similar number wounded, when Dennonville's main body of troops came up to support the ambushed lead division. Christian Iroquois from Kanawake played an instrumental role in the battle, setting the precedent for increased warfare between Christian and traditional Iroquois in the 1690s. When Denonville reached the site of the Seneca villages, he found them deserted. As the Mohawks 20 years prior, the Senecas retreated, choosing to live and fight another day rather than risk total defeat in defense of their homes and crops. Seneca warriors sought refuge in the forest, while sending their women and children to safety among the Cayugas. The remainder of the Five Nations had sent to Albany for assistance against the invasion, but governor Dongan, while resolving that the Iroquois "ought to be protected and defended by this government," provided no help.[26] Thus unopposed, Denonville's army waged an eight-day campaign against empty houses and defiant corn-fields, destroying the major Seneca towns of Ganondagan and Totiakton, along with two smaller villages. In addition, French troops burned an estimated 350,000 bushels of standing corn and another 50,000 bushels of stored corn.[27]

The winter of 1687–1688 proved bitter for the homeless Senecas, who never rebuilt their major towns and instead dispersed into smaller groups that settled along the Genesee River and among the Finger Lakes. Among the other Iroquois nations, confusion and indecision prevailed. Pro-English Iroquois again requested aid from New York Governor Thomas Dongan, but aside from advice and further twisting of the Covenant Chain, little material aid was forthcoming. "I put them off by giving them powder, lead, arms, and other things fitting and necessary for them," Dongan explained to his superiors in London, "and also by making such propositions as I thought would please them being unwilling actually to engage the French until I knew his Majesty's pleasure."[28] The English would not fight. Other Iroquois leaders, like neutralist Onondaga head-man Otreouti, tried to reach a peace accord with Denonville while keep-ing at bay Dongan's attempts to impose English rule over the Five Nations. Iroquois anger toward the French stemmed as much from the treachery of Denonville at Fort Frontenac as from his destruction of the Seneca towns. As a Mohawk headmen explained to the English at Albany, Denonville "has started an unjust war against all the [Five] Nations … that governor has taken prisoners from all the [Iroquois] nations to the west … therefor the [Five] Nations have desired to revenge the unjust attacks."[29] The peace movement seemed to be gaining momentum in 1688, until a del-egation of Onondaga negotiators was attacked by the duplicitous Wyandot war leader Kondiaronk, who desired war between New France and the Iroquois. Kondiaronk got his wish; after his attack the confederacy coun-cils of the Five Nations adopted a policy of unrestrained war against New France and its allies.[30]

The rage of the Five Nations quickly visited itself on the French and their allies. In late 1687, Iroquois warriors established blockades around

Forts Frontenac and Niagara, cutting off all traffic to and from the posts. French soldiers trapped inside the posts fell ill with scurvy from subsisting only on salted rations, and when spring arrived, a combined 180 soldiers from the two garrisons were dead. By 1689, the French had abandoned both forts. The same year sporadic raids against the French settlements gave way to a massed assault. In August 1689, an army numbering between 1,200 and 1,500 Iroquois descended on the settlement of Lachine on Montreal Island, killing 64 French soldiers, colonists, and allied Indians. More than 90 others were taken prisoner as the Iroquois ransacked and burned 56 of the 77 houses in the settlement. Yet in these and other attacks, the Iroquois suffered heavy casualties while inflicting only minimal damage on the French. Indeed, the arrival of measles and smallpox on ships from France eventually caused a great deal more death and suffering in New France than Iroquois raids.[31]

Even as the Iroquois struck back at New France, word arrived from Europe that war had been declared between England and France. The new rulers of England, William and Mary, had declared war against Louis XIV of France, news that the Five Nations hoped would finally compel the English to honor the Covenant Chain alliance. Pro-English Iroquois leaders such as the Mohawk headman Tahiadoris quickly offered their services against the French, proclaiming that "even if all our people should be ruined and cut in pieces, we will never make peace with them [the French]."[32] The Five Nations' war against France merged with the Anglo-French conflict known in North America as King William's War, but it was a dangerous union for the Iroquois. France and England fought to control the fur trade in North America and sought to bolster their Indian allies in the conflict, yet each also sought to expand its power at the expanse of Indian nations. For the Five Nations, close cooperation with the English would prove dangerous, as colonial officials tried to intertwine the war against France with efforts to demote the Five Nations from partners in the Covenant Chain to subjects of England.[33]

Internal discord in New York over the succession in England allowed the French to take the offensive first. Frontenac had returned to Canada as governor-general, and he badly wanted to attack his old enemies, the Iroquois. Frontenac scrapped plans for a grand attack against Albany, to be coordinated with a naval assault on New York City, in favor of a series of raids against the New York frontier, targeting both English colonists and the Iroquois. In February 1690, a party of more than 200 French and Christian Iroquois from Kanawake struck Schenectady, where French troops had been treated with kindness during the 1666 invasion of

Mohawk country. Those dealings were long forgotten by 1690, as the French and their allies killed 60 people, took 27 others prisoner, and burned the town. Thirty Mohawks who had been visiting the town escaped, or were allowed to escape, thanks to the intervention of the Christian Iroquois and their war leader, Kryn. Other raids struck the New England frontier, eliciting calls for retaliation from Boston to Albany.[34]

The English colonies planned for a grand invasion of Canada, to be coordinated between land and sea forces and featuring a prominent commitment of warriors from the Five Nations; but as often occurs in war, things did not go according to plan. Frontenac tried to neutralize the Iroquois by proposing peace in 1690 and returning the 13 surviving Iroquois who had been enslaved in Europe. But the Iroquois did not trust the French governor-general, and in the summer of 1690, the Onondagas made prisoner a party of French negotiators, all of whom except the leader the Iroquois subjected to the gauntlet, then tortured and burned. That August, 125 Iroquois warriors, primarily Mohawks, joined New York and New England militia under Captain Johannes Schuyler in an attack against the Canadian settlement of La Prairie. The other four nations of the Iroquois could offer little support, as the smallpox that ravaged New France had made its way into their villages as well. Although the mixed English-Iroquois struck its target, killing or capturing 25 French colonists and inflicting heavy property damage, the campaign was poorly managed and far behind schedule, and the primary objective of drawing French strength away from Quebec so that a new England naval squadron could capture the city was not achieved.[35]

A second English-Iroquois campaign in 1691 proved equally ineffective. A total of 80 Mohawks joined 120 New York militia and 66 Mahicans under Peter Schuyler in a second assault on La Prarie. An additional 500 Iroquois were expected to participate in the campaign, but lacking confidence in the English, they failed to appear. More than 40 French colonists died in the attack, but Schuyler's force quickly found itself overmatched and withdrew. The real battle took place on the march home, as the Iroquois and English were forced to fight their way through several ambushes and battles with Canadian militia and French soldiers. Nearly 70 of Schuyler's troops were killed or wounded before they reached the relative safety of Albany. As the Iroquois returned home, the New Yorkers fortified Albany and the outlying settlements in expectation of a French counterattack. The failure of two unified raids left bitter impressions on both the Five Nations and New York, and colonists from the Albany region would not again attempt an offensive during the war.[36]

After the failed Iroquois-English offensives, the war turned against the Five Nations. In December 1691, a Mohawk and Oneida war party returning with captives from a raid in Canada crossed paths with a much larger force of French and Christian Iroquois near Lake Champlain. In all, 15 Mohawks and Oneidas died, including two prominent pro-English war leaders, and another 14 Iroquois were taken prisoner. In March 1692, more than 300 French and allied Indians attacked a hunting party of 50 Senecas, 40 of whom were either killed or captured. Throughout 1692, approximately 800 Ottawas, Illinois, Wyandots, and other western Indians attacked the Iroquois in and around their villages, killing at least 42 people. Yet the deadliest blow fell in February 1693, when more than 600 French soldiers, Canadian militia, and allied Indians destroyed two small Mohawk villages. Most of the Mohawk warriors were out hunting, so the French and their allies faced little opposition as they entered the settlements. The Catholic Iroquois, who extracted promises from the Mohawks that they would join them at Kanawake, prevented a general slaughter, and the French soon moved out with their captives in tow. Four days later, a belated Iroquois-English relief force led by Peter Schuyler managed to overtake the French and Indians as they withdrew, killing or wounding more than 30 French and Indians, and freeing 40 to 50 of the 300 Mohawk prisoners. Still, the damage had been done. A generation after the 1666 invasion destroyed the Mohawk villages, their homes once again lay in ruins.[37]

The mounting losses took a terrible toll on the Five Nations. The Iroquois warrior population had been significantly reduced, especially among the Mohawks, since the beginning of the war. The suffering Iroquois vented much of their frustration at the English, whom they felt were not upholding their end of the alliance in the Covenant Chain, forcing the Five Nations to be bear an unfair portion of the fighting. "You tell us we are one heart, one flesh, and one blood," complained an Iroquois spokesman to the English, "pray let us know the reason why you do not come to our assistance according to your former promise the we may live and die together."[38] New York Governor Benjamin Fletcher was less than conciliatory toward the Iroquois, blaming poor scouting and defense by the Mohawks for the destruction of their villages. Yet his stance was on par with that of other New York leaders. Even under Thomas Dongan, New York had been lax in upholding its end of the Covenant Chain. The English in New York never provided the Five Nations with adequate assistance in war, although that did not stop the continual pressure the colony's leaders put on the Five Nations to accept a subordinate status to England.[39]

It is not surprising, then, that the Five Nations again entertained thoughts of peace with New France. In June 1693, Tarriha, a pro-French Iroquois headman from the Oneida nation, traveled to Quebec to explore the possibility of peace between New France and the Five Nations. His embassy began a two-year process during which pro-French leaders among the Five Nations tried to convince the rest of the Iroquois to make peace with the French. Meanwhile, Peter Schuyler and other English dignitaries lobbied pro-English Iroquois to keep the Five Nations in the fight. Indecision within Iroquois councils prolonged the negotiations, as pro-French, pro-English, and neutralist factions argued with each other. In addition, a potential deal breaking standoff arose when Frontenac announced that he intended to rebuild and re-garrison the French fort at Cataraqui. Few among the Five Nations welcomed the reestablishment of Fort Frontenac, and they sternly reminded the French governor-general of their dislike for the post. "Ononntio your fire shall burn no more at Cataraqui," Iroquois negotiators told Frontenac, "It shall never be kindled again. You did steal that place from us and we quenched the fire with the blood of our children.... We will never suffer you to kindle your fire at Cataraqui."[40]

Nevertheless, the Five Nations were in no position to block Frontenac's plans. By 1696, French officials had lost their patience with Iroquois indecisiveness and terminated the peace process. Believing the Five Nations' talk of peace to be a ploy to delay an invasion of other Iroquois nations, the French punctuated the failure of peace by invading Onondaga in 1696. Frontenac assembled 2,000 French and allied Indians, then pushed into the heart of Iroquoia after restoring Fort Frontenac. As the French army approached, the Onondagas burned their village and retreated. The French finished the job by destroying the Onondagas' fields of standing corn, then moved into Oneida country, where a delegation pleaded with the French to spare their village. The Oneidas had been the most active, and perhaps the most sincere, in pursuing peace with the French from 1694 to 1695, but it did not save them. After the Oneidas pledged to move to Canada so that they might be closer to the French, a detachment of 600 French soldiers burned the Oneida's village and destroyed their fields, justifying their actions by asserting that the Oneidas no longer had need of either, as they would soon be relocated to Canada.[41]

On the heels of the destruction imposed during Frontenac's invasion, the Iroquois received word that the French and English had made peace with one another in England. The Treaty of Ryswick in 1697 resulted in a cessation of hostilities between New France and the English colonies, but it did not end the war between the French and the Iroquois. Instead, the treaty presented yet another challenge to the Iroquois, as the formal end of King Williams' War mandated that the English colonies discontinue their support of the Five Nations' war against Canada. The Iroquois were again without allies, a condition the French and their Indian associates did not fail to exploit. French authorities in Canada encouraged the Great Lakes and Midwestern Indians to attack the Five Nations, presenting powerful incentives in the form of firearms and other trade goods. In the fall of 1697, the Miamis attacked the Senecas, killing 40 and capturing nearly 100 others. In 1699, an even more damaging assualt took place, as a well-armed army of French allied Indians from the west swept through Iroquoia, killing at least 90 Senecas and 70 Onondagas. Losses among the Iroquois were as bad if not worse the next year. In 1701, the French marked their victory over the Iroquois in the west by the unopposed construction of Fort Detroit, a bastion that would become central to the Great Lakes fur trade during the eighteenth century.[42]

The Five Nations' war against the French and their Indian allies, begun by the Senecas in 1680, had been lost. During the 20-year struggle, the Iroquois lost perhaps half of their warrior population, although a figure closer to one-fourth is more likely. The primary villages in four of the five Iroquois nations had been destroyed, as were countless acres of crops brimming with hundreds of thousands of bushels of corn, squash, and beans. Only the Cayugas' villages were spared. On the heels of the loss of homes and crops came the inevitable ravages of hunger and starvation. The Iroquois population, which was estimated at 8,600 during the period, declined by almost 25 percent, with as many as 2,000 people dead, captured, or removed to the Christian mission towns in Canada. It had been a supremely costly war, and "as the century closed, the peoples of the Longhouse faced the greatest political and cultural crisis since the founding of the League."[43]

In response, the Iroquois League found a diplomatic solution that allowed them to retain their autonomy. In 1701, the Five Nations concluded separate but equally important treaties with the French and the English that ended the fighting which had so devastated Iroquoia. These agreements, together often referred to as the "Grand Settlement of 1701," allowed the Iroquois League to avoid complete capitulation to the French and their Indian-allies while simultaneously renewing the Covenant Chain alliance with the English. Reaching this conclusion after years of being pummeled by their French enemies and ignored by their English allies proved no easy task. It was the work of a coalition of Onondaga leaders representing all three political factions within the league: Aradgi, a pro-French headman who secured the Iroquois surrender to the French and their Indian allies in the war; Sadekanaktie, a pro-English leader who soothed English concerns and reaffirmed the Covenant Chain relationship; and Taganissorens, a neutralist who performed the hard work of making two apparently divergent peace agreements mesh together in a unified settlement that allowed the Iroquois League to maintain its autonomy. To appease the English, the Five Nations accepted English political control over their western hunting lands, territory the Iroquois themselves had proven unable to administer during the previous two decades of war with the western Indian nations. The measure likely amounted to little more than show for the Iroquois, but it kept the Covenant Chain in tact even as the Five Nations reached accommodation with the French. The real key to the success of the Grand Settlement, however, was Iroquois acceptance of neutrality, a policy urged by the French and one that the Five Nations now adopted as their guiding principle in all future relations with the French and English. In exchange for peace and trade with the French, the Iroquois vowed to remain uninvolved in any future conflicts between New France and the English colonies. The Iroquois also earned the right to hunt and trade in the west, although the Indian nations of the Great Lakes would not always abide by the deal.[44]

The Grand Settlement was born from desperation. Over the previous two decades of war, the military might of the Five Nations had failed, rival Indian nations had humbled Iroquois warriors, and the French had sowed destruction throughout Iroquoia. But the Five Nations were not conquered. Iroquois leaders used diplomacy to secure what war could not, the continued autonomy of the Iroquois League. That autonomy was now subject to certain conditions imposed by the French and English, but for the most part, the Iroquois continued to maintain control over their territory and freedom of action. But the Iroquois also learned that they occupied a very dangerous position, caught between two aggressive colonial powers who seemed quite content to tear the Five Nations apart in their rivalry to dominate North America. The neutrality that the Iroquois adopted in 1701 was more than a ploy to appease the French; it was a necessity. For the Iroquois League to survive, their only choice was to steer a middle course between the French and the English and hope that they did not find themselves crushed between the two.

6

●

The Long Neutrality

After the Grand Settlement of 1701, the Five Nations began the difficult process of rebuilding the economic, political, and military strength of the Iroquois League. The hardships of the 1680s and 1690s had convinced many Iroquois leaders that only disaster could come from involvement in disputes between the French and the British, as the English were more commonly known in the eighteenth century. To restore themselves to their once powerful position, Iroquois leaders embarked on a policy of neutrality in their dealings with the French and the British, hoping to maintain balance in their relationship with the colonial powers. But neutrality proved to be a difficult strategy. Both the French and the British tried to entangle the Five Nations in their disputes, and various factions and nations within the Iroquois League often gravitated toward one colonial power or the other. Yet the Iroquois managed to secure their place among the colonial powers by pursuing several complementary policies over the first half of the eighteenth century. They established peace with the Great Lakes and Midwestern Indians, found new Indian enemies to satisfy mourning war and other military necessities, and entered into an alliance with Pennsylvania that extended Iroquois authority over other Indian peoples. The Five Nations' avowed neutrality allowed them to pursue these agendas, although the Iroquois did not hesitate to cast aside their neutrality if they saw an opportunity to advance their own interests.[1]

IROQUOIS NEUTRALITY

The Five Nations' neutrality was by no means passive. Pro-French and pro-British factions continued to exert influence over their constituents, and they vied with one another to pull the Five Nations into closer alignment with the colonial powers. Senecas, for example, tended to favor accommodation with the French, as their position at the western end of the Iroquois League left them most vulnerable to attack from New France's Indian allies in the Great Lakes. Mohawks, on the other hand, sought alliance with the British, on whom they depended for trade, and Onondagas wavered back and forth between French and British influence. Yet in time, factionalism gave way to a broad consensus that the Five Nations could prosper only by balancing the two colonial powers against one another, while avoiding becoming too dependent on either. Thus, "the fragile agreement to stand aloof from Anglo-French disputes grew into a robust consensus that everything could be gained by playing off one European group against the other and preventing either from gaining preeminence."[2]

Almost immediately after the Grand Settlement of 1701, both the French and the British began to test the limits of Iroquois neutrality. From their new post at Detroit, the French actively encouraged the Great Lakes and Midwestern Indians to relocate closer to French outposts, leading numerous Indian nations to settle on lands precariously close to the Five Nations. The Mississaugas, in particular, menaced the Iroquois homeland by occupying territory along the northern shore of Lake Ontario that had once been the preserve of the Hurons and other Iroquoian speakers, and more recently had been home to the villages of the *Iroquois du Nord.* The migrations of the Great Lakes and Midwestern Indians posed a threat to hunting and trading rights the Iroquois had obtained from the treaties at Albany and Montreal, not to mention an outright military threat against the Five Nations. The number of warriors in these nations was far greater than those of the Iroquois, and although they were technically at peace with the Five Nations, the long history of bitter enmity between the two peoples made the renewal of war a strong possibility. Not surprisingly, Iroquois leaders asked the French to guarantee the terms of the Grand Settlement, specifically the peace between all of New France's Indians allies. But in 1702, the outbreak of the War of the Spanish Succession, known in the British colonies as Queen Anne's War, severely complicated matters. Indeed, with war once again directing French-British relations, the French could not be expected to restrain their Indian allies, and instead the French enouraged them to attack the British. In August 1703, the new governor-general of France, Philippe de Rigaud, marquis de Vaudreuil, sent an army of 500 Abenakis against British settlements on the Maine frontier. The next year, 50 Canadians and 200 French-allied Indians attacked Deerfield, Massachusetts, burning half the town and killing or capturing nearly 60 percent of the 250 residents.[3]

These raids, and others like them, put the Five Nations in a difficult position. If the French-allied Indians attacked Albany, it was likely that the Iroquois would be drawn into the conflict. Even more problematic was the continued hostility of the Great Lakes and Midwestern Indians toward the Iroquois. Miami warriors ambushed a Seneca hunting party near the Great Lakes during the spring of 1704, and other Midwestern Indians killed five Oneidas, including a headman. Calls for revenge had many Oneidas and some Senecas on the brink of war as Iroquois leaders scrambled to maintain the fragile peace. The situation became even more critical when a large party of Ottawas attacked a pro-French Seneca village near Fort Frontenac, taking 30 prisoners before falling on an Onondaga diplomatic delegation headed to a meeting with Vaudreuil. The French governor worked diligently to defuse the situation, compelling the Ottawas to return their Seneca prisoners, but the Iroquois had learned a great deal about the precarious nature of their peace settlement. "Remember, Father, the promise which was given us at the peace, that if any of your children struck another, we would form a union in order to exterminate the nation which might have struck the blow," angry Iroquois orators reminded Vaudreuil, "nevertheless we have been repeatedly struck without it appearing that our father has taken our part; had we acted as the Outtauois [Ottawas] has done, our father would soon have resented it."[4]

Keeping the Great Lakes and Midwestern Indian nations from attacking Iroquoia was vitally important to Iroquois aspirations to reclaim their power and position in northeastern North America, but if the French could not restrain their Indian allies, then the Five Nations would have to look elsewhere for assistance. The British offered no help. Relations between the Iroquois and recently appointed New York Governor Edward Hyde, Viscount Cornbury, had not gotten off to a good start, as Cornbury made little attempt to adopt the diplomatic protocols necessary to ensure smooth Indian relations. In addition, the efforts of the new administration to limit and control the fur trade at Albany produced tensions, not only with the Iroquois but with colonial traders who thought their livelihood was being threatened. Yet despite Cornbury's lack of decorum and the strong-arm economic policies of his administration, the answer to the Five Nations' western dilemma lay in trade. Vaudreuil could not control the western Indian nations and the British were unwilling or unable to protect the Iroquois, which left only the Five Nations to act on their own behalf.[5]

The Iroquois turned to an economic strategy. They used trade to entice the Great Lakes and Midwestern Indians to make a separate peace with the Five Nations, and the enticement was the cheaper and more plentiful trade goods available at Albany. Since the 1680s, British officials in New York had encouraged the Five Nations to allow western Indian nations to travel through Iroquoia to trade at Albany, but the Iroquois refused, not only because they were at war with these Indian peoples but because they recognized that the blind ambition of the British traders might cut the Iroquois out of the economic picture all together. In the years after 1701, however, the Five Nations came to the conclusion that peace with the French-allied Indians to their west could be established only on economic grounds. The violence of 1704 reinforced this position, and during the next six years Iroquois negotiators worked to secure a new arrangement with the western tribes based on access to trade at Albany. As the western Indians and the Five Nations reached agreements that would allow Great Lakes Indians to travel through Iroquoia to trade at Albany, British traders proved eager to reach this new market. Yet the arrangement clearly was tailored to meet the security needs of the Five Nations. Before being allowed passage through Iroquoia, the Iroquois mandated that each of the western Indian nations had to conclude a formal peace treaty with the Five Nations, guaranteeing the Iroquois the right to hunt and travel throughout the Great Lakes and the Ohio Country in peace. Even then, only Iroquois or other appointed guides would be allowed to lead the westerners to Albany, serving also as peacekeepers should any trouble arise as these former enemies passed by and through Iroquois villages. The arrangement had a fair number of setbacks, but by 1709, the British were reporting a brisk trade at Albany with large numbers of Ottawas, Miamis, Wyandots, and Mississaugas.[6]

The new trade arrangements brought much-needed security to the Five Nations. By establishing themselves as middlemen in the Albany-based trade with the Great Lakes and Midwestern Indian nations, the Five Nations ensured that both the British and their new Indian customers needed good relations with the Iroquois to benefit economically. Thus, the new arrangement benefitted all parties involved, except the French, who viewed Iroquois actions as thinly disguised economic warfare. Indeed, the results were dramatic, as the French recorded that only 60 Indians came from the west to trade at Montreal in 1708, a figure drastically lower than usual. In response, French officials in Canada launched a diplomatic offensive against the Five Nations in an effort to induce the Iroquois to redirect the western trade to Montreal. Although the French lavished the Iroquois with gifts and worked to undermine the British traders at Albany, the effort failed to produce results, except perhaps among the Senecas, whose vulnerable position in western Iroquoia caused them to be more sympathetic to French requests. Still, even the Senecas would not agree to an outrageous French demand to kill Great Lakes and Midwestern Indians so that they would no longer seek to trade at Albany. Any such action would mean war, which was precisely what the Five Nations' economic strategy had been devised to prevent. Frustrated and desperate, the French then tried to undermine the new trade networks by murdering Alexander Montour, a half-blood Mohawk who was instrumental in leading parties of western Indians to trade at Albany.[7]

Rising Iroquois tensions with the French soon collided with shifting patterns of conflict in Queen Anne's War. The British government had placed a new colonial administration in New York, and the mother country had charged the colony with organizing the joint British-Indian conquest of New France. The plan called for the British navy to push up the St. Lawrence River while colonial land forces, including the Iroquois, invaded Canada from New York and New England. In May 1709, two British agents from Albany, Johannes and Abraham Schuyler, arrived at Onondaga to solicit the support of the Five Nations for the invasion of Canada. The overtures came at an opportune time, as resentment of the French was running high in Iroquoia after the murder of Montour. Despite the apparent wisdom of maintaining neutrality, many Iroquois were ready to strike a blow at the French. At Onondaga, Jesuit missionaries were asked to leave, after which the Iroquois burned their chapel. By midsummer of 1709, the majority of the Five Nations accepted the British call to war, pledging an army that would include almost every Mohawk warrior, two-thirds of the Cayugas and Oneidas, and a quarter of the Onondagas. The Senecas refused to participate, although they allowed British representatives to live with them in their villages during the campaign to ensure that they remained neutral during the fighting.[8]

Keeping a careful eye on the Senecas proved to be unnecessary, as the planned invasion never reached Canadian soil. An army of 1,500 American militia, including troops from New York, Connecticut, and New Jersey, and nearly 500 Iroquois warriors marched north from Albany and established camp near Wood Creek, along the southern end of Lake Champlain. There they remained through the summer and into the fall, awaiting word that the British fleet was ready to begin operations against Canada. That news never came, as the ships and sailors originally intended for the assault on Canada were diverted by the British government to lend assistance in fighting along the Iberian Peninsula in Europe. As the army sat at Wood Creek, provisions ran low, disease infested the camp, and desertions finally became so severe that the expedition utterly collapsed.[9]

The British were embarrassed by the failure of the expedition, and warriors from the Five Nations returned home disgusted with British incompetence. But more important, the Iroquois feared that the French would seek revenge for their support of the aborted British invasion. Divisions within the confederacy and within each nation had prevented many of the promised warriors from turning out for the campaign, but there was enough Iroquois presence to possibly draw a harsh rebuke from Canada. Seeking to head off any potential reprisals from New France, the Onondagas and Mohawks sent separate delegations to Governor Vaudreuil to seek forgiveness for their part in the affair and to reaffirm Iroquois neutrality. Iroquois spokesmen explained that only a handful of reckless young warriors had headed the British call to arms, and their actions did not represent the sentiments of the Iroquois League as a whole. Governor Vaudreuil did not necessarily agree with their assessment, but in the interests of peace he accepted the Iroquois apologies, although not without first issuing a stern warning that similar actions in the future would meet with a military response. Iroquois leaders understood the threat, and Onondaga speakers reminded their fellow members of the Five Nations that they lay "between two powerful nations each able to exterminate them and both interested in doing so when they no longer needed their help."[10]

Maintaining neutrality, however, proved difficult for many Iroquois. In 1710, the British again approached the Five Nations seeking support for another invasion of Canada. The Iroquois were dubious, but eventually three pro-British Mohawk chiefs agreed to accompany a New York delegation to England to secure royal funding for another attack on New France. One of the Mohawks was Theyanoguin, a young headman known to the British as Hendrick, who would become an extremely influential pro-British voice among the Iroquois. The Mohawks were presented to the queen, sat for portraits, and given the grand tour of London high society. They returned to Iroquoia convinced that the British had the might and the means to conquer Canada and drive off the French once and for all. Other factors were also at work that tipped Iroquois sentiment toward favoring war against New France. In the spring of 1711, the French began construction of a blockhouse at Onondaga without Iroquois permission. The measure, which may have been motivated by continued French anger over western Indians trading at Albany, was clearly designed to demonstrate that the French held power in Iroquoia. The blockhouse was never completed, however, as the Onondagas invited the British at Albany to send troops to chase away the French and tear down the incomplete structure. The Five Nations had neatly avoided open conflict with the French over the issue, but by June 1711, Iroquois leaders were petitioning New York officials for "powder to defend ourselves against the common enemy."[11]

That summer more than 600 Iroquois warriors participated in a much larger and better organized British campaign against Canada. Unlike 1609, this time the largest contingent of Five Nations warriors was provided by the Senecas, who now seemed as convinced as their brethren that the British would destroy the French. Placing their own self-interest ahead of pro-French sympathies, the Senecas chose to join what appeared to be the winning side, but things again did not go as planned. An impressive British fleet, boasting 14 ships of the line and more than 30 transports, left Boston with 5,300 soldiers to strike at Quebec. The lead elements of the fleet ran aground after becoming lost in heavy fog in the Gulf of St. Lawrence, resulting in the loss of 9 ships and more than 700 men. Despite having more than 50 ships and more than 4,000 men remaining, the British aborted the invasion. Meanwhile, Iroquois warriors again advanced with an army of more than 2,000 American colonists to Wood Creek, where they awaited word from the British fleet to begin the land invasion. When word of the fleet's withdrawal reached the army, the expedition collapsed, leaving a furious British commander to tear off his wig and kick it in frustration.[12]

The Iroquois were again disappointed by British failures and fearful of French reprisal. As an Iroquois spokesman told the British, "having now twice failed in their designs against Canada in conjunction with the British they were ashamed and must cover their faces, and they expected that they must meet with their first punishment."[13] Fortunately for the Five Nations, French officials in Canada were disposed toward peace with the Iroquois, despite Governor Vaudreuil's earlier threats. As 1711 drew to a close, Vaudreuil accepted the apologies of individual Iroquois delegations from each of the Five Nations that came to Canada to seek pardon. Perhaps Vaudreuil recognized how close the British had come to conquering Canada and did not want to alienate the Iroquois Confederacy while Queen Anne's War still raged. By 1713, however, the war was over; and the failure of British military endeavors, combined with Iroquois-British disputes over the price of gunpowder and other trade goods, led to a quick resumption of neutrality politics among most of the Five Nations. Only the Mohawks remained firmly in the British orbit, as Theyanoguin and other pro-British Mohawk leaders welcomed the construction of a fort and the presence of Protestant missionaries in their territory.[14]

Relatively calm relations between the two colonial powers over the next 30 years would allow the seeds of Iroquois neutrality to germinate, and leaders of the Five Nations engineered their policy judiciously by making frequent visits to both Montreal and Albany to maintain the fruits of peace and balance. Both the French and British used the lull in their mutual antagonism to impinge on Iroquois power and prerogatives. When the Iroquois continued and even expanded their efforts to recruit the western Indian nations to trade at Albany in the 1720s, both the French and British moved to cut the Iroquois out of the western trade altogether. The French took the most aggressive step, rebuilding Fort Niagara at the western end of Lake Ontario and constructing two smaller satellite posts at Toronto and Quinte on the northern shore of the lake. Together the posts blocked the primary route by which the Great Lakes Indians reached Iroquoia, where they were met by their Iroquois guides and taken to Albany. Moreover, the French hoped to provision and trade with the Great Lakes Indians from these posts, thereby eliminating their need to travel farther east. By reestablishing Fort Niagara, however, the French had technically occupied Seneca territory. Although the French had obtained a dubious and highly suspect agreement from certain pro-French Senecas to build the fort, the majority of the Senecas protested against the fort, which they believed would "encroach on the Five Nations to hinder them of their hunting and debar them of the advantages they should reap by a free passage of the far Indians through their castles."[15] The British followed a similar plan in seeking to eliminate Iroquois management of the western Indian trade. In 1724, New York colonists began improving transportation routes to and from Oswego on the south shore of Lake Ontario. The British then built a trading post at Oswego, hoping to induce the Great Lakes Indians to bypass the inlet at Irondequoit (near Rochester, New York), which served as the primary location where trade convoys left Lake Ontario and traveled overland to the Seneca villages to obtain escorts through Iroquoia to Albany. Soon the bulk of commerce with the western Indians shifted to the new post at Oswego, ensuring higher profits for British traders by undermining the Iroquois' position as middlemen in the trade.[16]

The aggressive measures taken by the French and British at Niagara and Oswego revealed the perils of Iroquois neutrality. The Six Nations had kept their homeland free of violence for more than a generation, but they were still losing control over their territory. In earlier times, the Iroquois were respected by the colonial powers because of the threat and fear of Iroquois military force, but now neutrality betrayed their inability to militarily ward off the increasing pressure of European colonial expansion. In short, the Iroquois League was losing its autonomy as the French and British increasingly came to view their positions as superior to that of the Iroquois. This shift in power status was demonstrated when the Iroquois League protested the construction of both posts. "You appear to me on both sides so full of jealousy, the one against the other, that I have reason to believe you are inclined to come to blows," an Iroquois headmen lectured both the French and British about the forts, "I therefore interpose myself between you to put a stop to the impetuosity of your ill temper; . . . reflect, and remember that you are on soil of which we are the masters." But Iroquois warnings fell on deaf ears. During the late 1720s, the French expanded Fort Niagara into an imposing stone citadel and the British fortified Oswego to house troops. The forts were there to stay.

THE WARRIORS' TRAIL

Although the Iroquois League struggled with the implications of its neutrality policy, warfare against other Indian nations remained a central part of life for the Five Nations. The need to replace population losses and the desire of young men to prove themselves as warriors were important considerations. The Five Nations knew that they still very much needed enemies, but the lessons learned during the bitter defeats of the 1680s and 1690s produced a revised Iroquois military strategy. The destruction of Iroquois homes and agricultural fields had led to great hardships, and if the Five Nations were to rebuild themselves socially and demographically, future wars had to be waged in a manner that would not threaten the security of Iroquois daily life. This meant that new Indian enemies had to be found who could fulfill the needs of the Five Nations' mourning war traditions and provide outlets for the martial aspirations of young men, but who could not easily strike back at their Iroquois tormentors. Fortunately for the Five Nations, such enemies were readily available in the form of Indian peoples living far to the south along the western reaches of Virginia and the Carolinas, nations with whom the Iroquois had warred sporadically before 1700, but who now became the focus of Iroquois military activity.[17]

Iroquois warfare against southern Indians—particularly the Catawbas and Cherokees, whom the Five Nations called "flatheads" because of their practice of binding bags of sands to the foreheads of infants to flatten their skulls and widen their faces—began sometime before 1700. Yet the conflict intensified after the Grand Settlement of 1701, as Iroquois warriors increasingly traveled south along the warrior's trail, a route that paralleled the Appalachian Mountains, in search of distant enemies to satisfy mourning war traditions. The exact origins of the war with the southern Indian nations is unclear, although colonial officials in New York and the southern colonies noted by 1715 that the Iroquois and the southern Indians had long been at war. Their enmity perhaps linked back to the incorporation of the Susquehannocks into the Iroquois League in the 1670s, as the Susquehannocks were bitter enemies of numerous Indian nations in southwestern Virginia and western North Carolina. Or perhaps the wars began as a result of the expansion of Iroquois raids to new horizons. In 1662, Jesuits recorded that Iroquois war parties were "pushing their way further down toward the South, without well knowing against whom they bear a grudge, seeking they know not whom, and declaring war before they have any enemies."[18] Regardless of when the war began, before 1700 it was a sporadic conflict, motivated in part by continued mourning war needs and the desire to pillage and plunder the southerners' trade goods. Indeed, in 1682, Iroquois warriors, many of whom were former Susquehannocks, raided Indians near the mountains of southwestern Virginia, obtaining 35 captives and harassing them so badly that they were unable to plant or harvest their corn crop that year.[19]

Iroquois raids in the south declined over the next two decades as the French and their Indian allies invaded Iroquoia, but by 1701, the war in the south seems to have had resumed full-scale. That year an explorer and surveyor named John Lawson traveled through the western Carolinas where he found graves of Indians killed by the Iroquois, witnessed people fortifying their villages against future Iroquois raids, and reported that Indians everywhere were apprehensive about being attacked by invaders from the north. In turn, southern Indian nations obtained firearms from British traders and prepared to defend themselves or even strike back. In 1704, a war party of 40 southern Indians appeared along the upper Potomac River, where they declared to observers that they knew their enemies to be Senecas, a common term for all Five Nations Iroquois, and that "they were resolved to be revenged, and [to] that end three nations had joined and would shortly come up and will destroy or be destroyed by them."[20] Despite their boasting, there is no evidence that the southern

Indians struck directly at Iroquoia, nor is it likely that they could have forged a broad enough alliance to do so, as many southern nations, especially the Cherokees, lacked a central authority capable of championing coordinated military action. And that made them the preferred enemy of the moment, because the southern Indians "fit Iroquois needs admirably: small enough in size and far enough away to make massive retaliation upon Iroquoia unlikely, stubborn enough to resist peace overtures, they were the ideal antagonist."[21]

Additional considerations may also have led to increased Iroquois raiding in the south after 1701. Although the Five Nations' fragile peace with the western Indians allowed the Iroquois to serve as intermediaries in the growing fur trade between Albany and the Great Lakes, the Iroquois themselves may have been forced to come south in search of furs or deerskins to trade directly with the British. Indeed, worried Virginia traders complained that the Iroquois, if left unchecked, would soon "get the whole trade from our neighboring and tributary Indians."[22] Additionally, the French may have encouraged the Five Nations to attack southern Indian nations allied to the British in an effort to force southern tribes to trade with the French in Louisiana. The government of New France had grown increasingly concerned with British economic expansion in the south, and the French hoped to block further British encroachment into their trading sphere. In addition, the French hoped that prolonged and difficult Indian wars along the southern British frontier would make it impossible for the British colonies to consolidate control of their western borders and expand their colonies toward the Mississippi Valley. In June 1700, French officials at Detroit convinced several Great Lakes Indian nations to strike the southern Indians, and by 1701, warriors from the Five Nations had joined in the attacks. Perhaps the Iroquois believed that raiding the southern Indians would earn them good standing with New France and the French-allied Great Lakes Indians, thus protecting Iroquoia from potential attacks from either. Indeed, the Five Nations, still badly battered after the disasters of the 1680s and 1690s, needed peace with New France and the Great Lakes Indians in order to survive. In addition, the Five Nations could expect to obtain powder, shot, food, and other much needed presents from the French in exchange for waging war against the southern Indian nations.[23]

The British were well aware of the situation, and they labored with little success to keep the Five Nations out of the struggle for the southern frontier. The Five Nations' policy of neutrality demanded balance in their dealings with the two European colonial powers, and attacking

British-allied tribes in the south countered the Iroquois' role in cutting the French out of the Great Lakes Indian trade. Yet balance was less important than self-interest. When the British recruited among the Five Nations for the two failed invasions of New France in 1709 and 1711, the Iroquois suspended their hostilities against the southern Indians, even asking British officials at Albany to assist in forging peace. As long as it appeared the British would conquer Canada, the Five Nations set aside their policies of neutrality and balance, but after the invasions failed to subdue Canada, the Iroquois resumed their hostilities against the southern Indians in an effort to placate the French. Through it all, however, a genuine enmity seems to have developed between the Five Nations and their southern enemies. In 1710, a Seneca leader informed British authorities that "when I think of the brave warriors that have been slain by the Flatheads, I can govern myself no longer. The hatred I bare to the Flatheads can never be forgiven."[24]

Iroquois relations with at least one group of southern Indians took a different path. In 1710, a group of Tuscaroras came north to ask the Five Nations for peace, even offering to relocate to the Susquehanna Valley and live under Iroquois supervision. The Tuscaroras were an Iroquoian-speaking people living in the northern reaches of what is now central North Carolina. By 1700, the Tuscaroras had been engaged in trade with Virginia and other southern colonies for nearly 50 years; but the steady encroachment of North Carolina colonists onto their lands, along with the kidnaping of Tuscarora people by the colonists, who sold them into slavery in the Carribean, had forced the Tuscaroras to the brink of desperation. In September 1711, the Lower Tuscaroras, those closest to the North Carolina settlements, banded together with several smaller Indian nations to attack North Carolina. The allied Indians captured and killed Carolina Surveyor General John Lawson, then fell upon the Carolina settlements along the Neuse and Pamlico Rivers. The South Carolina government, seizing an opportunity to improve its trade relations with Indians on its western frontier—who were traditional enemies of the Tuscaroras—organized two joint colonial-Indian campaigns against the Tuscaroras. The expeditions ransacked Tuscarora villages, including those of the Upper Tuscaroras who had taken no part in the attacks against North Carolina. Hundreds of Tuscaroras were killed, and many more were captured and taken to the slave markets at Charles Town.[25]

The Five Nations had only a peripheral role in the Tuscarora War. Before 1710, the Tuscaroras had been among the southern Indian nations whom Iroquois warriors attacked during their raids in the south. Susquehannocks living among the Iroquois, along with the Susquehannock community at Conestoga that was theoretically under Iroquois control, had been raiding the Upper Tuscaroras since the 1670s as part of their continued war against Indians affiliated with Virginia. Yet in 1710, the Five Nations accepted the Tuscaroras' peace initiative. During a council with the Tuscaroras and other Indian nations at Conestoga in Pennsylvania, an Onondaga sachem proclaimed that peace now existed between the Iroquois, their affiliated Indian nations, and the Tuscaroras, adding that "none of the young people here should go to war against that nation [Tuscaroras]."[26] Some historians have argued that the Five Nations, under pressure from the French after their support of the failed British invasions of Canada during Queen Anne's War, also used the conference proceedings to urge the Tuscaroras to attack the colonial settlements in North Carolina. Yet it is more likely that the Tuscaroras made peace with the Five Nations a precondition for their war with the British, as two years later the Tuscaroras asked the Five Nations for military assistance against their enemies from South Carolina. In any case, Iroquois assistance, if there was any at all, came too late to prevent the destruction of the Tuscarora villages.[27]

As a result, the Iroquois accepted the Tuscaroras' proposal to relocate north, extending survivors of the southern Indian nation an invitation to join the Iroquois League. British authorities tried to block the union, fearing the effect that the incorporation of such a large group of anti-British Indians would have on Iroquois-British relations. The Five Nations ignored British protests, however, recognizing that they had now had a rare opportunity to strengthen the Iroquois League through the peaceful adoption of a fellow Iroquoian nation. As such, Iroquois leaders beseeched the British to "have compassion upon them [Tuscaroras]. The English have got the upper hand of them; they have abandoned their castles and are scattered hither and thither.... we request our brother Corlaer [Governor of New York] to act as mediator between the English of Carolina and the Tuscaroras, that they may no longer be hunted down, and we assure that we will oblige them not to do the English any more harm."[28] After the war, between 1,500 and 2,000 Tuscaroras migrated north and settled either among the Oneidas or at various locations in the Susquehanna River watershed. According to the Onondaga headman Teganissorens, the Tuscaroras would now "shelter themselves among the Five Nations ... as our children who shall obey our commands and live peacefully and orderly."[29] Indeed, by the 1720s, the Tuscaroras had become the sixth nation of the Iroquois League, joining the Oneidas and Cayugas as junior partners in the union, although the Tuscaroras were not allowed to send representatives to the central Iroquois council, nor could they vote in matters of importance to all members of the League.[30]

The Tuscaroras were not the only southern Indians to find protection and security among the now Six Nations during the first half of the eighteenth century. During the 1710s and 1720s, the Iroquois adopted numerous groups of refugee Indians. Most were not taken as captives in war, but rather adopted peacefully. Groups of Shawnees, Delawares, Naticokes, Conoys, and others, fleeing increased colonial pressures or war with British-allied Indians, accepted Iroquois guidance and relocated to the Susquehanna Valley, where they became subject to an evolving Iroquois-Pennsylvania alliance. In return for the protection of the Six Nations and security against British colonial encroachment, these refugees came to comprise a buffer zone protecting the southern flank of Iroquoia, lending their manpower to Iroquois wars against the southern Indians and forming an impediment against any counterattacks; but at best it was a marriage of convenience that would not last long. By the 1730s, the Iroquois would begin to sell the Susquehanna lands to Pennsylvania, forcing many of these refugees to again relocate to the Ohio Country, where they would become implacable foes of the Six Nations.[31]

For most southern Indian nations, particularly the Catawbas, war remained the primary form of interaction with the Iroquois. Renewed conflict came in 1715, when several southern Indian nations joined together and attacked South Carolina in what became known as the Yamasee War. Like the Tuscaroras five years earlier, the southern Indians were responding to the loss of their lands and what they considered unfair treatment by British colonists. With their former trading allies now in arms against them, British authorities reversed 15 years of policy and encouraged the Iroquois to attack the southern Indian nations. The Six Nations responded that they would consider the proposal, but only if the British agreed to finance the war. During a conference at Albany in 1715, New York governor Robert Hunter cemented the deal, presenting the Six Nations with gifts of gunpowder and ammunition, which he hoped the Iroquois would put to good use against "some Indians in the neighborhood of his Majesty's good subjects, our brethren of Carolina."[32] The Mohawks embraced the call to arms, destroying a Cheraw Indian village in September 1715. Mohawk warriors remained active in the south over the next year, inflicting casualties that helped bring the southern Indians to the negotiating table. Indeed, South Carolina officials surveying the military situation along the Catawba River reported that "the Mohawks have been very hard upon them [the southern Indians] of late, and they are almost starved."[33]

Iroquois warriors may have helped the British win the Yamasee War, but they did so for their own reasons, many of which did not align neatly with British designs. By 1717, British authorities had decided that the southern Indians had been suitably chastised, and they tried to arrange a peace conference near Fort Christiana, Virginia. During the negotiations, a party of Senecas snuck into the camp just before dawn, killed five unarmed Catawbas, wounded two others, and took several prisoners. The British were furious and Governor Hunter quickly ordered the Iroquois to cease their attacks on the southern Indians. The Iroquois refused, citing their hatred of the Catawbas. Pressure from the French to maintain the war against the southern Indian nations also factored into the Iroquois decision, as French envoys had distributed presents among the Iroquois in 1717 as incentives to maintain the war. Among the most active French agents was Louis-Thomas Chabert de Joncaire, a former captive of the Senecas who maintained a good deal of influence with the westernmost Iroquois nation. It is was not mere coincidence that the Senecas violently disrupted the peace conference at Fort Christiana shortly after having been visited by Joncaire.[34]

The Iroquois attack on the Catawbas at Fort Christiana led to increased hostilities between the Six Nations and their southern enemies over the next several decades. Precise details of the war are scarce, as most altercations occurred beyond the view of British or European witnesses. What is more clear, however, is that the Catawbas often gave as good as they got. As they raided the southern Indian nations, Iroquois warriors developed a strategy in which they preferred to attack hunting camps, solitary travelers, or villages where the men were currently absent. The Catawbas countered by organizing strike forces that could quickly pursue and punish their Iroquois tormentors. The best recorded example occurred during the spring of 1729, when 100 Oneidas attacked a Catawba town while its men were away from their homes. The Catawbas quickly organized a party of 200 warriors to give chase. They overtook the Iroquois and a furious battled ensued. At the start of the second day, the Catawbas offered to discuss terms for a peaceful conclusion, but then treacherously killed the Oneidas sent to discuss peace. The Oneidas had little choice other than to surrender after 59 warriors were killed, including the famed war leader Currundawawnah. This episode was a famous, but by no means isolated, incident. In May 1745, Pennsylvania Indian agent Conrad Weiser crossed paths with an Onondaga warrior returning home from a raid against the Catawbas. Weiser reported that the Onondaga man "has lost everything but his life. He had no shoes, no stockings, no shirt, no gun, no hatchet, no fire-flint, no knife—nothing but an old torn blanket and some rags." Similarly, Virginia officials noted that the Catawbas "are generally victors over the parties of the Six Nations sent to war with them, being in their phrase great warriors."[35]

Still, Catawba victories did not stem the attacks flowing south out of Iroquoia. On the contrary, if anything Catawba victories stiffened the resolve of the Iroquois to rout their southern enemies, whom they viewed as treacherous and deceitful. Throughout the long conflict, British officials periodically tried to intervene to mediate a settlement, but they had little success. Indeed, the Iroquois informed the British that their war against the Catawbas "will last until the end of the world, for they molest us and speak contemptuously of us, which our warriors will not bear."[36] Yet by 1740, the war had begun to turn against the Catawbas, largely as a result of factors beyond their control. Large numbers of Shawnees, whom Pennsylvania authorities had managed to keep mainly out of the Catawba war, left the Susquehanna River in the late 1730s and early 1740s for new homes in the Ohio Country, from which they renewed their attacks on the Catawbas without Pennsylvania interference. At the same time, the French, sensing that another war with England was not far off, stepped up their campaign to influence Indian nations in their trading orbit to attack and harass Indians allied to the British, including the Catawbas. Perhaps most devastating was a peace agreement reached between the Six Nations and the Cherokees in 1742. After concluding peace with the Iroqouis, the Cherokees allowed Iroquois warriors to use their lands and villages as staging grounds for their assaults on the Catawba River valley. The British had long sought to end the Iroquois-Cherokee conflict, but it is unlikely that they anticipated that the Cherokees would facilitate Iroquois attacks on the Catawbas. Rounding out the list of troubles for the Catawbas was epidemic disease, which decimated southern Indian populations during the 1730s.[37]

All of these factors combined to give the military edge back to the Six Nations, who once again began to win more battles with the Catawbas than they lost. The shift in the war also marked renewed British efforts to mediate a peace agreement, as the British needed the Catawbas as a brace against French-allied Indians in the south. Throughout the late 1730s and early 1740s, British authorities in New York and Pennsylvania tried to convince the Six Nations to come to peace with the Catawbas. They failed. Occasionally, an Iroquois sachem from one or another of the Six Nations would promise to call off the war, but the promises never bound all of the Iroquois League, allowing one or more Iroquois nations to continue fighting. Moreover, continued intrigue by the French ensured that the Senecas, whose lands were the easiest target of New France's Great Lakes Indian allies, would remain on the warpath in an effort to maintain good relations with the French. Yet as the 1740s wore on, the prospects of peace increased. In 1751, South Carolina Governor James Glenn managed to convince the influential Catawba leader Hagler and five other Catawbas to travel to New York to discuss peace with the Six Nations. Those discussions eventually produced a cease-fire, although like the furtive peace initiatives that preceded the 1751 meeting, the agreement would not long hold back Iroquois warriors. Within two years Iroquois warriors again attacked the Catawbas, restarting a war that would eventually merge with a much larger struggle for control of colonial North America.[38]

THE AMBIGUOUS IROQUOIS EMPIRE

While Iroquois warriors followed the warrior's trail south, Six Nations' leaders were pursuing an alternate means of expanding Iroquois power over other Indian nations. The relationship between the Six Nations and Indian peoples residing in the British colony of Pennsylvania, especially the Delawares and Shawnees, was controversial. Its roots lay in the diplomatic efforts of the Six Nations to assert their authority over Indian peoples living in regions allegedly conquered by the Iroquois League during the great mourning war of the seventeenth century. Although the Iroquois took physical possession of little additional territory during that time, they did assert dominion over numerous Indian nations, either by assimilating them into the Iroquois League or by driving them away. Additionally, the Six Nations maintained that they held political authority over the lands once inhabited by the Susquehannocks, Eries, Petuns, Neutrals, Hurons, and others, regardless of whether the Iroquois settled there or not, an assertion bolstered by the Covenant Chain relationship between the Iroquois League and the British colonies.[39]

The military reverses of the late 1600s and the occupation of the northern portion of these lands by Great Lakes Algonquians demonstrate that the Six Nations' claims of lordship were thin at best. Yet to the south of Iroquoia, in the Susquehanna Valley and the eastern Ohio Country, Iroquois pretensions were bolstered by an elaborate treaty relationship that developed between the Six Nations and Pennsylvania. In 1722, a conference was held at Albany to address the issue of Virginia colonists who had been attacked or had property stolen during Iroquois raids against the southern Indians. A subplot of the meeting involved the efforts of

Pennsylvania Governor William Keith to secure an alliance with the Six Nations that might ease Indian relations in his colony and smooth the way for the transfer of lands in the Susquehanna Valley to Pennsylvania. The Six Nations had acted as representatives or spokesmen for the Indian peoples living along the Susquehanna River since 1710, when they began offering asylum in the Susquehanna Valley to numerous refugee Indian groups. These refugee Indian nations, which by 1722 included some Delawares and Shawnees, were in the way of Pennsylvania expansion, and Keith hoped to forge a deal with the Six Nations that would undercut refugee claims to the land and secure their orderly removal further west. Moreover, at least one member of the Six Nations, the Cayugas, maintained direct claim to the lands in the western Susquehanna watershed, necessitating that Keith work with the Iroquois to secure Pennsylvania's possession of the region.[40]

To accomplish its goal, the government of Pennsylvania created the fiction, as least in legal terms, that the Six Nations were not only spokesmen for the refugee Indian nations along the Susquehanna, but in fact their political masters. During the 1722 treaty, the Iroquois had agreed to recognize a boundary line running from the upper Potomac River south along the Blue Ridge mountains as border between their claims and those of the British colonies. The stated intention of the boundary was to keep Iroquois warriors traveling south to attack the Catawbas from straying into colonial settlements, but the Pennsylvanians seized on the agreement as a precedent to assert that the Iroquois held political control over all Indian groups living north and west of the line, or more specifically, those refugee peoples inhabiting the Susquehanna Valley. Many Delawares and Shawnees denied that they fell under the jurisdiction on this imaginary Iroquois empire, but Pennsylvania authorities insisted that "the Five Nations have an absolute authority over all our Indians, and may command them as they please."[41] For Pennsylvania, it was a pleasant fiction, as this construction of Iroquois power allowed the colony to formulate its Indian policy and secure land transfers through a single entity, the Six Nations, rather than having to negotiate with various refugee nations one at a time. Similarly, the Iroquois accepted their elevated status in the alliance as a means of perpetuating their power and authority over the Pennsylvania Indians and the lands of the Susquehanna Valley and the Ohio Country. In addition, the new relationship with Pennsylvania offered the Six Nations a new economic partner. Trading with Pennsylvania made the Six Nations less economically dependent on New York or Canada, as the Iroquois could now turn elsewhere for supplies.[42]

Conceptually, the Iroquois-Pennsylvania alliance was mutually beneficial, but time would test that theory. Beginning with the 1722 agreement,
the Six Nations periodically ceded vast tracts of land in the lower Susquehanna watershed to Pennsylvania. Already hard pressed on their eastern
border by expanding New York settlements, the Iroquois hoped to secure
their southern flank by selling land to Pennsylvania in exchange for promises that the colony would not make land claims against Iroquoia proper.
In the process, however, the Six Nations sold away lands occupied by
Delaware, Shawnee, and other refugee Indian peoples. The legality of the
transactions was questionable, although both Pennsylvania and the
Iroquois maintained that they were valid, and their combined pressure
forced the refugee groups to move off the lands. The low point of this
process occurred during the infamous 1737 Walking Purchase, in which
Pennsylvania officials and Iroquois representatives defrauded the
Delawares out of a vast tract of land along the Delaware River. Scores of
Delawares went into the west in protest after the Onondaga sachem
Canasatego confirmed the legality of the Walking Purchase in 1742. In
an antagonistic speech, Canasatego informed Delaware leaders that "You
ought to be taken by the hair of the head and shaken severely till you
recover your senses ... We [the Iroquois] conquered you, we made women
of you, you know you are women ... for all these reasons, we charge you
to remove instantly. We don't give you the liberty to think about it. You
are women; take the advice of a wise man and remove immediately."[43]

The policy of giving away other Indians' land carried with it the seeds
of Iroquois destruction. In 1744, representatives from the Six Nations,
including Canasatego, met in Lancaster, Pennsylvania with agents from
the British colonies of Virginia, Maryland, and Pennsylvania to discuss
grievances related to the Iroquois's continuing war with the southern
Indians. In exchange for the right of free passage through Virginia to
strike the Catawbas, the Six Nations' representatives agreed to revoke
their claim to any lands understood to be in the colony of Virginia. What
Canasatego and other Iroquois spokesmen did not understand, however,
was that Virginia's colonial charter defined the western border of the
colony as the Pacific Ocean, while also defining the northern and
southern terminuses as opening in a pie-shaped wedge from Point Com-
fort on Chesapeake Bay. A liberal interpretation of Virginia's colonial
charter could place the majority of North America under Virginia's jurisdiction. Most important, in the minds of Virginians, the Iroquois had
signed over their claim to the strategically vital Ohio Country, allowing
the British colony to pursue its own interests in the region.[44]

The consequences would not become clear for nearly a decade, fore-stalled by the renewal of war between England and France. The War of the Austrian Succession, called King George's War by the British colonists, began in 1744 and quickly came to involve the Six Nations on a deeper level than any European-sponsored war since the 1690s. Initially, most Iroquois maintained their neutrality, citing concern over the possibility of having to fight against Catholic Iroquois from the French mission towns. Moreover, the war caused a severe disruption in the French trade network, offering the Six Nations an opportunity to bring even more of the Great Lakes and Midwestern Indian nations into the Iroquois-managed trade network at Albany, an objective that seemed more beneficial to the Six Nations than war. In return, the French and their Indian allies in Canada kept most of their attacks away from the New York frontier, and they even allowed a small party of Mohawk scouts captured near Lake Champlain to return home unharmed. By the summer of 1746, however, repeated British appeals to war began to have an effect, especially among the largely pro-British Mohawks, whose connections to the British had deepened considerably with the arrival in New York of William Johnson. A young Irishman, Johnson had come to New York in 1738 to manage his uncle's estate, but he quickly struck out on his own as a trader and cultivated a beneficial relationship with the Mohawks, who referred to him as Warraghiyagey, meaning "big business" or "doer of great things." New York settlements were increasingly encroaching on Mohawk lands, and some Mohawk leaders hoped an alliance with Johnson, who had been appointed Colonel of the Six Nations, could gain them a powerful ally in future land disputes with New York. Other Iroquois nations also seemed ready to fight with the British, having informed Governor Clinton of New York in 1746 that they were ready to strike the French. In the end, however, only the Mohawks openly fought in King George's War, aided by a scattering of warriors from the other Iroquois nations. The vast majority of the Iroquois remained neutral, possibly because of a French threat to call on their Indian allies to attack the Iroquois if they aided the British.[45]

During the fall of 1746, two Mohawk war parties moved north into Canada. The first raided the settlements north of Montreal, and the second, under the leadership of Theyanoguin, parleyed with the Catholic Iroquois at Kanawake, where they urged their Mohawk relatives to take no part in the war, before attacking a party of French workers near Lake Champlain. Mohawk fortunes in the war went steadily downhill from that point. Although the Mohawks killed 14 French and took 25 prisoners the next spring, they suffered heavy casualties in the battles, including the loss of several prominent warriors. In June, the 66-year-old Theyanoguin led a Mohawk war party into an ambush near Montreal. Although Theyanoguin escaped, most of his party was killed or captured. British promises to invade Canada with a grand army again floundered, as the French and their Indian allies declared war on the Mohawks but not the other Iroquois. By 1748, the war was over and the Mohawks were angry. While the remainder of the Six Nations moved again to restore good relations with the French, the Mohawks stewed in bitter resentment over having supported a losing cause.[46]

King George's War resulted in the first large crack in the unified Iroquois policy of neutrality after 1701. The Mohawks had fought for the British against the French while the rest of the Six Nations left them to their fate. It was an ominous sign that one of the bastions of the Iroquois restoration, unified neutrality, was crumbling. Other elements of Iroquois policy were also coming unraveled, especially in the Ohio Country, where Indian migrants forced out of the Susquehanna Valley by Iroquois-brokered treaties with Pennsylvania arrived along the watersheds of the Allegheny and Upper Ohio Rivers. Here Shawnees, Delawares, and other Indian peoples mingled with a scattering of Iroquoian peoples already occupying much of what is now the border between eastern Ohio and western Pennsylvania. Although they called themselves Mingos (Iroquoian speakers), they were primarily Senecas who had drifted southwest to seek their own destinies semi-independently of the Iroquois League. Together these Indian newcomers began to rebuild their societies, and in the process they negotiated directly with the French or the British colonies for trade and alliances, bypassing their supposed overlords in the Iroquois Confederacy. Although the Six Nations sent regents, or half-kings, to assert control over the migrants, they soon found that anti-Iroquois sentiment ran very high in the Ohio Country, and many of the regents soon defected to their new charges. Thus, even as the policy of neutrality was failing, the Six Nations also were losing control over the very people whose political domination had helped fuel the Iroquois resurgence.[47]

To make matters worse, both the French and British had taken an active interest in the Ohio Country. The British recognized the region's latent potential for trade and settlement, and they quickly moved to seize both assets. Colonists from Virginia, seizing on the Lancaster Treaty as a valid deed for the region, began plotting settlements and constructing trade storehouses even before King George's War was over, without gaining any additional permissions from the Six Nations. Even more alarming to the Iroquois, Pennsylvania colonists used their connections to refugee

Delawares and Shawnees to establish direct trading relationships with the Midwestern Indian nations, threatening to cut deeply into the Iroquois-brokered trade out of Albany. The French took even bolder steps, recognizing the strategic importance of the Ohio River as a link in the sweeping arc of French colonies stretching from Louisiana through the Illinois Country to Canada. In 1749, the French sent a military expedition into the Ohio Country to assert their dominion over the region; then in 1752, after it became clear that many Ohio Country Indians were shifting their trade to the British, the French recruited Ottawa warriors to attack and destroy a Miami village where British traders had set up an outpost. The next year the French sent 1,500 men along the northern frontier of Iroquoia to the Allegheny River, where they began the construction of a network of forts intended to force the Midwestern Indians into submission and block British expansion into the Ohio Country. All the while, the Six Nations, who were at least in British eyes the rulers of the Ohio Country, were being cut out of the west completely.[48]

The world around them was about to erupt into war and the peoples of the Iroquois League stood on very uncertain ground. Wars with the southern Indians had produced modest gains in population and prestige, while the adoption of the Tuscaroras bouyed the Iroquois League by expanding its official membership to six Indian nations. But on all other fronts, the Iroquois were in trouble. Iroquois prestige was on the decline, a reflection of the lack of respect given to the league's military capabilities by the French, British, and other Indian peoples. The devolution of Iroquois strength came at a critical period, for ahead lay the final colonial struggle between the French and British for mastery of North America, and beyond that an uprising of the American colonists against England. Both conflicts would prove critically important to the Six Nations, testing the unity of the Iroquois League and stretching the bonds of their association to the breaking point.

7

•

The Longhouse Divided

In the years after the end of King George's War, all of colonial North America teetered on the brink of a major war, even if few clearly saw it coming. The Seven Years' War, sometimes called the French and Indian War in North America, would be of crucial importance to the Six Nations, as it would take place in and around Iroquoia and the lands of Indian nations supposedly subservient to the Iroquois. Moreover, the war threatened to unravel the Iroquois League, as the Mohawks chose to support the British even though the consensus among the Six Nations favored neutrality. The Six Nations emerged from the conflict intact, but the Iroquois faced unprecedented challenges in the aftermath of the Seven Years' War. The League had lost its control over Indian peoples living in Pennsylvania and the Ohio Country, the seeds of internal disunion had been planted, and British expansion into the Ohio Country and along the western reaches of Iroquoia was becoming increasingly difficult to bear. When Ohio Country and Great Lakes Indians precipitated a massive uprising against the British in 1763, Senecas were among the Indian peoples who declared war.

THE GREAT WAR FOR EMPIRE

As war loomed between the French and the British, the Iroquois once again faced difficult decisions. At the eastern edge of the Iroquois League, the Mohawks, closest to the British at Albany, generally were sympathetic to British interests, although trouble was brewing in their relationship. New York colonists were encroaching on Mohawk lands and straining the nation's relationship with the British. In the west, the Senecas, most likely to face attacks from Great Lakes Indians if the Six Nations sided with the British, supported an alliance with the French. In the center, Onondagas, Oneidas, Cayugas, and Tuscaroras were divided and uncertain over their future course of action. Each nation continued to send representatives to the central confederacy council at Onondaga during the early war years, but the only consistent policy that emerged from these meetings was a common determination among all Iroquois nations to prevent any further encroachments onto their territory by the French or British.[1]

Thus, as the war loomed, the Iroquois League was divided. In 1754, the Iroquois sent a delegation of 200 Oneidas, Cayugas, and Tuscaroras to Montreal to meet with the French and the Catholic Iroquois in an effort to mend relations, which had been become strained because of the imperious stance of the French governor-general, Ange Duquesne, Marquis de Menneville, toward the Six Nations. Duquesne had been charged by his superiors in France with driving the British out of the Ohio Country and divesting the Iroquois of any pretensions they had to the region. Duquesne had treated the Six Nations abrasively since his arrival in 1752 and had taken several measures that upset the Iroquois. He authorized the expeditionary force of more than 1,500 French and Canadian troops that passed through Iroquois territory on its way to build forts along the Allegheny River, and he ordered the Iroquois to "recall the dogs of their villages" who had migrated to settle in the Ohio Country.[2] In an effort to maintain the neutrality of their Six Nations cousins during the impending war, the Catholic Iroquois held their own secret council with the Iroquois representatives outside of Montreal. Catholic Iroquois had accompanied the French expedition to the Allegheny in 1753, and more of their warriors were in the process of strengthening the French garrison at Fort Duquesne at the forks of the Ohio River. Not wanting to potentially fight against their cousins from the Iroquois League, the Catholic Iroquois urged the Six Nations to take no part in the fighting, while reminding their cousins of the differences between the French and British:

> Brethren, are you ignorant of the difference between our Father and the English? Go see the forts our father has erected, and you will see that the land beneath his walls is still hunting ground, having fixed himself in places we frequent only to supply our wants; while the English no sooner

get possession of a country than the game is forced to leave it, the trees fall down before them, the earth becomes bare, and we find among them hardly wherewithal to shelter ourselves when night falls.[3]

Tensions decreased precipitously in 1755 after the arrival of a new governor-general, Pierre de Rigaud de Vaudreuil, who had been given new instructions to repair relations with the Six Nations and secure their assistance in the confrontation with the British over the Ohio Country. Vaudreuil interpreted Iroquois neutrality as sufficient to secure French interests, and throughout negotiations with the Six Nations from 1754 to 1756 he reinforced the position that France accepted Iroquois neutrality and would work to support it. Although some Iroquois would offer limited support to the French during the war, including a party of Senecas who accompanied the French expeditionary force in 1753 as guides and hunters, the majority of the Six Nations gratefully accepted French recognition of their neutrality and promised that "our arms shall be between you [the French and British] endeavoring to keep you asunder."[4] Vaudreuil played his part well in the accord, even making a grand gesture by ceding the lands around Oswego to the Six Nations after French troops captured the post from the British in 1756.[5]

Reconciliation with the French kept most of the Six Nations out of the early phases of the Seven Years' War. Only the Mohawks chose to forge a different path, although their road to alliance with the British was fraught with difficulties. In the aftermath of King George's War and the aborted British invasions of Canada, Mohawk relations with the colony of New York came under heavy duress. The Mohawks had not been pleased with the conduct of their British allies during the war, believing that British ineptitude had placed all the Iroquois nations in danger of French retaliation. There were also troubles between the Mohawks and British over land, as New York colonists were deep into a scheme to deprive the Mohawks of 800,000 acres of their territory. Moreover, the Mohawks were angry that the British had taken little action to oppose the presence of the French along the Allegheny River, where the new French forts threatened Iroquois control over lands the Six Nations claimed as their hunting grounds. The recalcitrance of the Indian peoples living there, including a large contingent of Mingo separatists, made the matter more acute. The failure of the British to defend the Ohio Country, which the Iroquois League expected, as the 1713 Treaty of Utrecht had designated the Iroquois as subjects of the British crown, seemed to provide more proof that the British were no friends of the Iroquois.[6]

In June 1753, Theyanoguin and 16 of his fellows from the pro-British Mohawk village of Canajoharie traveled to New York City seeking redress of their grievances from Governor George Clinton. Theyanoguin accused Clinton of neglecting the covenant chain alliance, pointing out that the Mohawks had remained faithful to the British when the other Iroquois nations had not. But now the Mohawks demanded action; otherwise they would break the Covenant Chain. Governor Clinton responded with vague assurances of nonspecific aid, referring Mohawk land disputes to British authorities at Albany. Theyanoguin responded angrily:

> Brother when we came here to relate our grievances about our lands, we expected to have something done for us, and we have told you that the Covenant Chain of our forefathers was like to be broken, and brother you tell us that we shall be redressed at Albany, but we know them so well, we will not trust to them, for they are no people but devils ... as soon as we come home we will send up a belt of wampum to our brothers the five nations to acquaint them [that] the Covenant Chain is broken between you and us. So brother you are not to expect to hear of me any more, and brother we desire to hear no more of you."[7]

With that statement, the meeting ended and the Mohawks returned home, apparently intent on ending their long relationship with the British and perhaps seeking new accommodations with the French. But the British government, on learning of Theyanoguin's speech, ordered its colonies to hold a special council at Albany, where the agenda would include concerted efforts to win back the friendship of the Mohawks and the rest of the Six Nations.[8]

The Albany Congress of 1754 served many purposes in the eyes of the British government, including the facilitation of colonial cooperation for the coming war with France, but mollifying the Mohawks was of special importance. The British needed the Iroquois to maintain a claim to the Ohio Country, as the Iroquois were recognized by treaty as British subjects, and the Ohio Country was considered Iroquois territory by right of conquest. Thus, the British government ordered its colonies to make the Six Nations happy by any means necessary, including providing payment for any questionable land deals and handing out prodigious gifts. In all, 30 wagon loads of trade goods, procured at royal expense, were distributed to Theyanoguin and the 150 Iroquois in attendance; but they did not address the central complaint leveled by Theyanoguin the previous summer, as the French still had possession of the Six Nations' hunting preserve in the Ohio Country. Indeed, those in attendance at the conference soon received news of the French victory over George Washington at Fort Necessity, which seemed to confirm the inability of the British to protect their Iroquois subjects. Theyanoguin chastised the British for their military weakness, urging them to "look at the French, they are men, they are fortifying everywhere—but, we are ashamed to say it, you are like women, bare and open without any fortification."[9] Additional evidence of Iroquois displeasure with the British was evident in the relatively small number of Iroquois attending a major council meeting with seven British colonies. Only 150 Iroquois were present, a surprisingly low turnout that guaranteed there would be no general reconciliation between the Iroquois League and the British concluded at Albany. Although the British promised to be more aggressive in contesting the French presence in the Ohio Country, much of the good work at the Albany Congress was buried under an avalanche of land schemes, which included getting Mohawk headmen drunk and convincing them to sign away lands in Pennsylvania's Wyoming Valley to Connecticut.[10]

Yet Theyanoguin, who perhaps informed the British that the Covenant Chain was broken as a means to spur them into action, seemed satisfied that the British were genuinely prepared to resist the French. The Mohawks needed a strong British presence to assert their dominance over the Iroquois League, a position that had been steadily eroding throughout the eighteenth century. Now, as word reached the Mohawks that the British were sending armies to North America to punish the French, Theyanoguin positioned the Mohawks under his influence to support the British war effort. In June 1755, William Johnson, recently appointed as the British Superintendent for Indian Affairs in the northern colonies, held a meeting at his Mohawk Valley home that was attended by more than 1,000 Iroquois headmen, warriors, women, and children. Johnson acquainted the assembled Iroquois with British military plans for the year, which included campaigns against French fortifications at Duquesne, Niagara, and Fort St. Frederic on Lake Champlain. Johnson asked for Iroquois warriors to support the attack on Duquesne, although it was already too late in the game for them to reach general Edward's Braddock's ill-fated army, which was crushed by a combined French and Indian force. Instead, he added the Iroquois to his own campaign against Fort St. Frederic. For the most part, the Iroquois vacillated back and forth between pledges of support and expressions of concerns about crossing the French, potentially fighting Catholic Iroquois who supported the French, and the poor results of past British military initiatives. In the end, Johnson won support for Braddock's campaign, though the Iroquois sent no warriors because of the lateness of the season, and secured the support of Theyanoguin's faction of Mohawks for his own campaign. Reflecting on the proceedings, Johnson realized that he had largely failed at his first task as Superintendent of Indian Affairs. "I found all the nations except the Mohawks extremely adverse to taking any part with us in the present active measures against the French," Johnson noted, a stance he attributed to "their fear of the French, owing to our long passiveness ... [and] from a real attachment in many of their most leading men to the French interest."[11]

Late in the summer of 1755, Theyanoguin led 200 Mohawk warriors into William Johnson's camp near the southern end of Lake George in preparation for the campaign against Fort St. Frederick, an impressive stone fort with a four-story tower commanding the narrow section of southern Lake Champlain that the British called Crown Point. Johnson originally intended to lead 3,500 militia from New York and New England, along with the Mohawks, against the fort, but not wanting to repeat Braddock's stunning defeat in the wilderness, Johnson contented himself mostly with having his men build supply posts and improve the roads between Lake George and the Hudson River. But when a party of Mohawks, who had recently returned from Canada, warned Johnson that a large number of French soldiers had recently arrived in Canada, Johnson stepped up the pace of his activities. As his men hurried to finish construction of Fort Edward on the upper Hudson, Johnson led the core of his army forward to the southern end of Lake George, where they began laying out a second fort, William Henry. Little did Johnson know that the French were already moving. Concerned by reports that overestimated the size and strength of Johnson's army, Governor-General Vaudreuil diverted nearly 3,000 French soldiers, Canadian militia, Abenaki Indians, and Catholic Iroquois from the French mission towns to protect Fort St. Frederic, whose walls were in such poor condition that the French feared the fort could not withstand even a modest artillery barrage. By early summer, the French had reached Fort St. Frederic, scouted the British position, and decided to strike the only partially completed Fort Edward.[12]

On September 7, an expeditionary force of 1,500 French and Indians, led by Jean-Armand, Baron de Dieskau, arrived in the vicinity of Fort Edward. The Catholic Iroquois refused to attack the fort, however, because it sat in what they considered to be British territory, and the Abenakis also balked at the prospect of laying siege to the fort. Both Indian groups preferred to strike the less-defended British camp near Lake

George, and as the 700 Indians amounted to nearly half of the French force, Dieskau had little choice other than to concur. At the camp along Lake George, Mohawk scouts informed William Johnson that they had discovered the tracks of a large body of French and Indians moving south toward Fort Edward. Recognizing the peril the incomplete fort and its small garrison faced, Johnson quickly organized a force of 1,000 militia to send to the fort's relief. The force would be guided and supported by nearly all of the 200 Mohawks in Johnson's camp, including the aged Theyanoguin.[13]

Early in the morning on September 8, the British and Mohawks set out for Fort Edward at a quick pace. The Mohawks took the lead with Theyanoguin mounted on horseback at the front of a single-file column, a formation often used by Iroquois warriors trying to cover ground quickly where they did not fear surprise attack. Indeed, neither the Mohawks nor the British had any idea that the French and their Indian allies had left the vicinity of Fort Edward, and they stumbled blindly into an ambush in a wooded ravine just four miles outside Johnson's Lake George camp. Learning of the column's approach from a captured British deserter, Dieskau had orchestrated an ambush in which his 200 French regulars blocked the road through the ravine while the Indians and Canadians massed in the woods to either side of the road. The only glitch in the plan occurred when Catholic Iroquois revealed themselves to Theyanoguin as the Mohawks entered the ravine, perhaps trying to warn the Mohawks to escape. Yet the warning came too late, as a single shot rang out before the Mohawk leader could fully assess the situation, leading to the beginning of an intense firefight. Most of the British militia fled after their leader, Colonel Ephraim Williams, was killed, leaving the Mohawks to hold the road against the attackers. Thirty Mohawks, including the 75-year-old Theyanoguin, who was bayoneted and later scalped, were killed in the opening minutes of the fight. The Mohawks steadied themselves after the initial shock and conducted a skillful, fighting retreat back towards Johnson's camp. Their conduct in the battle, later named "The Bloody Morning Scout" by the British, prevented the ambush from turning into a total disaster.[14]

The French, Catholic Iroquois, and Abenakis pursued to within sight of Johnson's camp, where the Catholic Iroquois refused to attack because so many of their Mohawk cousins were trapped there. Dieskau ordered his regulars to attack anyway, hoping their example would motivate the Indians. Stiff fire from the British and Mohawks in the camp, however, along with a few well-placed blasts of grapeshot from four British artillery pieces, repulsed the French assault and drove off the attackers. Dieskau, who had been severely wounded, and 20 other injured French soldiers were left behind to become prisoners. Johnson, who had also been shot during the battle, eventually turned all of the prisoners except Dieskau over to the Mohawks as compensation for the loss of Theyanoguin and so many of their warriors. Apparently this was not enough to satisfy their grief, as British reports claimed that the Mohawks canvassed both battle sites, amassing plunder from both French and British bodies while scalping and disfiguring dead French and Indian enemies. Then they departed for home over the objections of Johnson, although the Mohawks assured him that they would soon return, warning Johnson "not [to] make up a sudden peace with the French as was done last war, and leave us in the lurch and disappointed of venting our resentments upon our enemies."[15]

Unfortunately for William Johnson, the battle had a more unsettling effect on the Mohawks than their warriors made known. At a council a month after the battle of Lake George, Mohawk clan mothers declined to call for revenge and replacement of dead Mohawk warriors, rejecting practices long associated with mourning war traditions. That meant that Mohawk warriors would not soon rejoin Johnson as promised. Aside for some adventurous young men, the majority of the Mohawks would abstain from the war for almost four years. Their decision, reached separately from the other Iroquois nations, reflected the consensus of the Iroquois League, which had earlier adopted a neutral position in the conflict. The Mohawks' open support of the British had produced tension with their Iroquois brethren, but now the rest of the Six Nations hoped that the Mohawks' refusal to rejoin the British war effort would bring the keepers of the eastern door back into alignment with the decisions of the central council. Indeed in 1756, a Cayuga speaker informed the French that the other Iroquois nations had previously "cut off from their cabin the Mohawks, whose heart was wholly British; yet he hoped, by dint of shaking their heads, to make them recover their lost senses and to bring them back to their Father [the French]."[16]

The Six Nations' decision to remain neutral reflected their attachment to their own best interests. Logically, the Iroquois had no desire to become entangled in a losing military effort, especially if there was any chance of retaliation against Iroquoia. Yet the Iroquois League was far from inactive during the middle period of the Seven Years' War. Direct military participation was out of the question, but that did not stop the Six Nations from pressing their interests on the diplomatic front. Of great concern to the Iroquois were the Delawares, Shawnees, and Mingos living in the Ohio Country and along the Susquehanna River, Indian nations who had cast off their supposed dependence on the Six Nations and waged war with the French against the British colonies of Pennsylvania and Virginia. The war had been difficult for these nations, and some, especially the Susquehanna Delawares, began to send peace overtures to British authorities in Pennsylvania as early as 1756. The Iroquois involved themselves in these negotiations, which expanded by 1758 to include the Delawares, Shawnees, and Mingos of the Ohio Country. Iroquois motivations were twofold: the Six Nations wanted to reassert their dominion over these Indian nations, and they hoped to refurbish the former alliance with Pennsylvania, whose colonial leaders in the years before the Seven Years' War had ignored their long-standing policy of centering their Indian policy through the Six Nations in favor of direct negotiations with the Ohio Country Indian nations.[17]

Leaders of the Six Nations' saw in the Seven Years' War an opportunity to regain at least some measure of power over the region and its peoples. Direct diplomatic involvement began in 1756 after William Johnson urged the Six Nations to order the Delawares to make peace. Iroquois leaders understood that the Ohio Country Delawares, who were a separate entity from the Susquehanna Delawares, had never paid much heed to rulings of the Iroquois council, so they focused their activity on the Susquehanna nation. At a February 1756 meeting with Johnson, Iroquois spokesmen informed the Indian superintendent that "[we] had already sent some of our people to take the hatchet out of the hands of our nephews the Delawares."[18] The next year, the Iroquois sent representatives to Easton, Pennsylvania, as observers during a council between Pennsylvania officials and Susquehanna Delaware leader Teedyuscung.

That meeting led to additional discussions during a much larger conference at Easton in 1758, one that also included representatives from the Ohio Country Delawares, who spoke on behalf of the Shawnees and Mingos as well. From the start, the Six Nations took a more direct role. Three prominent Iroquois headmen—the influential Oneida leader Thomas King, the Mohawk leader Nichus, and the Seneca sachem Tagashata—presided over a very large Six Nations contingent that had come to reassert Iroquois control over their former Indian dependents and reestablish their diplomatic partnership with Pennsylvania. Both goals were accomplished, at least on paper. During the proceedings, the Iroquois representatives chastised Teedyuscung, claiming he had no authority except that which the Six Nations allowed him. The Delaware leader broke under the pressure, and in the interests of a lasting peace, Teedyuscung recognized Iroquois authority over the Susquehanna Delawares. In return, the colony of Pennsylvania relinquished its claims to the lands west of the Susquehanna River, territory it had purchased from the Iroquois League in a shady transaction during the 1754 Albany Congress. The return of this enormous tract of land brought peace with the Ohio Country Indian nations, even though the land was not awarded to them. Instead, Pennsylvania officials returned the land to the Indians from whom they had purchased it, the Six Nations. Potential difficulties surrounding this distinction were averted when the Ohio Country peoples won recognition that they, unlike their Susquehanna relatives, were independent from the Iroquois League, but Pennsylvania's cession nonetheless reestablished Iroquois claims to the Ohio Country and reconfirmed the Six Nations' principal role in Pennsylvania Indian policy.[19]

The Six Nations' diplomatic coup paralleled dramatic changes of fortune in the Seven Years' War. In 1758 and 1759, the French suffered a string of military setbacks. Most of their difficulties can be linked to the British naval blockade of Canada and the fall of Fortress Louisbourg, guarding the water approaches from the Atlantic Ocean to the St. Lawrence River, which by mid-1758 seriously disrupted the flow of military supplies and trade goods to Canada. Unable to meet the provisioning needs of their Indian allies, the French watched in horror as their extensive network of Indian alliances began to crumble. Most Indian nations simply quit fighting, but a few others made matters even worse for the French by switching sides to the British, who stood ready to fulfill the Indians' economic need for trade. Without Indian support, the French found it difficult to hold onto their western posts. Fort Frontenac, at the eastern end of Lake Ontario, and Fort Duquesne, at the forks of the Ohio River, both fell to the British by the end of 1758. Only Fort Niagara and Fort Carillon, constructed by the French in on a rocky plateau at the southern foot of Lake Champlain known to the Iroquois as Ticonderoga, remained securely in French possession. Niagara had not been attacked, and French troops successfully defended Carillon against a badly bungled attack by British forces several times their number. But the tide was turning in favor of the British, and the Six Nations could feel the winds of change blowing. Perhaps anticipating the changing military climate, a small number of Oneida warriors had participated in the British capture of Fort Frontenac, and several hundred Mohawks had accompanied William Johnson to Fort Carillon, although they prudently abstained from most of the fighting during the British defeat.[20]

In 1759, the shackles of restraint were fully removed and Iroquois warriors joined the British war effort in large numbers. The Six Nations' neutrality during the war had always been calculated on what most ben-efitted themselves, and under the present evaluation, that meant alliance with the British, who seemed poised to drive the French out of North America. The Iroquois also may have saw an opportunity to expand the reconstruction of their power over the Ohio Country that had begun at Easton a year earlier. The Ohio Country Indian nations had gained rec-ognition of their independence from the Iroquois League, and there was some fear in Iroquoia that the Delawares and Shawnees might try to forge a confederation with Ottawas, Miamis, or other western Indians nations to exclude the Iroquois from the Great Lakes region. The Six Nations may have hoped that by helping the British defeat the French, the British, who by treaty were the custodians of Iroquois hunting lands in the Ohio Country, would bring the Ohio Country Indians back under Iroquois political jurisdiction. Regardless of their true motivations, the Iroquois were ready to fight. At an April 1759 conference with William Johnson, Iroquois leaders pledged to support British military initiatives, particu-larly if they involved an attack against Fort Niagara at the western end of Iroquoia. Even representatives of the Genesee faction of Senecas, those who lived along the Genesee River and were considered most sympa-thetic to the French, vowed that they were ready to march against Fort Niagara.[21]

Nearly a thousand warriors from all six of the Iroquois nations turned out for the Niagara campaign, led by British General John Prideaux, although William Johnson commanded the contingent of Iroquois war-riors. The Iroquois commitment represented nearly the full military mobi-lization of the Six Nations, a clear indication that they had cast aside neutrality and resolved to risk everything upon British victory in the Seven Years' War. It was a calculated but necessary gamble. If the British won the war, the Six Nations would no longer be able to follow a path of neutrality between the two colonial powers. Most Iroquois leaders saw more utility in actively attaching themselves to the winning side than passively sitting back and expecting the British to treat them well after the war. Instead, they argued it was better that the British owed the Iroquois a debt of grati-tude. In theory, that debt would be incurred at Niagara, although there would be an unexpected twist along the way. On July 6, Iroquois warriors commenced the assault on Fort Niagara by attacking a party of French soldiers working outside the fort. The French had been caught completely by surprise, but in their haste to escape, approximately 100 local Senecas had been hurried into the protective walls of the fort. These Senecas had long been employed by the French to portage supplies and baggage along the Niagara River, and they were apparently not among those Senecas prepared to make war against Fort Niagara. Indeed, a representative of the Niagara Senecas, Kaendae, came forth under a flag of truce and labored for several days to convince his Iroquois brethren to abandon the attack. After long deliberation, the Iroquois refused—thanks in no small part to Johnson, who promised the Iroquois first opportunity to plunder the fort— but Kaendae was allowed to take his band of Senecas and withdraw from the combat zone.[22]

Still, the Iroquois warriors apparently were so shaken by the prospects of having almost drawn the blood of their kinsmen that they later refused to take an active role in the siege of Fort Niagara, fearful that more Senecas might yet dwell within the fort's walls. Instead they withdrew to a camp at nearby La Belle Famile, content to let the British guns blast the French into submission. Soon, however, events conspired to draw them back into the fray. First, General Prideaux died in an errant British canon blast, leaving William Johnson in command. Second, the Iroquois learned that a large column of French and Indian reinforcements were rapidly approaching from the southwest. Johnson convinced the Iroquois to send a warning to the Indians accompanying the French column asking the warriors to leave. While Johnson hastily organized an ambush near the Six Nations' camp at La Belle Famile, Iroquois warriors convinced almost all of the Indians in the French column, mostly warriors from the Great Lakes nations, to abandon their allies before they were ambushed. As a result, Johnson's force routed the French column, and 400 Iroquois warriors cleaned up the mess by chasing down fleeing French soldiers. In the end, more than 300 French had been killed or wounded. Shortly thereafter, Fort Niagara surrendered, and as promised, Johnson allowed the Iroquois warriors to pillage the fort and its storehouse, which contained large quantities of furs and trade goods.[23]

Throughout the remainder of the Seven Years' War, warriors from the Six Nations proved more valuable as negotiators than fighters. In 1760, nearly 700 Iroquois accompanied the British army under General Jeffrey Amherst as it moved to capture Montreal, and although Amherst despised them as he hated all Indians, the Iroquois played an important diplomatic role in the British victory. In conjunction with William Johnson, the Iroquois visited the French mission towns, pleading with Catholic Iroquois and other mission Indians to stay out of the fight and accept the British offer of amnesty. Their diplomatic initiative was successful, as the Catholic Iroquois not only abandoned the French, but also guided the British army to its targets in the upper St. Lawrence Valley. Iroquois warriors also aided the British, albeit with more violent forms of persuasion, in ending a war between the Cherokees and the southern British colonies in 1760. With the fall of Montreal and the subjugation of the Cherokees, peace finally settled over most of North America. It would not last long. Trouble already was brewing again in the Ohio Country, and before the French and the British could finalize their treaty ending the Seven Years' War in 1763, a new conflict would begin in North America. In the coming war, the Six Nations would again find themselves divided.[24]

PONTIAC'S WAR

The causes of the Indian uprising of 1763–1764—more commonly referred to as Pontiac's War—were many and varied from one Indian nation to the next. At its most basic level, it was a war fought over economics and status. In 1762, General Jeffrey Amherst, pressured by the home government to economize his operations, decided to assert British authority over the Indians of the Ohio Country. Amherst, who disliked purchasing the Indians' good behavior with gifts and presents because he believed such practices made the British look weak, no longer saw any utility in the mutual peace agreement that had tied the Indians to British interests during the Seven Years' War. Instead, Amherst viewed the Indians as conquered peoples who needed to be brought properly into line as British subjects. Thus, early in 1762, Amherst ordered Indian superintendent William Johnson to revise the Indian trade, with specific instructions to sharply decrease the amount of gunpowder and ammunition made available to the Indians and to make the Indian nations barter for goods previously afforded to them as gifts. Amherst hoped these changes would not only cut costs but also keep the Indians busy at hunting and trapping, leaving them less time to think about war.[25]

Although considerations of fair play in trade and diplomacy were not paramount for every tribe involved in the war, Amherst's reorientation of British Indian policy produced resentment among Indians living in the Ohio Country, who suddenly found themselves denied the traditional presents their alliance with the British warranted, deprived of the trade goods they needed to survive, and relegated to the status of vanquished foe in their own lands. Moreover, the continued presence of British soldiers in former French forts west of the Appalachian Mountains, despite repeated assurances that the army would withdraw, escalated tensions. Further adding to the Indian's tapestry of discontent was widespread disease and economic dislocation that decimated their self-sufficiency.

A nativistic religious revival, based largely on the teachings of the Delaware prophet Neolin, wove these various threads together into a pattern of unity. Neolin stressed the need to purify Indian society of white influence and return to the traditional lifeways of past generations. His simple panacea for the problems facing the Indian nations called for the removal of all white people from Indian territory, if necessary by force.[26]

The peoples of the Iroquois League were not immune to these tensions. Amherst's policies displeased all the Six Nations, but among the Senecas, the situation had become dangerous. Trade restrictions mixed with land concerns to produce a violent reaction. The problems began with the Niagara portage, the land route taken by travelers and traders between the western end of Lake Ontario and the eastern terminus of Lake Erie. The Niagara River connected the two lakes but was unnavigable, owing both to Niagara Falls and powerful rapids below the falls. Dating back at least to the second construction of Fort Niagara in the 1720s, bands of Genesee Senecas—those settled farther west in New York and sometimes referred to as the Chenussio Senecas—had hauled goods along the Niagara portage route, amassing a respectable income from traders and military leaders alike. After the British capture of Fort Niagara in 1759, however, General Amherst authorized British settlements in the Niagara portage, and a former soldier, Walter Rutherford, began putting together a freight hauling company to service the portage between Fort Niagara and newly built Fort Schlosser on the Niagara River above the falls. The Genesee Senecas were outraged. In their estimation, the British intended to deprive them of their territory—the Niagara portage had long been Seneca country—and deprive them of valuable income at the same time.[27]

Moreover, many Senecas were growing increasingly concerned by the presence of so many British forts along the borders of their territory. From Niagara south to Pittsburgh, the British had occupied the former French forts and constructed several new posts, leaving many Senecas with the impression that they were being encircled by the British. They reasoned that this could only be intended to cut the Senecas and the rest of the Six Nations off from their hunting grounds in the Ohio Country, or even worse, that the forts were the first step in a planned British invasion of Iroquoia. These fears manifested themselves in 1762 at a conference in Lancaster, Pennsylvania. The meeting had been called by Pennsylvania to reconfirm the peace agreement made at Easton in 1758, but Pennsylvania Governor James Hamilton used the proceedings to seek Seneca permission for a Pennsylvania fort along the western branch of the Susquehanna River, which would put the post on the southeastern frontier of Seneca territory. Seneca headman Kinderutie denounced the proposal and reminded Hamilton that the British had promised to abandon their western forts:

> You may remember you told me, when you were going to Pittsburgh, you would build a fort against the French, and you told me you wanted none of our lands; our cousins [Ohio Country Mingos and Delawares] know this, and that you promised to go away as soon as you drove the French away, and yet you stay there and build houses, and make it stronger and stronger every day. For this reason we entirely deny your request; you shall not have a road this way.[28]

Kinderutie's rebuke was only a small expression of Seneca anger, which had grown very deep. The Genesee Senecas, in particular, engaged in more dangerous activities. Two Senecas—the Genesee leader Tahaiadoris, a blood relative of the influential Joncaires, longtime French agents among the western Senecas, and Kiasutha, variously described as a Seneca regent over the Ohio Country Mingos or a Mingo-Seneca himself—attempted to create a unified military uprising against the British among the Indian nations of the Ohio Country. Together, the two Senecas traveled to Detroit during the summer of 1761, where they attempted to enlist the Indian nations living around Detroit in a plan to strike the British forts along the Niagara portage and throughout the Ohio Country. Local Indians betrayed the plot to the British commander at Detroit, Captain Donald Campbell, who confronted the two Seneca envoys. Tahaiadoris and Kiasutha disavowed their plan, promising to return home and live in peace with the British. Although their plot failed, the Senecas' anger did not abate.[29]

Nor did that of many Indian nations throughout the Ohio Country and the Great Lakes region. Rumors of an uprising against the British riddled the Ohio Country in 1762, forcing Sir William Johnson to travel to Detroit to investigate the extent of the problem. Along the way, Johnson stopped at Niagara, where he chastised Seneca leaders for trying to stir up trouble in the Ohio Country. The Seneca leader Sonajoana assured Johnson that his people had nothing to do with such a plot, a reply that may have revealed a fracture among the Senecas. The main body of Senecas living near the Finger Lakes may have had no knowledge of the plot, but the Genesee Senecas were trying to start a war with the British. The extent to which they were involved in organizing a united Indian uprising is uncertain, especially as the Ohio Country Indians were simultaneously planning a united war against the British. Yet all those close to the situation agreed that the Genesee Senecas believed that the "British had a mind to cut them off the face of the earth" and that they were very angry over British actions along the Niagara portage.[30] Johnson confided to Amherst that he "was very apprehensive that something not right is brewing."[31]

The war began in 1763 when the Ottawa leader Pontiac organized an attack against Detroit, thus giving the conflict its generally accepted title of "Pontiac's War" or "Pontiac's Uprising." After the attack on Detroit, Indian warriors besieged nearly every British fort west of the Appalachain Mountains, quickly capturing or destroying most of them. Among the Six Nations, news of the uprising produced a divided reaction. In June 1763, Mohawk sachem Tekarihoga reported to Sir William Johnson that a war belt had arrived at the Mohawk town of Canajoharie. The belt urged the Mohawks to join a widespread Indian uprising in the west, but the Mohawks put little stock in the tale. Indeed, the majority of the Six Nations would not support the uprising. However, the western Senecas, perhaps because of their involvement in earlier intrigue, proved more receptive to calls for war from the west. Shortly after the attack on Detroit, Delawares and Shawnees in the Ohio Country sent a war belt to the Genesee Senecas, urging them to join the war. They accepted. Indeed, Sir William Johnson learned that the Genesee Senecas, despite their denials, had circulated additional war belts to the Ohio Country throughout the spring of 1763.

There is no way to be certain exactly how much the Senecas participated in the war, or from what towns or factions they originated. It is likely that only the Genesee Senecas took an active part in the fighting, and the majority of the Seneca nation abstained. Nonetheless, Seneca warriors were instrumental that summer in the destruction of three British forts along their borders. On June 16, a group of Senecas approached the unsuspecting small garrison at Fort Venango (Franklin, Pennsylvania), a small post that consisted of a two-story log blockhouse surrounded by earthen ramparts. The post had been constructed by the British during the later stages of the Seven Years' War after the French had destroyed a nearby installation known as Fort Machault. The Senecas approached the fort in peace and, according to some accounts, duped the soldiers into allowing them into the fort. Once inside, the Senecas quickly attacked the dozen or so defenders, overpowering them. No one was spared, although the post's commander, Lieutenant Francis Gordon, was kept alive to draft a manifesto outlining the Indians' complaints. The document explained that the Senecas had attacked because they had become convinced that the British intended to steal their lands, as evidenced by the presence of the so many British forts in their hunting territory. It is unknown whether Lieutenant Gordon attempted to justify the British occupation, but, if so, his rationale must have proved unsatisfactory: the Senecas slowly roasted him to death.[32]

Next the Senecas struck Fort Le Boeuf (near modern Waterford, Pennsylvania), just a short distance north of Venango. A former French fort occupied by the British after the Seven Years' War, Fort Le Boeuf consisted of little more than a log blockhouse enclosed by walls of mounded earth with a few outbuildings strewn about. The British garrison was made up of 13 enlisted men under the command of Ensign George Price, and there was also a solitary women at the post. Unlike the troops at Fort Venango, the Le Boeuf garrison was on alert, having heard rumors of possible Indian troubles in the west. Rumor became reality on June 18, when a small party of Senecas approached the fort, claimed to be en route to strike the Cherokees in the south, and asked for powder and ammunition to support their campaign. Price refused, and the Senecas departed. They soon returned, however, in a larger party of at least 30 warriors, accompanied by other Indian warriors, perhaps Delawares or Ottawas. After Price again refused requests for material aid, this time a cooking pot, the Senecas and their allies forced entry into a nearby storehouse and began firing on the fort. The Senecas rained flaming arrows down on the roof of the wooden blockhouse, which soon was engulfed in flames. The British garrison worked valiantly to manage the blaze, but had to abandon the structure and make a run for the forest. The British chopped their way through the rear of the blockhouse and fled under cover of darkness, escaping pursuit. Although the party became separated, both groups, including the woman, eventually made their way south to Fort Pitt (present-day Pittsburgh) with minor casualties, passing the ruins of Fort Venango and the mutilated bodies of its garrison along the way. The Senecas burned Le Boeuf to the ground.[33]

Forts Venango and Le Boeuf were small, poorly defended wilderness posts, but nonetheless they were symbols of British power sitting along the border between the Six Nation's claimed hunting grounds in the Ohio Country and the southwestern frontier of Seneca territory. The Senecas had expressed their displeasure with the British occupation by reducing each post to ashes. Tackling Fort Presque Isle, which sat atop a bluff overlooking a fishhook shaped peninsula on Lake Erie, was not as easy. The post housed 29 soldiers, under the command of Ensign John Christie, as well as small contingent of civilian laborers and one woman for a total of perhaps 60 persons. The fort itself boasted a strong blockhouse attached to the corner of a palisaded fort. The post's strength was reflected by the

Indian attack force, which included 250 Senecas, Delawares, Ottawas, Chippewas, and Wyandots. Demonstrating a clear understanding of siege warfare, the Indian warriors dug trenches, established strategic firing positions, and tunneled under the fort's palisade, gaining entry to the parade ground. The walls and most of the structures were set on fire, leaving the garrison huddled in the blockhouse. The defenders' spirits were lifted briefly when an British vessel, the *Huron*, was cited a few miles off the coast; but the ship's crew could not maneuver close enough to shore to bring the ship's guns into play, nor would the captain risk sending in a shore party without covering fire. Finally, Ensign Christie surrendered to the Indians on condition that he and his men be allowed to march south to Fort Pitt. They never got close. As soon as the garrison came out of the fort, the Indians attacked them, killed or wounded many men, and took the remainder captive. Christie and five others went west with the Detroit Indians, and the others were divided among the Senecas and Delawares. The fort was burned.[34]

The Genesee Senecas also attacked the British along the Niagara portage. The British presence there had been one of the Senecas' major concerns in the years leading up to the war, and there was little chance the region would escape the violence of the uprising. In September 1763, as many as 500 Seneca warriors ambushed a British supply convoy, consisting of 25 wagons, as it wound its way from Fort Schlosser north toward Fort Niagara. The attack was perfectly coordinated to occur along a thin road that wound along the Niagara River, at a spot where high cliffs overlook a deep gorge highlighted by a spectacular whirlpool that dominates a sharp bend in the Niagara River. The spot, today known as Devil's Hole, earned its name. The Senecas opened fire on the supply caravan from cover, scattering the 20 or 30 British soldiers escorting the convoy, then rushed forward and began hacking into British with tomahawks and knives. Frightened horses plunged over the cliffs in their panic to escape the tumult, and the Senecas sent most of the wagons, reluctant draft animals, and more than a few British over the side as well. Two members of a wagon team were the only British survivors. The noise of the battle was heard two miles downstream at a small fortified station called Fort Demler. The post's commander, Lieutenant George Campbell, hurriedly organized the two companies of redcoats under his command, about 80 men, and rushed to the relief of the supply convoy. The Senecas spotted the approaching troops and organized a second ambush, killing Campbell and most of the British officers in the opening volley. Again the Senecas surged forward with tomahawks and scalping knives, crashing into the stunned British soldiers and driving the relief column back down the portage road. Only a handful of men survived. A relief force from Fort Niagara reached Devil's Hole the next day, but the Senecas had withdrawn, leaving 76 dead British soldiers stripped and scalped along the portage road. At least 32 British men had been tossed over the cliffs to the Niagara River below, along with a large number of horses, oxen, and wagons. It was a symbolic and poignant reminder of the Genesee Senecas' displeasure over having been cut out of the portage business.[35]

From his home in the Mohawk Valley, British Indian Superintendent William Johnson desperately tried to discover the extent of the Senecas' involvement and to draw other members of the Six Nations into the war on the British side. In July, Johnson met with more than 300 Iroquois at German Flats. The Senecas were notably absent, but Johnson urged the representatives from the other Iroquois nations to remain neutral and asked that the Iroquois League pressure the Senecas into giving up the fight. Four Mohawks, including the prominent spokesmen Little Abraham, agreed to talk with the Senecas. Two months later, Johnson opened a larger conference at his home in the Mohawk Valley. Little Abraham brought along six Seneca representatives, who explained that their villages near the Finger Lakes supported peace, but the Genesee Senecas and their Mingo relatives in the Ohio Country remained at war. This revelation left Johnson with little choice but to ask the Iroquois to send war parties to punish the rebellious Indian nations. Johnson understood that the other Iroquois nations would not fight the Senecas, so instead he asked that they attack the Delawares and Shawnees in the Ohio Country. When General Amherst learned of Johnson's plans to employ the Iroquois against the Ohio Country Indians, he squashed the plan. A British army was already moving across southern Pennsylvania toward the Ohio Country, and Amherst wanted no part of using Indians, whom he distrusted and despised, to rescue the beleaguered British forts.[36]

Amherst's recall to England in October 1763 removed this obstacle, and his replacement, General Thomas Gage, approved the use of Iroquois warriors to chastise the rebellious Indian nations. A British army had already broken the Indian siege of Fort Pitt, and another expedition was planned to relieve Detroit, although Pontiac would call off his attack on the fort long before the British expedition arrived. This left the Iroquois warriors free to strike at the Susquehanna Delawares, who had attacked British settlements after the suspicious death of Teedyuscung, who burned to death in his cabin. Johnson urged the warriors of the Six Nations to punish Captain Bull, Teedyuscung's son and the war leader responsible for the Delaware raids. It was a target readily acceptable to the Six Nations, as it allowed the Iroquois to demonstrate their allegiance to the Covenant Chain while simultaneously reasserting their control over the wayward Susquehanna Delawares. In late February, a large expedition of 200 Mohawks, Oneidas, and Tuscaroras commanded by Andrew Montour, a mixed-blood interpreter, and John Johnson, Sir William's son, set out toward the Susquehanna to attack the Delawares. In late February, the expedition halted near the village of Oquaga (near present-day Windsor, New York), a mixed community of Oneidas, Tuscaroras, and Mohawks on the Susquehanna. At Oquaga, the Iroquois encountered a large party of Delawares headed north. The Iroquois seized seven of the warriors who entered Oquaga in peace, then surrounded the main Delaware camp outside the village. Accounts of what followed are confusing, but either through a surprise attack or via voluntary surrender, the Iroquois captured upwards of 40 Delawares, including the notorious Captain Bull. Fourteen warriors, including Captain Bull, were sent to William Johnson, who promptly shipped them off to prison in New York City. Most of the remaining Delaware were women and children, whom the Iroquois claimed by right of war. By then, news of the Iroquois attack had reached the Delawares, who abandoned their Susquehanna villages and fled. Nonetheless, the Iroquois moved along the west branch of the river, destroying fields and stores of corn while burning more than 130 houses in three villages and a number of smaller, outlying settlements.[37]

By the spring of 1764, the war had turned in favor of the British, revealing that the Indian uprising had been a spectacular failure. The Six Nations had taken up the British cause, British armies were preparing to advance on the Ohio Country and Detroit, and the most important British forts—Detroit, Pitt, and Niagara—remained firmly under British control. On the other side of the war, the belligerent Indian nations were somewhat in disarray, having suffered through a long, cold winter without achieving their objectives of driving the British out of the Ohio Country. Sensing that the time for armed resistance had past, the Genesee Senecas used the lull in fighting occasioned by the winter to make peace. The terms arranged by Johnson were far from lenient. He required the Genesee Senecas to cede their claims to the land along the Niagara portage, return any white captives in their villages, break off all relations with the Ohio Country Indians, and reconfirm their attachment to the Covenant Chain alliance. The Senecas begrudgingly agreed, and they confirmed their acceptance of Johnson's terms during a July 1764 meeting at Fort Niagara, where they delivered up 13 British captives in their possession and agreed to send 23 warriors with the British expedition headed to punish the Indian nations around Detroit. Johnson accepted the agreement and tried not to embarrass the Genesee Senecas too terribly, as the British needed the Senecas to return willingly to the fold of the Six Nations.[38]

The British campaigns of 1764, which fought no major battles against Indians, restored order to the British imperial world. With few exceptions, Ohio Country and Great Lakes Indian nations agreed to tentative peace accords to avoid the destruction of their villages. The British would now formally replace the French as their principal economic and political ally. To further the new arrangement, the British government put in place what became known as the Proclamation Line, a ruling actually adopted in London before the uprising began that forbid British colonists to settle west of the Appalachian Mountains, reserving the interior of the continent for the Indian nations. The measure was a step toward guaranteeing Indian sovereignty over their lands, but it soon became apparent that the proclamation would not curb colonial expansion or offer any real protection for the lands of the Six Nations or any other Indian people. In 1768, the line was moved farther west to the Ohio River by the Treaty of Fort Stanwix, an agreement to which the Six Nations were principal signatories. The new boundary protected Iroquoia from settlement, but enforcement of the boundary lapsed after 1772, when the British abandoned their western forts and transferred the garrisons to the Atlantic coastal cities to monitor the activities of their increasingly rebellious colonists. By 1774, the scent of war once again was in the air as the American colonies threatened to break away from England. Although the peoples of the Iroquois League had little concern for the white man's family quarrel, few people in eastern North America would escape the coming storm. Indeed, for the Iroquois League, the war of the American Revolution would prove especially disastrous.

8

•

The Longhouse in Flames

The American Revolution was the most devastating war in Iroquois history. American armies rampaged through Iroquoia, burning villages and destroying crops, forcing thousands of Iroquois people to become refugees in their own lands. Perhaps even worse, the revolution sparked a civil war among the Six Nations, as many Oneidas and Tuscaroras sided with the Americans, and the majority of Mohawks, Senecas, Cayugas, and Onondagas took up the king's arms. While American colonists squabbled with their English king over taxation, the Iroquois fought each other, both as auxiliaries in American and British armies and directly as they raided each other's villages. Somehow, through it all, the Six Nations remained unbeaten. By the end of the war, the Six Nations were bloodied, battered, and divided, but they were still able to mount raids and attacks against their enemies. Only the British decision to cease hostilities after Yorktown took the Six Nations out of the fight, and even then not completely.

THE FAILURE OF NEUTRALITY

The Six Nations initially sought to return to the policy of neutrality during the American Revolution. The American colonies' split from England allowed the Iroquois to again balance diplomacy between two antagonistic entities on their borders. During discussions with both the British and the Americans in the years preceding the revolution, Iroquois representatives explained that the Six Nations desired "not to take any part [in the war], but as it is a family affair, to sit still and see you fight it out."[1] Neither the British nor the Americans were content with the Iroquois decision, and throughout 1775 and 1776, both struggled to win the support of the Six Nations. The Americans held the early advantage. They considered it a victory if the Iroquois abstained from participation in the conflict, so they requested only that the Iroquois hold firm to their pledge of neutrality. Major-General Philip Schuyler, commander of the Continental Army's Northern Department, explained that the revolution was "a family quarrel between us and old England," informing the Iroquois that "We don't wish you to take up the hatchet against the King's troops. We wish you to remain at home and not join either side, but keep the hatchet buried deep."[2] Iroquois leaders appreciated the American stance, as it coincided nicely with their policy, but they nonetheless warned Schuyler not to bring the war onto Iroquois lands. The Six Nations would not allow Iroquoia to be "defiled with blood," warned Mohawk leader Little Abraham, who also reminded the Americans that "we bear as much affection for the King of England's subjects on the other side of the water as we do for you born on this island."[3]

The Iroquois recorded that they were "well pleased that they could live on neutral ground, surrounded by the din of war, without being engaged in it."[4] But the Six Nations were perhaps naive to believe that they could remain completely aloof from the conflict. Their relationship with both antagonists was too deep to allow total isolation. Indeed, the Six Nations' new American friends soon took a number of actions that upset and con-cerned Iroquois leaders. Late in 1775, American armies invaded Canada, disrupting the flow of British trade goods up the St. Lawrence. The Sen-ecas, who traded at Fort Niagara, were severely affected as trade goods quickly dried up. The inability of American traders to adequately supply the Iroquois during the early war years spread the economic malaise to rest of the Six Nations. American harassment of suspected loyalists in the Mohawk Valley, many of whom had long associations with the Mohawks and Cayugas, further damaged the colonies' relationship with the Iroquois. In 1775, overzealous American patriots murdered a Mohawk headman known as Peter Nickus, whom they suspected of Loyalist activities. The killing might have been smoothed over as a minor misunderstanding had the Americans not hacked his body to pieces with swords. The attempted arrest of John Johnson, eldest son of Sir William Johnson, was another particularly damaging episode. American authorities suspected that Johnson was organizing loyalist militia units, but rather than asking the Mohawks to intercede with Johnson, the Americans twice sent troops through Mohawk territory to arrest him. Johnson eventually escaped to Canada, but these episodes greatly angered the Mohawks, who needed little massaging to push them into the British camp.[5]

American actions were not the only forces pushing the Six Nations toward the British. As had been the case during previous conflicts, divisions riddled the Iroquois during the early years of the American Revolution. Many Oneidas and some Tuscaroras were pro-American, having become deeply attached to American missionary preachers, such as Samuel Kirkland and James Dean, who had been active in their villages since the 1760s. Most Mohawks, especially those under the influence of the increasingly influential war leader Thayendanegea, better known as Joseph Brant, were pro-British. Brant had been the star pupil of Sir William Johnson, who married Joseph's older sister Molly, and the Indian Superintendent had taken special measures to have Brant educated and indoctrinated in British values. Not surprisingly, Brant became a strong advocate of an alliance with the British, and late in 1775, he even traveled to England to seek the support of the British government. Some Onondagas, Cayugas, and Senecas supported Mohawk calls for war against the Americans, but the majority of these nations favored neutrality. Least influenced by either side, they believed abstaining from the war was the only way to provide security for their people.[6]

These divisions produced cracks in the Six Nations' wall of neutrality. In 1777, the British pushed hard to bring the Iroquois into the war against the Americans. The British needed Iroquois support for their military plans, which called for an invasion of New York from Canada, with one wing of the British army slotted to pass through the eastern reaches of Iroquoia to attack Fort Stanwix, an American post situated between the Mohawk River and Wood Creek in Oneida country. The author of the British invasion plan, Lieutenant-General John Burgoyne, intended this leg of his force to be composed of only 200 regulars and a body of loyalists under the command of Sir John Johnson. The vast majority of manpower for the expedition was to be provided by a "body of savages."[7] During the spring of 1777, British agents warned the Iroquois "what a wretched situation you must be in when the king attacks … and comes in earnest to sweep off the Americans, if he finds you supporting the Americans."[8] John Butler, a loyalist Indian trader from the Mohawk Valley and the newly appointed Indian agent at Fort Niagara, was extremely active, especially among the Senecas. But his appeals failed to sway the Senecas from neutrality. Despite worsening economic difficulties, Flying Crow, war leader of the Senecas living along the upper Allegheny River, asked Butler a deceptively simple question: "If you are so strong brother, and they but as a weak boy, then why ask our assistance?"[9]

As the spring gave way to early summer in 1777, a series of events began to pull the Six Nations apart. Joseph Brant had returned from England, and, after briefly participating in the British capture of New York City, he made his way back to Mohawk country in late 1776. There Brant quickly began recruiting a mixed force of Iroquois and white loyalists to join the British army descending from Canada. Fearing American reprisals, many Mohawks abandoned their villages and withdrew down the Susquehanna or moved west to Fort Niagara, where they found a fair number of Cayugas also prepared to join the British. Elsewhere, however, pro-American Iroquois moved closer to alliance with the rebellious colonies. Earlier in 1776, General Philip Schuyler had carried out a directive from the Continental Congress to enlist the Six Nations in the war. A number of Oneidas and Tuscaroras accepted the call to arms, and the Oneidas asked the Americans to repair and garrison Fort Stanwix, so that the fort might provide shelter for Oneida women and children should the Mohawks or the British strike their villages. Meanwhile, the Onondagas held fast to neutrality, but an epidemic disaster thwarted any influence or ability the nation may have had to keep other Iroquois out of the war. During the winter of 1777, the sacred Iroquois central council fire at the Onondaga capitol was accidentally extinguished after a powerful pestilence struck the town's residents, leaving upwards of 90 dead and many others grievously ill. Neglected because of the widespread sickness and suffering, the ceremonial fire that was symbolic of the Six Nations' unity died, perhaps foreshadowing the horror to come.[10]

At the western door of Iroquoia, the Senecas, most populous of all the Six Nations, remained uncommitted as the summer of 1777 approached. But the lack of trade goods at Fort Niagara had brought grave economic hardship to the Senecas, a situation British agents were only too happy to exploit. By the end of 1776, the British had expelled the Americans from Canada and reopened the St. Lawrence River to westward-bound commerce, which they used to leverage Seneca allegiance. Nearly 2,000 Senecas flocked to British councils at Irondequoit and Oswego, including large numbers of women and children, where they joined other Iroquois drawn by promises of generous gifts of food, clothing, and ammunition. Only the Oneidas were not represented. Provisions were abundant for the taking, the feasting was sumptuous, and presents were given out to every Iroquois individual. Moreover, the British appealed to the Six Nations' sense of tradition by presenting a massive wampum belt that commemorated the original covenant chain the Iroquois people and the King of England. The Great Covenant Chain, as the Iroquois named the belt, predated any agreements between the Iroquois League and the Americans, and it illustrated for all the undying friendship between the Great British father and his Iroquois children.[11]

Once the feasting and celebrating had concluded, the British asked for a formal military alliance with the Six Nations in their struggle against the Americans. Many Iroquois declared their support, but the Senecas were still uncertain. Gayentwahga, or Cornplanter, a headman of the western Senecas, counseled caution, warning that "war is war, death is the death, a fight is a hard business."[12] He argued that the Iroquois did not fully understand the conflict between the Americans and the British, having been told two different versions of dispute's origins, and he warned that the Six Nations should not become embroiled in someone else's war. Joseph Brant spoke for those Iroquois willing to fight. There would be no peace, he predicted, regardless of what the Senecas decided. Brant argued that the Americans could not be trusted, and he urged the Senecas to strike now before the Americans "cut our throat."[13] Brant then accused Cornplanter of cowardice, telling the rest of the Senecas that their leader was afraid to fight to protect their homes. Witnesses later testified that Cornplanter, only 25 years old and conscious of his status as a warrior, stood silent as if struck senseless after Brant concluded his verbal assault. The next day, the assembled Iroquois, including the Senecas, voted to enter the war against the Americans. Iroquois neutrality again had failed, but this time the unity of the Six Nations would die with it.[14]

CIVIL WAR

The Iroquois warriors who joined the British at Oswego were attached to the army of Lieutenant Colonel Barry St. Leger, whose objective was the capture of Fort Stanwix on the Mohawk River. St. Leger's campaign was designed to support the major British offensive for 1777, which targeted the Hudson River corridor in New York. General John Burgoyne, at the head of a large army of British regulars, Canadian militia, Hessian mercenaries, and Canadian Indians, would descend Lake Champlain from Montreal, capture Fort Ticonderoga from the Americans, and then advance on Albany. Meanwhile, the main British army, headquartered in New York City, would ascend the Hudson to rendezvous with Burgoyne in Albany. Once Fort Stanwix had been reduced, St. Leger would join the other British armies at Albany, leaving the British in firm control of the colony of New York. Theoretically, the stroke would sever the rebellious colonies in two, allowing the British to operate at their leisure against either George Washington's ragged Continental Army in eastern Pennsylvania or to invade and reduce the New England colonies, long considered the seedbed of the revolution.[15]

The British invasion from Canada would eventually end in disaster at Saratoga, but St. Leger's campaign would prove even more damaging for the peoples of the Iroquois League. By its end, the Iroquois would be entangled in a bloody civil war. St. Leger's army, a mixed force of British regulars, Canadian militia, Hessian riflemen, and loyalist partisans under John Johnson, advanced slowly toward Fort Stanwix, joined along the way by some 800 Indians. Most were Senecas, under their war leaders Cornplanter and Sayenqueraghta (Old Smoke), or Mohawks and Cayugas, headed by Joseph Brant. More than 100 Canadian Indians, including some Catholic Iroquois, were also present, as well as scattering of Great Lakes Indians. The army reached Fort Stanwix on August 3, where St. Leger found a repaired and refurbished structure garrisoned by more than 700 Americans. Owing to poor intelligence, St. Leger had not known that the Americans had rebuilt Fort Stanwix, and he had failed to bring along a large enough artillery train to reduce the fort. Left with little other choice, St. Leger settled in for a siege.[16]

From the start, the Iroquois warriors expressed their displeasure with this turn of events. They were reluctant to attack a well-manned and strongly fortified military post, a fact they made well known to St. Leger. Joseph Brant wanted to attack nearby American settlements in the Mohawk Valley, which would perhaps induce the defenders of Fort Stanwix to come to their aid, but St. Leger refused. Although the Indians helped build a series of breastworks to defend the attackers and fired on the fort alongside the British soldiers and militia, they grumbled constantly and talked openly of going home. Before that could happen, messengers arrived from Joseph Brant's sister, who still resided in the Mohawk Valley, that a large column of American militia was on the march to relieve Fort Stanwix. St. Leger decided to ambush the American militia rather than "subject myself to be attacked by a sally from the garrison in the rear, while the enforcement employed me in the front."[17] For this task he selected the Iroquois, freeing them from their unhappy participation in the siege, and the loyalist militia under John Johnson, who would command the endeavor. After scouting the road leading from the American settlements to the fort, Johnson and the Iroquois selected an ambush point where the road dipped through a ravine as it crossed a small creek near the Oneida settlement of Oriska. Johnson placed his loyalists in the road at the far end of the ravine, while the Iroquois fanned out in the woods along either side. The plan called for Johnson's men to attack the front of the Americans' column as it began to come up out of the ravine, while the Iroquois would hit the flanks and then circle around to cut off any potential escape routes. Their ambush in place, the Iroquois waited, in the words of a young Seneca warrior named Black-snake, to "shed our white brothers and ourselves blood over the earth."[18]

The column of 760 unsuspecting Americans entered the ravine on the morning of August 6. At their head were 60 Oneida warriors under 3 pro-American headmen, Thomas Spencer, Haunnagwasuke (Henry Cornelius), and Thawengarakwen (Honyery Doxtater). Normally, the Oneidas would have been well forward of the militia scouting the countryside, but the American commander, General Nicholas Herkimer, was pressing his army forward with great haste after a confrontation with his officers, who accused the general of cowardice and loyalist sympathies after several delays along the march. When most of the American column was in the ravine, the Senecas opened fire. A chaotic melee then ensued as the Senecas and Mohawks poured out of the woods and slammed into the Americans, attacking with tomahawks, clubs, and knives. Thomas Spencer was killed and Thawengarakwen was shot in the arm, although he stayed in the fight thanks to his wife, who had accompanied him on the campaign and stood beside her husband furiously reloading his musket and helping him fire at approaching enemies. A fierce Oneida warrior named Blatcop ran back and forth through the chaos, striking down Senecas, Mohawks, and British alike. American survivors eventually re-formed themselves into a defensive circle along a ridge on the ravine's western edge, where General Herkimer, wounded below his knee, continued to direct his troops. For three hours, the battle became a bloody stalemate. The Senecas made several assaults but could not break through the American lines, while the Mohawks abandoned the field to chase after fleeing American militia. Finally, a thunderstorm erupted over the ravine, turning the battlefield into a swamp and ending the fight. The Iroquois and British headed for Fort Stanwix, from which the sound of cannons had been heard earlier in the day, leaving the battered Americans to limp back toward their settlements to the east.[19]

The battle of Oriskany, as it came to be called, proved costly for both sides. Perhaps 200 Americans died, and another 150 were wounded, although estimates vary widely. It is unknown how many Oneidas were killed or wounded in the battle. Casualties on the British side were light by comparison, numbering just over 20 killed and wounded, although 33 Indians lay dead and another 29 had been wounded. Of these, more than 30 were Senecas, including 6 dead war chiefs. To the Senecas, these were horrifying losses. "There I have seen the most dead bodies all over it that I never did see," recalled Blacksnake, "I thought at that time the blood shed a stream running down on the descending ground."[20] Sayenqueraghta, whose son died during the battle, wanted to pursue the Americans and finish them off, but St. Leger refused, preferring instead to continue the siege of Fort Stanwix, much to the disdain of the Iroquois warriors. Yet they reluctantly agreed to maintain the siege, which went on without success for another two weeks, until word reached the fort that another American relief column was approaching. The Iroquois initially agreed to conduct another ambush, this time accompanied by St. Leger and the British regulars. They changed their minds, however, when a young loyalist, Han Yost Schuyler, who was well known to the Mohawks in St. Leger's army, appeared in the British camp claiming that the approaching American army was as numerous as the leaves of the trees, a gross exaggeration arranged by Benedict Arnold, who commanded the American column. There is some debate concerning whether the Iroquois believed Schuyler's tall tale, but in any case, the Iroquois used the news as justification to abandon the siege. St. Leger was powerless to stop them from leaving, and without the Iroquois to protect his siege lines, he had little choice but to withdraw as well. The arrival of Arnold's supposedly massive army hastened the entire process, and in the confusion of the disorganized retreat, some Iroquois attacked and pillaged British and Hessian troops to replenish themselves for their journey home.[21]

The campaign against Fort Stanwix was a British failure, but for the Iroquois it was a monumental disaster. The Senecas were shocked at the outcome. Mary Jemison, a white woman raised among the Senecas, recalled that "our town exhibited a scene of real sorrow and distress, when our warriors returned and recounted their misfortunes, and stated the real loss they had received in the engagement. The mourning was excessive, and was expressed by the most doleful yells, shrieks and howlings, and by inimitable gesticulations."[22] More important, however, Senecas, Mohawks, and Oneidas had killed one another at Oriskany, beginning a civil war that would shake the foundations of the Iroquois League. So angry were the Senecas over the participation of the Oneidas in the battle that they paused long enough in the vicinity of Fort Stanwix to sack the Oneida village of Oriska, burning it to the ground, destroying crops, and driving away cattle. That October, during a conference at Onondaga, the pro-British Iroquois recommitted themselves to the war, although they followed the suggestion of Joseph Brant that their warriors must fight according to their own traditions, by executing raids against the settlements and towns of their enemy. No longer would the Iroquois serve as auxiliaries for British armies; instead they would harass and destroy the Americans and their Oneida allies by driving them off their lands. The Onondagas and a handful of neutralists from the other Iroquois nations resolved to remain uninvolved, but their position was becoming increasingly difficult to maintain. The Iroquois civil war had begun.[23]

After the British defeat at Fort Stanwix, the Oneidas from Oriska avenged themselves on Mohawks who had not yet fled the valley. Oneida warriors under Honyery Doxtater invaded the largely abandoned Mohawk village of Canajoharie, forcing Molly Brant and the few remaining Mohawks into exile in the west. Indeed, Doxtater and other Oneida leaders pillaged Brant's considerable property, with Doxtater taking possession of her house. The attack fractured the Oneidas, not all of whom supported the Americans, but to those who were pro-American, victory seemed within their grasp. More than 150 Oneidas and Tuscaroras joined American armies fighting against the large British army that had descended from Canada, which had advanced as far as the upper reaches of the Hudson River. Under the leadership of Louis Atayataghronghta, Peter Beard, and Doxtater, who according to their American companions "were all brave men and fought like dogs," the Oneidas and Tuscaroras fought at the battles around Saratoga that defeated the British push.[24]

The onset of winter, during which most Iroquois warriors, pro-British and pro-American alike, returned to their villages to hunt, halted hostilities until the spring of 1778. The Iroquois were content to wait. "As those people whom we intend to attack in the spring are asleep," explained Sayenqueraghta, "we do not choose to awaken them until we strike the blow."[25] In the interim, Joseph Brant and Sayenqueraghta collaborated with British Indian agent John Butler to develop a three-headed war plan. Brant would lead Mohawks and Cayugas against the American settlements in the Mohawk Valley. He also hoped to move into Oneida territory and attack the Oneidas' principal village of Kanwolohale, then reoccupy Oswego, which had been abandoned after the Fort Stanwix fiasco, as a base for future operations. Simultaneously, Sayenqueraghta and Cornplanter would take the Senecas from the Finger Lakes to raid the American settlements situated along the Susquehanna River in Pennsylvania's Wyoming Valley. The Susquehanna, especially its western branch, provided a gateway into Seneca territory, and the Seneca war leaders considered disrupting American activities on the river a matter of the utmost importance. Meanwhile, western Senecas living along the Genesee and upper Allegheny Rivers would move down the Allegheny to attack the American settlements around Pittsburgh and in northwestern Virginia (modern West Virginia). The British, under John Butler and his son Walter, would lend assistance wherever and whenever possible. The consistent goal of all three offensives was the removal of Americans from lands claimed by the Iroquois and the destruction of their homes and property. Settlers who resisted would be killed, but otherwise the Iroquois hoped to force the Americans off the land without an overwhelming cost in lives, especially their own.[26]

The western Senecas struck first. In April, 1778, a war party of 125 Senecas and Cayugas descended on the Derry settlements, southeast of Pittsburgh in Westmoreland County, Pennsylvania. The Iroquois ambushed a party of 20 American militia in the vicinity of a stockaded homestead known as Fort Wallace. Nine Americans and four Indians died during the brief skirmish, after which the Iroquois attacked the fort. Some time thereafter another engagement took place when a large party of settlers sallied forth from a nearby fortified farm called Fort Barr to relieve the besieged Fort Wallace. The Iroquois ambushed the advancing militia as they crossed a bridge over a deep gully, although the Americans managed to retreat back to their stockades. Fifteen Americans were killed and two others were captured before the Senecas withdrew. The same war party may then have moved further south, killing 13 Americans and capturing 2 others in northwestern Virginia. During the next two months, however, the western Senecas shifted their attention to the west branch of the Susquehanna River, raiding numerous settlements from Lycoming to Bald Eagle Creek. The raids left 15 settlers dead, while the Senecas withdrew with more than 50 prisoners. The attacks precipitated what frontier Pennsylvanians termed "the Big Runaway," when hundreds of frightened settlers abandoned the region from Bald Eagle Creek to the forks of the Susquehanna.[27]

As spring wore into summer, the rest of the Senecas readied their attack on the Wyoming Valley. Sayenqueraghta and Cornplanter established a base of operations at Tioga, a mixed Indian community at the intersection of the Chemung and Susquehanna Rivers. They assembled 464 warriors, primarily eastern Senecas along with some western Senecas, Cayugas, and even a few Onondagas. They were joined at Tioga by 110 loyalist partisans, known as Butler's Rangers after their commander, John Butler.

In late June, the raiders moved down the Susquehanna in a flotilla of 50 canoes, reaching the outskirts of the Wyoming Valley three days later. From there, the Iroquois and loyalists advanced by foot toward the settlements, which were defended by seven forts, most of which were little more than stockaded homesteads. On July 1, Iroquois scouting parties encountered a group of 12 settlers working in the fields near Sutton Creek, 4 of whom were killed and 2 others captured. The rest fled and sounded the alarm, sending panicked Americans fleeing into their stockades throughout the valley. The largest of these was Forty Fort, situated across the river from the main settlement of Wyoming. The fort was garrisoned by 450 men, including a detachment of 60 Continental soldiers under Colonel Zebulon Butler. When word of the attacks reached Forty Fort, Butler gathered 400 men and led them forth to meet the enemy.[28]

As was their strategy, Sayenqueraghta, Cornplanter, and John Butler had been busily negotiating the surrender of two settler forts on the western side of the valley, where there was a strong loyalist presence in the region. The two posts, Wintermoot Fort and Jenkins Fort, surrendered; and the settlers were allowed to leave unharmed, although the Senecas nonetheless began burning and plundering vacated homes and farms in the surrounding countryside. Scouts soon reported the approach of the American militia, and the Iroquois settled on their favorite strategy, an ambush. Sayenqueraghta ordered the two captured forts set on fire to fool the Americans into thinking the Senecas were withdrawing, then divided his warriors into six groups and concealed them in trees alongside a large open field, while Butler's rangers took up a position beyond a log fence that bordered the pasture. As Zebulon Butler led the Americans into the field, the loyalists crouched down behind the log fence. Thinking they had their enemy trapped, the Americans opened fire. After three volleys failed to force the loyalists from their position, they stood up, returned fire, and then began to retreat. Believing victory was at hand, the Americans surged forward, only to be taken completely by surprise when the Senecas fired on them from the woods, then rushed forward and smashed into the Americans' left flank. A fierce battle raged as the Americans struggled to fight off the assault, but in the confusion the American militia misunderstood an order to re-form their lines and instead began to retreat. The Senecas chased the Americans toward an island in the Susquehanna, where they shot or tomahawked many of them as they tried to wade across the river. Some Americans, including Zebulon Butler, fought their way out of the ambush and fled south to the safety of Forty Fort, but more than 300 Americans died. The Senecas and Butler's Rangers lost perhaps 10 men each.[29]

Some Senecas paused to take scalps and torture American prisoners, but most accompanied Butler's rangers to besiege Forty Fort. When they reached the post, Sayenqueraghta and Butler offered the Americans a chance to surrender. Staying with their strategy to force the Americans from the land, the attackers demanded the surrender of the fort and all other stockaded homes in the valley, promising that the inhabitants would be spared if they left in peace. Faced with little other alternative after the debacle the previous day, the Americans accepted the terms. Formal surrender was delayed long enough to allow Zebulon Butler and his remaining Continental soldiers to escape, then the settlers handed over the fort to John Butler. The inhabitants were allowed to leave the region without harm, but the Senecas destroyed their homes and looted their possessions as they withdrew. Hundreds of homes were burned, and nearly a thousand head of cattle, a large number of horses, and several flocks of sheep and pigs were butchered or driven into the forest. The Senecas and loyalists then departed the valley with 227 scalps and 5 prisoners.[30]

When the Senecas reached Tioga, Butler detached most of his rangers and sent them under Captain William Caldwell to reinforce Joseph Brant's Mohawk company of warriors. Brant had not been idle. In February 1778, he had established bases of operation at Oquaga and Unadilla, two mixed Iroquois communities on the banks of the upper Susquehanna River, where many pro-British Mohawks had intermixed with the Tuscaroras, Oneidas, and Delawares already living there. The villages initially tried to remain neutral in the conflict, but the arrival of the pro-British Iroquois and Brant's intention to use the towns as his headquarters erased any possibility of neutrality. Brant raised the British flag, convinced the residents that supporting the British was in their best interests, and began recruiting an army. He soon had more than 200 Iroquois warriors, mostly Mohawks from his home village of Canajoharie, assembled and ready for war. Brant recruited not only Iroquois warriors, however, but loyalists as well. By the time Brant launched his first raids in the summer of 1778, more than 100 loyalists had joined his cause, calling themselves "Brant's volunteers."[31]

Brant's target was the American settlements in the Mohawk Valley. On May 30, he sent a small scouting party toward the southern edge of Cobleskill, a community of some 20 families strung out over a three-mile stretch of the Mohawk Valley. The community had no fortified homesteads, but a detachment of 33 Continental soldiers under Captain William Patrick patrolled the region. Brant's plan was to draw the Continentals into a trap, which worked perfectly when Patrick led his detachment, along with a handful of local militia, in pursuit of the Iroquois scouts. Brant's main force ambushed the Americans about a mile outside the settlement, killing Patrick and two of his officers in the initial exchange of fire. The Americans immediately retreated toward Cobleskill, where several took refuge in a house at the southern end of the settlement. The Iroquois set fire to the house and then moved into Cobleskill, burning 10 house and barns and killing cattle that would not be driven off. The Iroquois killed 22 Americans, wounded 8 others, and took 5 prisoners, whom Brant later turned over to British officials at Niagara. The Iroquois began an operation against the neighboring settlement of Durlach (modern Sharon, New York), but Brant withdrew his force after setting fire to a single house when he learned that American militia were heading his way.[32]

Brant did not allow the Mohawk Valley to rest long, returning in mid-July to attack Springfield, a small settlement at the northern tip of Otsego Lake, and Andrustown (now Jordanville, New York), a settlement of seven families a few miles northwest of the lake. The Iroquois burned both settlements, killed 8 men, took 14 prisoners, and captured a large number of horses and cattle, which Brant ordered transported to Unadilla for the sustenance of his warriors. But again Brant withdrew, this time because Oneida scouts had warned the American settlements at German Flats to prepare for an attack. The Oneidas had been cautiously assisting the Americans in defending the region, although they mostly remained in the vicinity of their main village at Kanowalohale, where the Americans had erected a fort for their defense. Nonetheless, just about the time of the attack on Springfield, four Oneida and Tuscarora headmen approached General Philip Schuyler and requested commissions in the Continental Army so that they might more effectively combat Brant and the Mohawks.[33]

Oneida assistance was not enough to save German Flats, a string of scattered farms and homesteads along a rich grain producing region of the Mohawk Valley, which Brant struck in September. Although a party of five Oneidas scouting south of the settlements were captured by Brant's warriors before they could warn the Americans of the impending attack, the assault on German Flats did not catch the Americans by surprise. On September 16, advance elements of Brant's force attacked an American scouting detail, killing three men. Survivors warned German Flats settlers of the attack, and the inhabitants crowded into two defensive posts, Forts Dayton and Herkimer, to weather the attack. Brant reached the settlements that night with 152 Iroquois and 300 loyalists. His warriors demonstrated for a bit in front of Fort Dayton, but lacking artillery to reduce the post, Brant posted small parties to harass the forts while the remainder of the Iroquois and loyalists occupied themselves by destroying the settlements. With their militia too frightened to sally forth from the forts, the helpless Americans watched as Brant's forces ravaged a 10-mile long stretch of settlements on both sides of the Mohawk River. When they had finished, 63 houses, 57 barns, 3 gristmills, and 1 sawmill had been reduced to ashes, leaving 719 people without shelter. Only two houses, a church, and Fort Dayton remained intact on the north side of the river. Three houses, one belonging to a minister and the other two the property of loyalists, were unscathed on the southern shore. Satisfied with the devastation, the Iroquois withdrew, taking 235 horses, 229 cattle, and 269 sheep with them.[34]

Iroquois strategy was working perfectly: homes and property were being destroyed, making it difficult for the Americans to remain in possession of the land, while the loss of life had been kept to a minimum for both sides. There was only one flaw, and it proved fatal. Sayenqueraghta and Brant had hoped to minimize the killing of American settlers, believing low casualty totals would mute American cries for revenge. But the widespread destruction of property angered the Americans almost as much as if there had been a massive body count, leading to loud and persistent calls for retaliation. New York Governor George Clinton informed George Washington that he could not secure his state's frontier "until the straggling Indians and Tories who infest it are exterminated and drove back and their settlements destroyed. If, therefore, you can destroy the settlement of Achquago [Oquaga], it will in my opinion be a good service."[35] Washington agreed, although he could spare few troops to accomplish the task. All that he could allocate was Colonel William Butler and a portion of the Fourth Pennsylvania Regiment, which would have to be enough. On October 2, Butler set out from Fort Schoharie, 35 miles southwest of Albany, with 214 men from his regiment and 53 New York militia. On October 7, the Americans reached Unadilla, which they found deserted. A captured loyalist informed Butler that the inhabitants had withdrawn to Oquaga, which the Americans reached two days later. The village contained 40 well-built log houses, complete with shingled roofs, glass windows, stone fireplaces, and solid floors; but it, too, had been evacuated. The Americans put the settlement to the torch, burning houses on either side of the river and destroying stores of dried corn before withdrawing. During the march back to Unadilla, Butler sent out flanking parties to destroy several other small Iroquois villages. Finally, on October 10, the Americans burned Unadilla and then returned to Schoharie.[36]

Meanwhile, a similar campaign had been mounted from the Wyoming Valley in Pennsylvania. After the Wyoming raid, Washington sent Continental units to the Susquehanna Valley to protect settlers returning to their homes. On September 21, Colonel Thomas Hartley of the Eleventh Pennsylvania Regiment, led 200 men on a campaign to destroy Tioga. Hartley's detachment found the village abandoned, but learned that a large number of loyalists and Senecas had massed 12 miles upriver at Chemung. Accordingly, the Americans set fire to the structures at Tioga and the nearby village of Sheshecunnunk, and then began their retreat. They had almost reached the Wyoming Valley when they were attacked by 200 pursuing Senecas and loyalists at Wylusing. The Senecas advanced too quickly, however, and the Americans nearly surrounded them. The Senecas fought their way out of the trap, but suffered 10 killed and many others wounded. Hartley reached Wyoming without another major confrontation, although the small parties of Senecas shadowing his army killed and scalped three Americans who wandered too far astray in search of potatoes.[37]

That fall, Iroquois warriors, especially the Senecas, authored a powerful retaliation for the destruction of their villages when they attacked the American settlements at Cherry Valley, New York. On the night of November 10, more than 300 Iroquois, mostly Senecas under Cornplanter with about 30 Mohawks led by Joseph Brant, and 200 British regulars and loyalists, commanded by John Butler's rash and inexperienced son Walter, reached the outskirts of Cherry Valley under a blanket of heavy snow. The Americans knew the Iroquois were coming, having been warned by Oneida spies. Yet they had taken few precautions, largely because of the incompetence of the local Continental commander, Ichabod Alden, who refused to allow settlers or their private belongings to enter the recently constructed Fort Alden until he was certain the danger was real. Indeed, Alden and most of his officer corps, despite the danger, maintained their headquarters at a home owned by the Wells family some 400 yards outside the fort. As the Iroquois surveyed the situation, they decided to divide their forces, with one group slated to surround the Wells house, while the other moved against Fort Alden, which in reality was no more than a stockade surrounding the local church. Just as the plan was being put into effect, however, a few overeager warriors fired on two Americans cutting wood outside the settlements. One escaped, raising the alarm as he ran. A Seneca war leader named Little Beard immediately led an assault on the Wells House that prevented most of the American officers from escaping to the fort. A brief firefight ensued, in which three Senecas were wounded, before the Iroquois rushed the house and forced their way inside. In all, 26 Continentals died during the desperate struggle inside the house, including Ichibod Alden, whom the Senecas tomahawked as he tried to escape. Infuriated over the injuries suffered by their own warriors, the Senecas then killed the Wells family and their servants, 12 people in all.[38]

The scene was just as grim elsewhere in Cherry Valley. The attackers poured a heavy fire into Fort Alden, but again lacking artillery to bring down the stockades, the Iroquois quickly abandoned the effort. While the loyalists maintained a perimeter around the fort to keep its small garrison penned up, the Iroquois fell on the settlement in fury. They plundered and burned every structure in the valley, leaving only the church inside Fort Alden untouched. Unlike previous Iroquois raids, however, this time the American inhabitants became a target. The Senecas, in particular, burst into homes and attacked settlers despite the best efforts of some British officers and Joseph Brant to restrain them. By the time the attack was over, 33 Americans had been killed, most of whom were women and children, and more than 70 were taken prisoner, although more than half of these were later released. More than 180 people were left homeless, including many professed loyalists.[39]

The war had taken a decidedly ugly turn. The Senecas explained after Cherry Valley that they had reacted so violently because of false accusations made by the Americans that the Senecas had butchered the inhabitants of the Wyoming Valley. Moreover, among the Americans who burned Tioga were many men who had surrendered to Sayenqueraghta and Butler at Forty Fort in the Wyoming Valley. The Senecas had allowed these men to go free after extracting promises that they would no longer fight against the Iroquois. Obviously they lied, which was not uncommon in wars of the period, but it convinced the Senecas that American troops could not be trusted and thus should not be given quarter in battle. The greatest reason for the escalation of violence that occurred at Cherry Valley, however, lay in the destruction of Oquaga, Unadilla, and Tioga, which infused the Senecas and Mohawks with a powerful desire for revenge. "Your rabbles came to Oughquago [Oquaga] when we Indians were gone from our place, and you burned our houses," Mohawk war leader William Johnson explained, "which makes us and our brothers, the Seneca Indians, angry, so that we destroyed men, women, and children at Chervalle [Cherry Valley.]"[40] A vicious cycle had begun. The Senecas' actions at Cherry Valley raised the stakes of the war to a dangerous level and intensified further the Americans' desire for revenge. A storm was gathering, and soon it would deluge the people of the Iroquois League in a torrent of violence and destruction, the likes of which had not been felt in Iroquoia for nearly a century.[41]

IROQUOIA IN FLAMES

After the raid on Cherry Valley, George Washington decided enough was enough. He had been reluctant to divert large numbers of troops for a campaign against the Six Nations because he believed he needed all his manpower to contend with the main British army occupying New York City, or because he thought there were better military targets elsewhere. But the killing on the New York and Pennsylvania frontiers in 1778 changed his mind. Now the American commander resolved to "carry the war into the heart of the country of the Six Nations; to cut off their settlements, destroy their next year's crops, and do them every other mischief of which time and circumstances will permit."[42] The campaign against the Iroquois would involve three thrusts. The main attack force of 3,000 troops under General John Sullivan would move up the Susquehanna River from Pennsylvania. Another 1,000 men led by General James Clinton would move down the Susquehanna from the Mohawk Valley, and a third army of 500 soldiers headed by Colonel Daniel Brodhead would advance north from Pittsburgh by way of the Allegheny River. All three would rendezvous in Seneca country, where they would destroy villages and burn crops. To facilitate these goals, the campaign was set to begin in June, so that the Americans would reach Iroquoia just as the fields were beginning to ripen.[43]

Under pressure from Philip Schuyler, Washington also agreed to supply men for an assault on the Onondagas. Schuyler believed that by subjugating the keepers of the Iroquois League's central council fire, the rest of the Six Nations could be brought to the bargaining table. Washington disagreed, but he allowed the attack to placate Schuyler. This secondary campaign was the first of the American attacks to get moving in 1779. On April 19, a force of more than 500 Continental solders, drawn primarily from the Schoharie and Mohawk Valley settlements, departed Fort Stanwix to attack the Onondagas. After a hard day of travel, the Americans, commanded by Colonel Goose Van Schaick, reached the Onondaga villages. The Onondagas were caught by surprise, and though there was some armed resistance, most fled into the woods, having little time to gather either provisions or precious possessions. Van Schaick ordered his troops to burn every home they could find, including the 80-foot long longhouse that held the central council fire of the Iroquois League. The fire, which had been rekindled after the epidemic of 1777, once again was snuffed out. All told, 12 Onondagas died during the eight hours it took the Americans to destroy the villages, and another 34 were taken as prisoners. The Americans suffered no military casualties, although their standing with their Oneida allies suffered a blow. The Oneidas were outraged that the Americans had attacked the Onondagas, the bulk of whom had honored their neutrality during the war, and the Oneidas demanded that the Onondaga prisoners be released into their custody. Those that were paroled, along with the bulk of the nation who had eluded capture, eventually found their way to Fort Niagara, where they belatedly took up arms against the Americans.[44]

Meanwhile, Sullivan's main army, which included more than 3,000 Continental regulars and Pennsylvania militia, along with a small detachment of Oneida scouts led a war leader named Hanyost Thaosgwat, began its ascent up the Susquehanna River from the Wyoming Valley on the last day of July. The army reached Tioga without encountering any meaningful opposition, and on August 14, Sullivan ordered an assault on Chemung. The Iroquois abandoned the village to the Americans without a fight, although some Munsee Delawares in the region inflicted 13 casualties on an advance unit that pushed too far beyond Chemung. Fearing a larger assault on his army, Sullivan ordered the 39 houses at Chemung set on fire and pulled back to Tioga, where he awaited the arrival of General Clinton's army. Clinton had not left the Mohawk Valley until August 9, but his column made good time as it descended the north branch of the Susquehanna. Clinton paused at the ruins of Oquaga as detachments burned several smaller villages in the region, including two abandoned Tuscarora settlements, but his 2,000 troops reached Tioga and united with Sullivan's army during toward the end of August.[45]

In the face of the overwhelming show of American force, Iroquois leaders held their warriors back and allowed the Americans to advance mostly unhindered. Although they avoided battle with Sullivan or Clinton's large army, the Iroquois were not completely idle. Joseph Brant believed that raids against the American settlements behind Sullivan's line of advance would induce the general to break off a portion of his army and send troops to defend the settlements. On July 20, Brant led 60 Iroquois warriors and 27 loyalists in a raid against Minisink, a small American town on the Delaware River in lower New York. The attackers burned 10 houses, 11 barns, a gristmill, and a church, but spared most of the inhabitants. Brant's forces then ambushed a militia detail sent after them, killing more than 40 Americans. Meanwhile, Cornplanter led 120 Senecas and Cayugas, along with 50 loyalists, into the Muncy Valley along the west branch of the Susquehanna River in Pennsylvania. The attackers besieged Fort Freeland, a stockaded, two-story log house defended by 33 Americans. The garrison agreed to surrender on the condition that the 52 women and children inside the fort be allowed to go free. As negotiations were being finalized the next day, a relief force of 34 men hastened up from the south and surprised the Iroquois and British, killing more than two dozen of them during a mourning raid. The Iroquois quickly fought off the attack, killing 12 Americans in the process, but the enraged warriors then proceeded to burn every house along the full 30-mile length of the valley. Leaving the devastated valley in ashes, they departed with 116 captured cattle.[46]

If Iroquois leaders hoped these attacks would distract Sullivan from his main purpose, they were disappointed. Despite pleas for assistance, Sullivan did not detach troops to help the settlements. This left the Iroquois with little choice but to attack Sullivan's 5,000 man army directly, hopefully inflicting enough damage to cause the Americans to withdraw. On August 19, more than 700 Iroquois, affiliated Indians, and British rangers under John Butler planned an elaborate ambush of Sullivan's army at the Munsee Delaware village of Newtown, 14 miles up the Chemung River from the American camp at Tioga. The trail that Sullivan's army would likely be following passed alongside the foot of a mountain on one side and small flat landing on the other, at a place where the Chemung River made a sharp bend to the north. On the left, Butler's men took up positions behind a three-foot high breastwork of logs, concealed from the road by uprooted pine trees and saplings. To the right the main body of Iroquois waited in the forest at the base of the mountain. With any luck, they would catch the vanguard of Sullivan's army in their trap, inflict heavy casualties, and force them to retreat back into the main body of Americans, sowing chaos and confusion.[47]

Luck was not with the Iroquois. American scouts discovered the ambush sight and gave plenty of notice to Sullivan, who devised a three-prong attack to defeat the Iroquois and cut off their escape. One body of Americans advanced up the road to keep the British and Indians in their positions, while two flanking parties circled around to come at the Iroquois and British positions from the rear. A small detachment of artillery initiated the attack by bombarding the British breastwork. But one of the American flanking parties, commanded by Enoch Poor, failed to get into position on time because it had to go around a swamp in the forest, allowing many of the Iroquois to withdraw once the cannonade began. Those that remained attacked Poor's column in the forest as they came up the mountain, killing 8 men and wounding another 33 before American reinforcements forced the Indians to retreat. Skirmishing parties pursued the fleeing Indians for two miles, killing eight warriors, but overall the attack failed because the Iroquois escaped. Butler claimed the Iroquois and British had 10 killed and 12 wounded, although the Americans claimed to find the bodies of 14 dead Indians on the field, a pair of which some enterprising American militiamen skinned to make boots. The Americans otherwise contented themselves by burning Newtown's 20 houses and destroying its ample agricultural fields.[48]

While the Iroquois, British, and Americans fought at Newtown, the third prong of the American invasion, under Colonel Daniel Brodhead, attacked western Seneca and Munsee Delaware villages on the Upper Allegheny River. On August 11, Brodhead led 600 Continentals, augmented by a scattering of poorly equipped local militia, up the Allegheny. A few miles south of Conewago (modern Warren, Pennsylvania), the American scouts came across a war party of 30 to 40 Senecas headed down river, apparently intent on attacking the American settlements around Pittsburgh. The scouts flanked the unsuspecting war party, which lay directly in the path of Brodhead's slowly advancing column. After the Senecas collided with the main body of American troops, the scouts moved to close off their retreat. Several Senecas were killed as the war party fought its way out of the trap, but the majority escaped. When his army reached the Seneca village of Bucktooth (now Salamanca, New York), Brodhead found only deserted lodges. For three days, Brodhead's troops sacked the empty village. The Americans burned 130 houses and cut down 500 acres of near-ripe corn. After the devastation, Brodhead wanted to push deeper into Seneca territory to link up Sullivan and Clinton's army, but supply shortages and the resistance of the militia forced him to withdraw. On the return march, the Americans discovered and destroyed three more abandoned villages along French Creek, putting an additional 35 houses to the torch.[49]

The destruction imposed by Brodhead was only a small sample of the devastation Sullivan's army would impose as it moved unopposed into Seneca country. From Newtown the Americans crossed overland to the bottom of Seneca Lake, then marched alongside the water toward Canadesaga, Sayenqueraghta's town at the northern tip of the lake. Cornplanter wanted to make a stand at Canadesaga, but Brant and Butler convinced the Seneca leader to retreat toward Fort Niagara, where the British could more easily resupply them. Thus, the Senecas fled while the Americans burned at least six villages around the lake, including Canadesaga, the place where the Council fire of the Iroquois League had been moved after the destruction of Onondaga. In many cases, the Senecas effected their escape just moments before the Americans reached their villages, as American soldiers discovered the fires still burning and food cooking on the hearths. One some occasions, Senecas too old or sick to flee were left behind, as were numerous adolescent white children taken captive by the Senecas. The Senecas must have reasoned that the Americans would spare these unfortunates, which for the most part held true, although on at least one occasion impetuous American militiamen shot a Seneca women and then locked several others in a house they promptly set on fire.[50]

From Seneca Lake the Americans advanced to and destroyed Canandaigua, a village of 23 houses at the northern end of Canandaigua Lake, then prepared to attack Chenussio, also known as the Genesee castle, a large village on the Genesee River where Sullivan believed the Iroquois were gathering for a final showdown. Indeed, a force of 400 Indians and loyalists under Sayenqueraghta and Joseph Brant had prepared an ambush where the path to Chenussio ran between two ravines before ascending a steep hill onto the western New York plain. But an American scouting detail, which included the Oneida lieutenant Hanyost Thaosagwat, inadvertently foiled the trap by attacking a small party of Indians they encountered near the now empty Chenussio. Fearing the Americans had flanked them, a large number of Iroquois and British abandoned the ravines and attacked the American scouts, killing 13 Americans and taking 3 prisoners, including Thaosagwat. But 11 other Americans escaped to warn Sullivan of the ambush, which the Iroquois now abandoned, fleeing north to the village of Canawaugus. Along the way, Seneca war leader Little Beard killed Thaosagwat with a single blow to the head, executing the Oneida for his role in leading the Americans into Seneca country. The enraged Senecas then hacked Thaosagwat to pieces.[51]

The Americans promptly burned Chenussio, but the failed Iroquois ambush convinced Sullivan that the time had come to begin his withdrawal. He still had to destroy the Cayuga villages around Cayuga Lake, which his army reached during the third week of September. A delegation of Oneidas intervened on behalf of the Cayugas, whom they claimed wanted nothing more than peace with the Americans. Sullivan refused to spare their villages, however, citing orders from Washington not to make peace with any of the Six Nations until after he had devastated their country. Accordingly, two detachments of soldiers canvassed both sides of the lake and burned more than 130 houses spread among at least six towns, including the Cayuga's principal settlement at Goiogouen on the eastern shore of the lake. The army then resumed its march back to the Wyoming Valley, fanning out to destroy small hamlets and isolated houses discovered along the way. In all, Sullivan's army had burned 32 distinct Iroquois villages, not including isolated houses, and destroyed thousands of fruit trees and an estimated 160,000 bushels of corn, not to mention uncounted amounts of squash, beans, and potatoes.[52]

Yet in retrospect the campaign was what one historian has called "a well-executed failure."[53] The villages of the Onondagas, Cayugas, and Senecas lay in ruins; but rather than compel the Iroquois to seek peace, the devastation renewed their determination to fight. And their fighting capacity was largely undiminished, for the Iroquois decision to retreat in the face of Sullivan's numerically superior army meant that few warriors had died during the campaign. "Although we have received a severe blow, our hearts are still good and strong, and our arms are not feeble, neither are we at all discouraged," proclaimed Sayenqueraghta in December 1779. "We lost our country it is true, but this was to secure our women and children; and we do not look upon ourselves as overcome."[54] The Iroquois had not been conquered, but they had been dealt a serious blow. In October 1779, there were more than 5,000 Indians, mostly Iroquois, camped near Fort Niagara; the majority were refugees from the villages destroyed by Sullivan's army. Some eventually filtered back into Seneca country to rebuild their lives, but in November British officials reported that 2,628 Iroquois remained at Niagara in several squalid refugee camps. The refugees, huddled in poorly built shelters around the fort, suffered terribly during the winter of 1779–1780, which was bitterly cold, with snow piling up to five feet in many places. There was little food, as many game animals froze to death under the deep snow, and the British garrison at Fort Niagara struggled to meet the needs of so many refugees. More than 300 died from exposure and disease, which became a frequent visitor to the refugee camps.[55]

Despite their suffering, the Iroquois refugees gathered around Fort Niagara were not ready for peace. In February 1780, a delegation of two Oneidas and two pro-American Mohawks from Fort Hunter visited Niagara to beseech the Iroquois there to make peace with the Americans. The Niagara refugees refused, and their leaders offered only cursory objections when the British arrested the ambassadors and jailed them in an unheated dungeon in Fort Niagara. One of the negotiators, Little Abraham, the Mohawk leader who years before had outlined the policy of neutrality for the Six Nations, died during his confinement. The others were eventually released, but only after agreeing to join the war against the Americans, which the Niagara Iroquois renewed with vigor. From February to September 1780, 59 war parties departed Fort Niagara to attack the American settlements. By September, they had killed 142 Americans and taken 161 others prisoner, although 81 women and children were later released to British custody. All told, the warriors burned 157 houses, 150 granaries, and 2 churches and abducted 247 horses and 922 cattle. The fighting continued in 1781, with 75 war parties outfitted for combat at Fort Niagara.[56]

Although details are not available for every raiding party, the Mohawk Valley seems to have been the primary target for these warriors, in part because of the determination of Joseph Brant to revenge himself on the American settlers who had taken Mohawk lands there, but also because of the presence of many pro-American Iroquois in the region. Indeed, the Oneidas became a special obsession of the Niagara Iroquois, who blamed them for the success of Sullivan's campaign. Despite the divisions in the Iroquois League, however, those Iroquois who had supported the Americans or remained neutral were given one last opportunity to join the pro-British faction at Niagara. In 1780, Wagondenage, an influential Onondaga war leader, convinced many Tuscaroras to migrate to Niagara. He then orchestrated the secession of the Onondagas who had been taken in by the Oneidas after the Americans destroyed their villages the year before. Mohawk and Seneca warriors, along with British agents, furthered these efforts. In early July, 294 neutral or pro-American Iroquois migrated to Niagara, where they pledged themselves to the British.[57]

Of those who departed, few were Oneidas. There were only 34 Oneidas in the large group of migrants that left in July, the remainder having refused to abandon their attachment to the Americans. Their recalcitrance caused Wagondenage to threaten them with the destruction of their villages if they did not comply. Indeed, those Oneidas who failed to recant their pro-American sympathies were attacked. In late July 1780, Joseph Brant led more than 300 Niagara warriors on a campaign against the Oneidas. Among Brant's force were 59 Onondagas, Oneidas, and Tuscaroras who had recently migrated to Niagara. The attackers burned every building in the abandoned village of Kanowalahale, the main Oneida settlement, including the church built by American missionary Samuel Kirkland. Many Oneidas and Tuscaroras now agreed to join their fellows at Niagara, but more than 400 still refused and instead took refuge in nearby Fort Stanwix. Brant's force then moved to attack the former Mohawk village of Canajoharie. The village had been Brant's home before the revolution, but now it was occupied by Americans and Oneidas from the former village of Oriska. At Canajoharie, Brant's force was joined by a large group of Seneca warriors under Sayenqueraghta and Cornplanter, as well as some Cayuga and Tuscarora warriors. Although most of the inhabitants of Canajoharie escaped to a local stockaded homestead, 29 died and 40 others were captured. In all, 53 houses, numerous barns, a church, a gristmill, and 2 fortified homesteads scattered throughout the district were destroyed.[58]

Like the Iroquois at Niagara, the Oneidas who refused to abandon the Americans now became refugees. The 406 Oneidas who took shelter in Fort Stanwix eventually found their way to Schenectady, where they endured tortuous conditions in a wretched refugee camp outside of town. Lacking adequate food, clothing, and shelter, 93 Oneida men, 44 women, and 259 children lived in abject poverty. American promises of aid never materialized, and scores of Oneidas died during the winter, many from a smallpox outbreak that ravaged their camp in December 1780. General Philip Schuyler labored to ease the Oneidas' suffering, moving the refugees into the army barracks at Schenectady, but after an American soldier brutally murdered an Oneida, Schuyler had no alternative but to send them back to their squalid camp. Yet the time in the barracks proved a blessing in disguise, for the transfer of the Oneidas saved them from enduring another attack. Joseph Brant, who never forgave the Oneidas for evicting his sister Molly from Canajoharie in 1777, had planned to attack their camp to finish them off but, on learning they had been moved inside the town, called off the operation. Some Oneidas eventually obtained relief among the Stockbridge Indians to the east, and a few others served with American troops defending the New York frontier, but for most, there was no place to go and no hope. Unfortunately, it was only the beginning of their mistreatment at the hands of their American friends.[59]

For all the peoples of the Iroquois League, the violence slowly ground to a merciful halt at the end of 1781. The American victory at Yorktown induced the British government to open peace negotiations with the rebellious colonies, and the British military command ordered all offensive operations, including British supported Indian raids, to cease immediately. Only defensive measures would be sanctioned, pending the outcome of negotiations. With the British at Niagara no longer willing to provide Iroquois warriors with guns or ammunition, the raids against the American settlements gradually ceased. Although fighting did not entirely disappear from the Iroquois landscape in 1782 and 1783—Iroquois warriors fought with other British-allied Indians in the Ohio Country and continued sporadic raids in New York and Pennsylvania—the violence was greatly diminished from previous years. It was an opportune time for hostilities to end. The Iroquois were exhausted: warriors on both sides had been waging war for almost four years without interruption; much of Iroquoia lay in ruins—only the three Seneca towns north of Chenussio had escaped destruction—and the people of the Six Nations had been reduced to refugees. Yet despite their suffering and internal turmoils, the Iroquois had not surrendered. They remained unconquered—in spirit if not in reality—and they would now play on that concept as they waged a diplomatic battle to find a place for themselves in a world where everything had changed.[60]

Epilogue: The Longhouse Endures

Despite the suffering, dislocation, and despair wrought upon the Six Nations during the American Revolution, the Iroquois League endured. Indeed, the long recovery of the Iroquois began even before the American Revolution came to a close. In the spring of 1780, more than 1,000 Iroquois refugees began the long process of rebuilding their lives when they resettled along Buffalo Creek (today known as the Buffalo River) in western New York. Here Sayengeraghta and other Iroquois leaders rekindled the central council fire of the Iroquois League, seeking to restore the political and cultural union that had been ruptured by civil war. Other Iroquois began to pick up the pieces of their shattered lives by returning to their ruined villages. The Senecas reoccupied the upper Allegheny River villages and Chenussio; and Oneidas, Onondagas, and Tuscaroras effected a partial return to their homelands. Some Iroquois, however, saw no future in returning to their homelands and instead migrated elsewhere, notably to Canada. In 1784, Joseph Brant negotiated a land grant for the Iroquois along the Grand River in Ontario, where today a separate council fire serves the people of the Six Nations Reserve.[1]

Rebuilding their lives was made all the more difficult after the British betrayed the Six Nations in the 1783 Treaty of Paris, which formally ended the Revolutionary War and recognized the independence of the

United States. As one historian has noted, "three thousand miles across the ocean, in Paris, negotiators at the conference table dealt the Iroquois a blow more fatal than any they ever suffered on the battlefield."[2] Indeed, the Treaty of Paris was a severe setback for the Six Nations. In the treaty, England ceded to the United States all the lands east of the Mississippi River, from the Great Lakes to Florida and the Spanish possessions in Louisiana. In essence, the deal gave away the Iroquois homelands without permitting the Iroquois a voice in the discussion.

The peoples of the Iroquois League responded to this betrayal by demonstrating the resiliency that had characterized them through all the long years of their military struggle to survive in colonial America. At first individually, and later collectively, the Six Nations concluded treaties with the state of New York and the U.S. government that allowed them to maintain at least some of their lands. It is not easy to find the seeds of Iroquois success in some of these treaties, marked as they were by massive cessions of Iroquois lands to the United States and a diaspora of some Iroquois people throughout North America. But the treaties allowed most of the Iroquois to remain in New York while almost every other Indian people was forced west of the Mississippi River. Moreover, the treaties provided the framework for the reformation of the Iroquois League. Although it took much time and effort, the central council fire of the Iroquois League burns anew. In the early nineteenth century, the Seneca prophet Handsome Lake inspired a revitalization movement among the Six Nations survivors that led to the reformation of the Iroquois League and the rekindling of the central council fire. First reestablished at Buffalo Creek, the council fire now has been moved back to its traditional home among the Onondagas.[3]

In addition, the peoples of the Iroquois League have continued to wage war on their own grounds. Iroquois warriors have fought in nearly every American war since the Revolution, from the major wars of the nineteenth century, including the War of 1812 and the American Civil War, through the modern wars of the twentieth century, including both world wars, the Vietnam War, and the recent conflicts in the Persian Gulf. Iroquois warriors have played both large and small roles in these conflicts, which on occasion have included large-scale Iroquois involvement, such as the Iroquois warriors who fought on both sides during the War of 1812. These later wars have also witnessed the rise of individual Iroquois warriors to positions of extraordinary rank and authority in the American military, best highlighted perhaps by the success of Ely Parker, a Tonawanda Seneca sachem who became Ulysses S. Grant's military secretary during the American Civil War and later commissioner of the Bureau of Indian Affairs. Although the conflicts of the nineteenth and twentieth centuries were organized and fought under the stewardship of the U.S. government, the Iroquois participated as allies of the United States, not as conquered, dependent peoples or colonial subjects. Just as they had done during the colonial era, the Iroquois fought for themselves and to protect their culture, land, and autonomy as an independent people. Indeed, during both World War I and World War II, the Six Nations issued their own declarations of war against Germany and fought alongside the Allied powers as partners, an emphatic illustration of the continued autonomy of the Iroquois people.[4]

Today, the Six Nations continue to occupy a unique place among Indian peoples in the United States, having maintained their autonomy and position in New York State. Indeed, the population of most of the Six Nations has regenerated to pre-contact levels, while the Mohawks have even exceeded the high end estimates of their seventeenth century population. Moreover, the unity and flexibility of the Iroquois League is still intact. The Six Nations continue to send the traditional 50 representatives to the central council at Onondaga, yet each member nation and local community retain the traditional autonomy to follow their own course of action. Thus, the people of the Iroquois League remain unconquered. Nearly 200 years of warfare in colonial America disrupted their world, destroyed their villages, and damaged their union, but war did not destroy them. The Iroquois endured and learned to adapt, a process that continues today as they move forward with new economic and political agendas—including the construction of gaming facilities—designed to help preserve their sovereignty and position in a still rapidly changing world. Although war no longer defines their efforts to maintain their autonomy and culture, the struggle to remain unconquered continues.

Notes

BORN FROM BLOOD

1. Daniel K. Richter, *The Ordeal of the Longhouse: The Peoples of the Iroquois League in the Era of European Colonization* (Chapel Hill: The University of North Carolina Press, 1992), 1; Michael Johnson, *Tribes of the Iroquois Confederacy* (Oxford, UK: Osprey Publishing, 2003), 5–7.

2. Richter, *Ordeal*, 11–13.

3. Richter, *Ordeal*, 9–10; Dean R. Snow, *The Iroquois* (Malden, MA: Blackwell Publishing, 1994), 3–4.

4. Richter, *Ordeal*, 10–11; Snow, *Iroquois*, 3–4.

5. Richard Aquila, *The Iroquois Restoration: Iroquois Diplomacy on the Colonial Frontier, 1701–1754* (Lincoln: University of Nebraska Press, 1983), 30–31; Richter, *Ordeal*, 11–15; Colin G. Calloway, *First Peoples: A Documentary History of American Indians*, 2nd ed. (New York: Bedford St. Martin's Press, 2003), 4–6.

6. Quoted in Snow, *The Iroquois*, 40.

7. Richter, *Ordeal*, 18; Snow, *Iroquois*, 40–46; William N. Fenton, *The Great Law and the Longhouse: A Political History of the Iroquois Confederacy* (Norman: University of Oklahoma Press, 1998), 23–24.

8. Richter, *Ordeal*, 17; Snow, *The Iroquois*, 88–89; Fenton, *The Great Law*, 21.

9. Thomas S. Abler, "Longhouse and Palisade: Northeastern Iroquoian Villages in the Seventeenth Century," *Ontario History* 62 (1970): 24–28; Elisabeth Tooker, ed., *An Iroquois Sourcebook,* 3 vols. (New York: Garland, 1985–86), 1:217; Richter, *Ordeal,* 17–18.

10. Anthony F. C. Wallace, *The Death and Rebirth of the Seneca* (New York: Vintage Books, 1972), 44–46; Snow, *Iroquois,* 54–57; Alan Taylor, *American Colonies* (New York: Viking, 2001), 102–103.

11. Richter, *Ordeal,* 35–36; Taylor, *American Colonies,* 102–103.

12. Richter, *Ordeal,* 32; Taylor, *American Colonies,* 103.

13. Taylor, *American Colonies,* 103.

14. Arthur C. Parker, *The Constitution of the Iroquois; or, The Iroquois Book of the Great Law,* New York State Museum Bulletin, no. 184 (Albany, NY: 1916), 16–17.

15. Barbara Graymont, *The Iroquois* (New York: Chelsea House Publishers, 1988), 14;

16. Graymont, *Iroquois,* 14–19.

17. Quoted in Richter, *Ordeal,* 32.

18. Graymont, *Iroquois,* 19–21, 28–30; Richter, *Ordeal,* 39; Fenton, *The Great Law,* 51–103.

19. Snow, *Iroquois,* 60–61.

20. Aquila, *Iroquois Restoration,* 32–33; Taylor, *American Colonies,* 103.

21. Aquila, *Iroquois Restoration,* 33–34; Taylor, *American Colonies,* 104.

22. Richter, *Ordeal,* 33.

23. Richter, *Ordeal,* 36.

24. E. B. O'Callaghan, ed., *Documents Relative to the Colonial History of the State of New York, Procured in Holland, England, and France,* 15 vols. (Albany, NY: Weed, Parson, and Company, 1857), 4:22 [hereafter cited as NYCD].

25. Richter, *Ordeal,* 33; Jose Antonio Brandao, *"Your fyre shall burn no more":* Iroquois Policy toward New France and Its Native Allies to 1701 (Lincoln: University of Nebraska Press, 1997), 32.

26. Quoted in Brandao, *"Your fyre shall burn no more,"* 32.

27. Richter, *Ordeal,* 35; Brandao, *"Your fyre shall burn no more,"* 32.

28. NYCD, 5:274 (quotation); Richter, *Ordeal,* 36–37.

29. Snow, *Iroquois,* 54; Brandao, *"Your fyre shall burn no more,"* 33.

30. Snow, *Iroquois,* 54; Brandao, *"Your fyre shall burn no more,"* 33–34; Jeffrey P. Blick, "The Iroquois Practice of Genocidal Warfare (1534–1787)," *Journal of Genocidal Research* 3 (2001): 416.

31. Richter, *Ordeal,* 37–38; Snow, *The Iroquois,* 54; Brandao, *"Your fyre shall burn no more,"* 34–35.

32. Snow, *Iroquois,* 54–55; Brandao, *"Your fyre shall burn no more,"* 35–36.

33. Richter, *Ordeal,* 38.

34. This terminology is borrowed from Richter, *Ordeal,* chap. 2.

GUNS AND FURS

1. H. P. Biggar, ed., *The Works of Samuel de Champlain*, 6 vols. (Toronto: Champlain Society Publications, 1922–1936), 1:137 [hereafter cited as *Works of Champlain*]; Jose Antonio Brandao, *"Your fyre shall burn no more": Iroquois Policy toward New France and Its Native Allies to 1701* (Lincoln: University of Nebraska Press, 1997), 62–67, 71; William A. Starna and Jose Antonio Brandao, "From the Mohawk-Mahican War to the Beaver Wars: Questioning the Pattern," *Ethnohistory* 51 (2004): 726.

2. *Works of Champlain*, 1:137 (quotation); Daniel K. Richter, *The Ordeal of the Longhouse: The Peoples of the Iroquois League in the Era of European Colonization* (Chapel Hill: University of North Carolina Press, 1992), 53–54; Dean R. Snow, *The Iroquois* (Malden, MA: Balckwell Publishers, 1994), 75–76; Starna and Brandao, "Mohawk-Mahican War," 726–727.

3. Richter, *Ordeal*, 53.

4. Alan Taylor, *American Colonies* (New York: Viking, 2001), 94.

5. John Hopkins Kennedy, *Jesuit and Savage in New France* (New Haven, CT: Yale University Press, 1950), 70–71; Taylor, *American Colonies*, 92–94.

6. Taylor, *American Colonies*, 94.

7. Quoted in Taylor, *American Colonies*, 97.

8. Quoted in Taylor, *American Colonies*, 98.

9. Taylor, *American Colonies*, 96–98.

10. Richter, *Ordeal*, 86.

11. Richter, *Ordeal*, 86–87; Taylor, *American Colonies*, 92–93, 98.

12. Reuben Gold Thwaites, ed., *The Jesuit Relations and Allied Documents: Travels and Explorations of the Jesuit Missionaries in New France (1610–1791)*, 73 vols. (Cleveland: Burrows Brothers Company, 1896–1901), 6:19 [hereafter cited as *Jesuit Relations*].

13. Kennedy, *Jesuit and Savage*, 70–71; Taylor, *American Colonies*, 98–99.

14. Taylor, *American Colonies*, 93, 100.

15. Bruce G. Trigger, *The Children of Aataentsic: A History of the Huron People to 1660*, 2 vols. (Montreal: McGill-Queen's University Press, 1976), 1:62–63; Francis Jennings, *The Ambiguous Iroquois Empire: The Covenant Chain Confederation of Indian Tribes with English Colonies from Its Beginnings to the Lancaster Treaty of 1744* (New York: Norton, 1984), 85–86; Taylor, *American Colonies*, 93, 100–101.

16. Richter, *Ordeal*, 52–53, 76–79.

17. Richter, *Ordeal*, 55.

18. Ian K. Steele, *Warpaths: Invasions of North America* (New York: Oxford University Press, 1994), 64.

19. *Works of Champlain*, 2:99–100.

20. *Works of Champlain*, 2:82–107; Trigger, *Children of Aataentsic*, 1:246–256; Steele, *Warpaths*, 64–65.

21. *Works of Champlain*, 2:130.

22. *Works of Champlain*, 2:122–134; Steele, *Warpaths*, 65.

23. Trigger, *Children of Aataentsic*, 1:308–315; Steele, *Warpaths*, 66–67.

24. *Works of Champlain*, 2:130.

25. Richter, *Ordeal*, 54–55.

26. *Works of Champlain*, 5:74.

27. Richter, *Ordeal*, 55–56.

28. Alan W. Trelease, *Indian Affairs in Colonial New York: The Seventeenth Century* (Ithaca, NY: Cornell University Press, 1960), 25–34; Jennings, *Ambiguous Iroquois Empire*, 47–49; Richter, *Ordeal*, 87–89; Taylor, *American Colonies*, 105.

29. Steele, *Warpaths*, 115; Taylor, *American Colonies*, 105.

30. *Works of Champlain*, 5:214.

31. Bruce G. Trigger, "The Mohawk-Mahican War (1624–1628): The Establishment of a Pattern," *Canadian Historical Review* 52 (1971): 276–279; Steele, *Warpaths*, 113–114; Starna and Brandao, "Mohawk-Mahican War," 725, 728–731.

32. *Works of Champlain*, 5:77.

33. *Works of Champlain*, 5:77–79; Starna and Brandao, "Mohawk-Mahican War," 733.

34. Snow, *Iroquois*, 81; Steele, *Warpaths*, 114; Starna and Brandao, "Mohawk-Mahican War," 739.

35. J. Franklin Jameson, ed., *Narratives of New Netherland: 1609–1664* (New York: Charles Scribner's Sons, 1909), 84–85 (quotations) [hereafter cited as *NNN*]; Trigger, "The Mohawk-Mahican War," 276–286; Steele, *Warpaths*, 114; Starna and Brandao, "Mohawk-Mahican War," 731.

36. *NNN*, 85–87.

37. *NNN*, 85–87; A.J.F. Van Laer, ed. and trans., *Van Rensselaer-Bowier Manuscripts: The Letters of Killiean van Rensselaer, 1630–1643, and Other Documents Relating to the Colony of Rensselaerswyck* (Albany: University of the State of New York, 1932), 258 (quotation); Jennings, Ambiguous Iroquois Empire, 49–50.

38. Van Laer, ed. and trans., *Van Rensselaer-Bowier Manuscripts*, 302.

39. Jennings, *Ambiguous Iroquois Empire*, 51–52; Richter, *Ordeal*, 90.

40. Jennings, *Ambiguous Iroquois Empire*, 89–90; Brandao, *"Your fyre shall burn no more,"* 95–96, 98.

41. E. B. O'Callaghan, ed, *Documents Relative to the Colonial History of the State of New York, Procured in Holland, England, and France*, 15 vols. (Albany, NY: Weed, Parson, and Company, 1857), 1:150.

42. Jennings, *Ambiguous Iroquois Empire*, 50, 53–57; Richter, *Ordeal*, 62, 93–94; Steele, *Warpaths*, 115; Brandao, *"Your fyre shall burn no more,"* 100; Jeffrey P. Blick, "The Iroquois Practice of Genocidal Warfare (1534–1787)," *Journal of Genocide Research* 3 (2001): 413–415.

43. Adrian van der Donck, "Description of the New Netherlands (1656)," trans. Jeremiah Johnson, *New York Historical Society Collections*, 2nd ser., 1 (1841): 209–210.

44. Richter, *Ordeal*, 57, 76.

45. *Works of Champlain*, 5:224–225.

46. *Works of Champlain*, 5:229–230.

47. Starna and Brandao, "Mohawk-Mahican War," 735–739.

48. *Jesuit Relations*, 24:273 (quotation); Richter, *Ordeal*, 56–57.

49. Richter, *Ordeal*, 56–57; Taylor, *American Colonies*, 105–106 (quotation).

THE GREAT MOURNING WAR

1. Alan Taylor, *American Colonies* (New York: Viking, 2001), 38–39.

2. Daniel K. Richter, *Ordeal of the Longhouse: The Peoples of the Iroquois League in the Era of European Colonization* (Chapel Hill: University of North Carolina Press, 1992), 58; Taylor, *American Colonies*, 40–42; Daniel K. Richter, *Facing East from Indian Country: A Native History of Early America* (Cambridge, MA: Harvard University Press, 2001), 60.

3. Richter, *Facing East*, 60–61.

4. Taylor, *American Colonies*, 43; Colin G. Calloway, *One Vast Winter Count: The Native American West before Lewis and Clark* (Lincoln: University of Nebraska Press, 2003), 416.

5. William Bradford, *Of Plymouth Plantation, 1620–1647*, ed. Samuel Eliot Morrison (New York: Knopf, 1952), 270–271.

6. J. Franklin Jameson, ed., *Narratives of New Netherland: 1609–1664* (New York: Charles Scribner's Sons, 1909), 139–162; Richter, *Ordeal*, 58–59; Jose Antonio Brandao, *"Your fyre shall burn no more": Iroquois Policy toward New France and Its Native Allies to 1701* (Lincoln: University of Nebraska Press, 1997), 146–151.

7. Richter, *Ordeal*, 60.

8. Brandao, *"Your fyre shall burn no more,"* 73–75.

9. Reuben Gold Thwaites, ed., *The Jesuit Relations and Allied Documents: Travels and Explorations of the Jesuit Missionaries in New France (1610–1791)*, 73 vols. (Cleveland, OH: Burrows Brothers Company, 1896–1901), 6:145, 7:213–215, 8:69, 115, 149 [hereafter cited as *Jesuit Relations*]; Richter, *Ordeal*, 60.

10. *Jesuit Relations*, 26:175.

11. Richter, *Ordeal*, 60–61.

12. Richter, *Ordeal*, 62–64.

13. Francis Jennings, *The Ambiguous Iroquois Empire: The Covenant Chain Confederation of Indian Tribes with English Colonies from Its Beginnings to the Lancaster Treaty of 1744* (New York: Norton, 1984), 87–88.

14. Jennings, *Ambiguous Iroquois Empire*, 87–89, 100; Ian K. Steele, *Warpaths: Invasions of North America* (New York: Oxford University Press, 1994), 70.

15. *Jesuit Relations*, 22:305.

16. *Jesuit Relations*, 12:181–183; 15:171–173; 17:63–65, 71–77; 22:305 (quotation).

17. *Jesuit Relations*, 33:259–261; 34:87–91, 99; Bruce G. Trigger, *The Children of Aataentsic: A History of the Huron People to 1660*, 2 vols. (Montreal: McGill-Queen's University Press, 1976), 2:617–664; Dean R. Snow, *The Iroquois* (Malden, MA: Blackwell, 1994), 115; Richter, *Ordeal*, 61.

18. *Jesuit Relations*, 34:27, 123–137, 213, 217; Trigger, *Children of Aataentsic*, 2:617–664; Snow, *Iroquois*, 115; Richter, *Ordeal*, 61–62, 64.

19. *Jesuit Relations*, 34:197.

20. *Jesuit Relations*, 35:37–41, 187–191; 36:123, 181–189; Snow, *Iroquois*, 115; Brandao, "Your fyre shall burn no more," 77–78.

21. *Jesuit Relations*, 35:45, 201–203.

22. *Jesuit Relations*, 36:127, 135; 37:101, 105; 38:51, 57.

23. *Jesuit Relations*, 33:55. 59; 38:49–51.

24. *Jesuit Relations*, 24:297.

25. Richter, *Ordeal*, 61; Brandao, "Your fyre shall burn no more," 77.

26. Jennings, *Ambiguous Iroquois Empire*, 95.

27. *Jesuit Relations*, 36:183.

28. *Jesuit Relations*, 42:253.

29. Brandao, "Your fyre shall burn no more," 79–80.

30. Richter, *Ordeal*, 66–68.

31. *Jesuit Relations*, 43:293–295 (quotation); Richter, *Ordeal*, 68–69.

32. Trigger, *Children of Aataentsic*, 2:840.

33. *Jesuit Relations*, 43:265.

34. *Jesuit Relations*, 35:219 (quotation); 45:207; 51:123, 187; Richter, *Ordeal*, 65–66.

35. Brandao, "Your fyre shall burn no more," 74.

36. *Jesuit Relations*, 35:107–113; 41:121; Jennings, *Ambiguous Iroquois Empire*, 101–102; Helen Hornbeck Tanner, ed., *Atlas of Great Lakes Indian History* (Norman: University of Oklahoma Press, 1987), 30, 32–34 (maps 6 and 7); William N. Fenton, *The Great Law and the Longhouse: A Political History of the Iroquois Confederacy* (Norman: University of Oklahoma Press, 1998), 245–246.

37. Turner, *Atlas*, 30, 31–32 (Map 6); Fenton, *The Great Law*, 246.

38. *Jesuit Relations*, 15:159; 16:253; 17:25–29; 33:81–83; Snow, *Iroquois*, 116; Fenton, *The Great Law*, 246.

39. *Jesuit Relations*, 36:199–121, 141–143, 177; 37:97; Fenton, *The Great Law*, 246.

40. *Jesuit Relations*, 40:89; 41:77–81, 111–113, 121; 42:31, 57–59, 113, 177–183; 45:209; Fenton, *The Great Law*, 247.

41. *Jesuit Relations*, 37:97, 103–105, 111; *NYCD*, 12:431–432; Jennings, *Ambiguous Iroquois Empire*, 121; Steele, *Warpaths*, 117–118; Fenton, *The Great Law*, 247.

42. Jennings, *Ambiguous Iroquois Empire*, 91–92.

43. *Jesuit Relations*, 22:275–279; 24:23, 281; 25:69, 28:123; 31:31; Brandao, "*Your fyre shall burn no more*," 98–101.

44. *Jesuit Relations*, 27:221–225; Brandao, "*Your fyre shall burn no more*," 93–95, 101.

45. *Jesuit Relations*, 23:247–249, 267; 24:205–207, 231–233, 255–261, 275–279, 289–291; 27:63–65.

46. Jennings, *Ambiguous Iroquois Empire*, 92–93; Steele, *Warpaths*, 70; Brandao, "*Your fyre shall burn no more*," 85–86, 102.

47. *Jesuit Relations*, 31:115–119; Jennings, *Ambiguous Iroquois Empire*, 96–97; Richter, *Ordeal*, 112–113; Brandao, "*Your fyre shall burn no more*," 102–103.

48. *Jesuit Relations*, 32:95–99, 157–159, 163–183; 35:41, 53, 211–213; 36:125, 165; Steele, *Warpaths*, 72.

49. *Jesuit Relations*, 41:87.

50. *Jesuit Relations*, 44:149–151 [quotation]; Jennings, *Ambiguous Iroquois Empire*, 104–107; Brandao, "*Your fyre shall burn no more*," 105–108.

51. *Jesuit Relations*, 43:117–119, 135, 187–189; Brandao, "*Your fyre shall burn no more*," 108–109.

52. Jennings, *Ambiguous Iroquois Empire*, 107–109; Snow, *Iroquois*, 117; Brandao, "*Your fyre shall burn no more*," 110–111.

53. Joyce Marshall, ed. and trans., *Word from New France: The Selected Letters of Marie de l'Incarnation* (Toronto: Oxford University Press, 1967), 255.

THE LONGHOUSE IN PERIL

1. E. B. O'Callaghan, ed., *Documents Relative to the Colonial History of the State of New York, Procured in Holland, England, and France*, 15 vols. (Albany, NY: Weed, Parson, and Company, 1857), 13:175 [hereafter cited as *NYCD*]; Reuben Gold Thwaites, ed., *The Jesuit Relations and Allied Documents: Travels and Explorations of the Jesuit Missionaries in New France (1610–1791)*, 73 vols. (Cleveland, OH: Burrows Brothers Company, 1896–1901), 45:157, 245–261 [hereafter cited as *Jesuit Relations*]; Francois Dollier de Casson, *History of Montreal, 1640–1672*, ed. and trans. Ralph Flenley (London: J.M. Dent and Sons, 1928), 253–265; Ian K. Steele, *Warpaths: Invasions of North America* (New York: Oxford University Press, 1994), 72–73.

2. *Jesuit Relations*, 45: 161–163; 46:121, 219–21; Steele, *Warpaths*, 73; Jose Antonio Brandao, "*Your fyre shall burn no more*": *Iroquois Policy towards New France ands its Native Allies to 1701*, (Lincoln: University of Nebraska Press, 1997), appendix D, table D.1.

3. *Jesuit Relations*, 47:303; 48:77–75, 99–111.

4. Francis Jennings, *The Ambiguous Iroquois Empire: The Covenant Chain Confederation of Indian Tribes with English Colonies from Its Beginnings to the Lancaster Treaty of 1744* (New York: Norton, 1984), 127–128.

5. NYCD, 12:357, 431; *Jesuit Relations*, 47:71, 77–79; Daniel K. Richter, *Ordeal of the Longhouse: The Peoples of the Iroquois League in the Era of European Colonization* (Chapel Hill: University of North Carolina Press, 1992), 98.

6. Neal Salisbury, "Toward the Covenant Chain: Iroquois and Southern New England Algonquians, 1637–1684," in Daniel K. Richter and James H. Merrell, eds., *Beyond the Covenant Chain: The Iroquois and Their Neighbors in Indian North America, 1600–1800* (Syracuse, NY: Syracuse University Press, 1987), 63–64; Richard I. Melvoin, *New England Outpost: War and Society in Colonial Deerfield* (New York: Norton, 1989), 42–43; Richter, *Ordeal*, 98–99.

7. NYCD, 3:67–68; 13:226–227, 308–309, 355–356, 378; *Jesuit Relations*, 47:191–141, 279; 48:233–235; 49:139–147; Salisbury, "Toward the Covenant Chain," 66–67; Melvoin, *New England Outpost*, 44–46; Richter, *Ordeal*, 99.

8. Salisbury, "Toward the Covenant Chain," 67–68; Melvoin, *New England Outpost*, 46; Steele, *Warpaths*, 119–120; Richter, *Ordeal*, 99–102; Alan Taylor, *American Colonies* (New York: Viking, 2001), 258–260.

9. Jennings, *Ambiguous Iroquois Empire*, 102; Brandao, *"Your fyre shall burn no more,"* appendix C, table C4.

10. Brandao, *"Your fyre shall burn no more,"* 111–113.

11. *Jesuit Relations*, 46:189, 217–219; 47: 71–73, 95; Casson, *History of Montreal*, 275–277; William N. Fenton, *The Great Law and the Longhouse: A Political History of the Iroquois Confederacy* (Norman: University of Oklahoma, 1998), 277–278.

12. *Jesuit Relations*, 47:217.

13. *Jesuit Relations*, 46:241 (quotation); Steele, *Warpaths*, 73–74.

14. NYCD, 3:121–125; *Jesuit Relations*, 50:139, 189, 193; Jennings, *Ambiguous Iroquois Empire*, 131; Steele, *Warpaths*, 74.

15. NYCD, 3:118–121; *Jesuit Relations*, 50:127–135, 181–187; Richter, *Ordeal*, 103; Steele, *Warpaths*, 74; Fenton, *The Great Law*, 253.

16. NYCD, 3:135; *Jesuit Relations*, 50:139–147, 199–205; Richter, *Ordeal*, 103–104; Steele, *Warpaths*, 74–75; Fenton, *The Great Law*, 275.

17. Richter, *Ordeal*, 102–103; Steele, *Warpaths*, 121.

18. *Jesuit Relations*, 52:117 (quotation); Richter, *Ordeal*, 107–116; Steele, *Warpaths*, 121.

19. Richter, *Ordeal*, 119–128; Steele, *Warpaths*, 121–122; Fenton, *The Great Law*, 253.

20. Richter, *Ordeal*, 134–135; Steele, *Warpaths*, 122–123.

21. Richter, *Ordeal*, 135; Steele, *Warpaths*, 123.

22. Richard L. Haan, "Covenant and Consensus: Iroquois and English, 1676–1760", in Richter and Merrell, eds., *Beyond the Covenant Chain*, 42–44; Taylor, *American Colonies*, 261–262.

23. Richter, *Ordeal*, 135.
24. NYCD, 3:255; Melvoin, *New England Outpost*, 116–121.
25. Richter, *Ordeal*, 135–136.
26. Richter, *Ordeal*, 120–121; Steele, *Warpaths*, 122.
27. Jennings, *Ambiguous Iroquois Empire*, 139–147.
28. Jennings, *Ambiguous Iroquois Empire*, 154–164; Richter, *Ordeal*, 136.
29. *Jesuit Relations*, 49:251 (quotation); Jennings, *Ambiguous Iroquois Empire*, 165–166; Richter, *Ordeal*, 136, 145; Steele, *Warpaths*, 123–124.

THE LONGHOUSE UNDER SIEGE

1. Jose Antonio Brandao, *"Your fyre shall burn no more"*: Iroquois Policy towards New France and Its Native Allies to 1701, (Lincoln: University of Nebraska Press, 1997), 117.
2. Ian K. Steele, *Warpaths: Invasions of North America* (New York: Oxford University Press, 1994), 75–77.
3. Reuben Gold Thwaites, ed., *The Jesuit Relations and Allied Documents: Travels and Explorations of the Jesuit Missionaries in New France (1610–1791)*, 73 vols. (Cleveland, OH: Burrows Brothers Company, 1896–1901), 54:263–265 [hereafter cited as *Jesuit Relations*].
4. Brandao, *"Your fyre shall burn no more,"* 117–119.
5. Steele, *Warpaths*, 76–77; Brandao, *"Your fyre shall burn no more,"* 119.
6. E. B. O'Callaghan, ed., *Documents Relative to the Colonial History of the State of New York, Procured in Holland, England, and France*, 15 vols. (Albany, NY: Weed, Parson, and Company, 1857), 9:80 [hereafter cited as NYCD].
7. NYCD, 3:534.
8. Daniel K. Richter, *Ordeal of the Longhouse: The Peoples of the Iroquois League in the Era of European Colonization* (Chapel Hill: University of North Carolina Press, 1992), 130–131; Brandao, *"Your fyre shall burn no more,"* 119–120.
9. NYCD, 9:95–114; Richter, Ordeal, 131; Steele, Warpaths, 76–77, 122; Brandao, *"Your fyre shall burn no more,"* 120; William N. Fenton, *The Great Law and the Longhouse: A Political History of the Iroquois Confederacy* (Norman: University of Oklahoma, 1998), 253–254.
10. Richter, *Ordeal*, 131, 138–139; Steele, *Warpaths*, 77; Brandao, *"Your fyre shall burn no more,"* 120–121.
11. Richard White, *The Middle Ground: Indians, Empires, and Republics in the Great Lakes Region, 1650–1815* (New York: Cambridge University Press, 1991), 29; Steele, *Warpaths*, 124.
12. NYCD, 3:252; *Jesuit Relations*, 60:165–167, 185; George M. Hunt, *The Wars of the Iroquois* (Madison: University of Wisconsin Press, 1940), 150–153; Richter, *Ordeal*, 144; Eric Hinderaker, *Elusive Empires: Constructing Colonialism in the Ohio Valley, 1673–1800* (New York: Cambridge University Press,1997), 13.

13. White, *Middle Ground*, 29–31; Hinderaker, *Elusive Empires*, 13–14.

14. *Jesuit Relations*, 62:71, 153 (quotation), 159–161, 185; Richter, *Ordeal*, 144–148; Steele, *Warpaths*, 125; Hinderaker, *Elusive Empires*, 14.

15. Louise Kellogg, ed., *Early Narratives of the Northwest, 1634–1699* (New York: Charles Scribner's Sons, 1917), 305–311; Richter, *Ordeal*, 149–150; Steele, *Warpaths*, 125; Hinderaker, *Elusive Empires*, 16.

16. Jennings, *Ambiguous Iroquois Empire*, 184; Richter, *Ordeal*, 153; Steele, *Warpaths*, 125.

17. Quoted in Richter, *Ordeal*, 153, 155.

18. NYCD, 9:253.

19. Jennings, *Ambiguous Iroquois Empire*, 184–185; Richter, *Ordeal*, 153–155; Fenton, *The Great Law*, 256–257.

20. Lawrence H. Leder, ed., *The Livingston Indian Records, 1666–1723* (Harrisburg: Pennsylvania Historical Association, 1956), 103 [hereafter cited as *LIR*].

21. NYCD, 9:253–258; Jennings, *Ambiguous Iroquois Empire*, 180–184; Richter, *Ordeal*, 142–144, 150–153; Fenton, *The Great Law*, 278–280.

22. *LIR*, 103, 133, 148; Daniel K. Richter, "Ordeals of the Longhouse: The Five Nations in Early American History," in Daniel K. Richter and James H. Merrell, eds., *Beyond the Covenant Chain: The Iroquois and their Neighbors in Indian North America, 1600–1800* (Syracuse, NY: Syracuse University Press, 1987; reprint, University Park: Pennsylvania State University Press, 2003), 21–27; Richter, *Ordeal*, 169–170.

23. NYCD, 9:271–272.

24. Jennings, *Ambiguous Iroquois Empire*, 186–187; Steele, *Warpaths*, 137.

25. Richter, *Ordeal*, 156–157; Steele, *Warpaths*, 137–138.

26. Quoted in Richter, *Ordeal*, 157.

27. NYCD, 3:431–436, 444–447; 9: 334–341, 358–369; *Jesuit Relations*, 63:269–283; *LIR*, 126–133; Jennings, *Ambiguous Iroquois Empire*, 190–191; Richter, *Ordeal*, 158, 168; Steele, *Warpaths*, 138.

28. NYCD, 428–430.

29. *LIR*, 136–137.

30. Jennings, *Ambiguous Iroquois Empire*, 191–192; Richter, *Ordeal*, 158–159; Fenton, *The Great Law*, 258, 286–287.

31. NYCD, 9:434–439; Jennings, *Ambiguous Iroquois Empire*, 195–196; Richter, *Ordeal*, 159–160; Steele, *Warpaths*, 138–140.

32. *LIR*, 155.

33. Richter, *Ordeal*, 162–164.

34. Richter, *Ordeal*, 166–168; Steele, *Warpaths*, 140–141.

35. E. B. O'Callaghan, ed., *The Documentary History of the State of New York*, 4 vols. (Albany, NY: Weed Parsons, 1849–1851), 2:285–288; Richter, *Ordeal*, 165–166, 170–173; Steele, *Warpaths*, 141–142.

36. Richter, *Ordeal*, 166–167; Steele, *Warpaths*, 142.

37. NYCD, 3:815–817; Richter, *Ordeal*, 173–174; Brandao, *"Your fyre shall burn no more,"* appendix D, table D1; Fenton, *The Great Law*, 266.

38. Quoted in Richter, *Ordeal*, 175.

39. Richter, *Ordeal*, 173–175; Fenton, *The Great Law*, 266.

40. NYCD, 4:121–122 (quotation); Richter, *Ordeal*, 176–184; Fenton, *The Great Law*, 291–293.

41. *Jesuit Relations*, 65:27–29; Richter, *Ordeal*, 185–186; Fenton, *The Great Law*, 267.

42. NYCD, 4:294; Steele, *Warpaths*, 147–148; Richter, *Ordeal*, 187–188; Brandao, *"Your fyre shall burn no more,"* appendix D, table D1.

43. Richter, *Ordeal*, 188–189.

44. Daniel K. Richter, "Ordeals of the Longhouse," 26–27; Richter, *Ordeal*, 201–213; Fenton, *The Great Law*, 330–360.

THE LONG NEUTRALITY

1. William N. Fenton, *The Great Law and the Longhouse: A Political History of the Iroquois Confederacy* (Norman: University of Oklahoma Press, 1998), 363–364.

2. Richard Aquila, *The Iroquois Restoration: Iroquois Diplomacy on the Colonial Frontier, 1701–1754* (Detroit, MI: Wayne State University Press, 1983; reprint, Lincoln: University of Nebraska Press, 1997), 15–18; Fred Anderson, *Crucible of War: The Seven Years' War and the Fate of Empire in British North America, 1754–1766* (New York: Alfred A. Knopf, 2000), 15–16 (quotation).

3. Daniel K. Richter, *The Ordeal of the Longhouse: The Peoples of the Iroquois League in the Era of European Colonization* (Chapel Hill: University of North Carolina Press, 1992), 215–218; Ian K. Steele, *Warpaths: Invasions of Colonial America* (New York: Oxford University Press, 1994), 155; Aquila, *Iroquois Restoration*, 130–131.

4. E. B. O'Callaghan, ed., *Documents Relative to the Colonial History of the State of New York, Procured in Holland, England, and France*, 15 vols. (Albany, NY: Weed, Parson, and Company, 1857), 9:768 (quotation) [hereafter cited as NYCD]; Richter, *Ordeal*, 218–219.

5. Richter, *Ordeal*, 215–217.

6. Richard L. Haan, "Covenant and Consensus: Iroquois and English, 1676–1760," in Daniel K. Richter and James H. Merrell, eds., *Beyond the Covenant Chain: The Iroquois and their Neighbors in Indian North America, 1600–1800* (Syracuse, NY: Syracuse University Press, 1987; reprint, University Park: Pennsylvania State University Press, 2003), 53–54; Richter, *Ordeal*, 223–224; Aquila, *Iroquois Restoration*, 132–136.

7. Richter, *Ordeal*, 224–225.

8. Richter, *Ordeal*, 225–226; Aquila, *Iroquois Restoration*, 85–86.

9. Richter, *Ordeal*, 226; Aquila, *Iroquois Restoration*, 86–87.

10. Aquila, *Iroquois Restoration*, 87–88.

11. Peter Wraxall, *An Abridgement of the Indian Affairs Contained in Four Foilio Volumes, Transacted in the Colony of New York, from the Year 1678 to the Year 1751*, ed. Charles Howard McIlwain (Cambridge, MA: Harvard University Press, 1915), 87–89 (quotation); Richter, *Ordeal*, 227–228.

12. Richter, *Ordeal*, 228; Steele, *Warpaths*, 158; Aquila, *Iroquois Restoration*, 89–90.

13. Cadwallader Colden, "Continuation of Colden's History of the Five Indian Nations, for the Years 1707 through 1720," New York Historical Society, *Collections*, 68 (1935): 408.

14. Richter, *Ordeal*, 228–231; Aquila, *Iroquois Restoration*, 91.

15. *NYCD*, 550–551.

16. Richter, *Ordeal*, 246–250.

17. Richter, *Ordeal*, 237; James H. Merrell, "Their Very Bones Shall Fight: The Catawba-Iroquois Wars," in Richter and Merrell, eds., *Beyond the Covenant Chain*, 119–120.

18. Reuben Gold Thwaites, ed., *The Jesuit Relations and Allied Documents: Travels and Explorations of the Jesuit Missionaries in New France (1610–1791)*, 73 vols. (Cleveland, OH: Burrows Brothers Company, 1896–1901), 47:143.

19. James H. Merrell, *The Indians' New World: Catawbas and their Neighbors from European Contact through the Era of Removal* (New York: Norton, 1991), 41–42; Richter, *Ordeal*, 372n1; Merrell, "Their Very Bones Shall Fight," 117; Theda Purdue, "Cherokee Relations with the Iroquois in the Eighteenth Century," in Richter and Merrell, eds., *Beyond the Covenant Chain*, 137.

20. Samuel Hazard, ed., *Colonial Records of Pennsylvania, or Minutes of the Provincial Council of Pennsylvania*, 16 vols. (Harrisburg, PA: T. Fenn, 1838–1853), 2:138 [hereafter cited as *CRP*].

21. Merrell, *Indians' New World*, 5, 42; Merrell, "Their Very Bones Shall Fight," 117–120 (quotation from 120); Purdue, "Cherokee Relations," 137.

22. Quoted in Merrell, *Indians' New World*, 42.

23. Merrell, *Indians' New World*, 42; Aquila, *Iroquois Restoration*, 206–207, 227–228; Jon Parmenter, "L'Arbre de Paix: Eighteenth Century Franco-Iroquois Relations," *French Colonial History* 4 (2003): 67.

24. Colden, "Continuation," 382–383 (quotation); Richter, *Ordeal*, 237–238; Aquila, *Iroquois Restoration*, 207–209.

25. Richter, *Ordeal*, 238; Douglas W. Boyce, "As the Wind Scatters the Smoke: The Tuscaroras in the Eighteenth Century," in Richter and Merrell, eds., *Beyond the Covenant Chain*, 151–154; Merrell, *Indians' New World*, 53–54.

26. Quoted in Boyce, "As the Wind Scatters the Smoke," 153.

27. Aquila, *Iroquois Restoration*, 209–210; Boyce, "As the Wind Scatters the Smoke," 152–155.

28. *NYCD*, 5:376.

29. *NYCD*, 5:387.

30. Richter, *Ordeal*, 219; Boyce, "As the Wind Scatters the Smoke," 155–160.

31. Richter, *Ordeal*, 239–240.

32. *NYCD*, 5:442.

33. Merrell, *Indians' New World*, 78 (quotation) ; Richter, *Ordeal*, 240; Aquila, *Iroquois Restoration*, 210–212.

34. Merrell, *Indians' New World*, 89; Richter, *Ordeal*, 240; Aquila, *Iroquois Restoration*, 212–214.

35. Merrell, *Indians' New World*, 118–120; Merrell, "Their Very Bones Shall Fight," 121–123 (quotation from 121).

36. *CRP*, 4:733.

37. Merrell, *Indians' New World*, 135–137; Merrell, "Their Very Bones Shall Fight," 124–125; Purdue, "Cherokee Relations with the Iroquois," 137–140.

38. Merrell, *Indians' New World*, 154–160; Merell, "Their Very Bones Shall Fight," 125–132; Aquila, *Iroquois Restoration*, 217–227.

39. Aquila, *Iroquois Restoration*, 156–157.

40. Richter, *Ordeal*, 241–243; Aquila, *Iroquois Restoration*, 159–163.

41. Quoted in Richter, *Ordeal*, 243.

42. Francis Jennings, *The Ambiguous Iroquois Empire: The Covenant Chain Confederation of Indian Tribes with English Colonies from Its Beginnings to the Lancaster Treaty of 1744* (New York: Norton, 1984), 295–298; Richter, Ordeal, 243–244; Aquila, *Iroquois Restoration*, 166–182.

43. *CRP*, 4: 579–580 (quotation); Jennings, *Ambiguous Iroquois Empire*, 289–346; Richter, *Ordeal*, 273–276; Aquila, *Iroquois Restoration*, 183–186.

44. Jennings, *Ambiguous Iroquois Empire*, 356–362.

45. Ian K. Steele, *Betrayals: Fort William Henry and the "Massacre"* (New York: Oxford University Press, 1990), 18–21; Aquila, *Iroquois Restoration*, 95–100, 144.

46. Steele, *Betrayals*, 21–23; Aquila, *Iroquois Restoration*, 149–151.

47. Francis Jennings, *Empire of Fortune: Crowns, Colonies, and Tribes in the Seven Years War in America* (New York: Norton, 1988), 21–45; Richter, Ordeal, 256; Michael N. McConnell, *A Country Between: The Upper Ohio Valley and Its Peoples, 1724–1774* (University of Nebraska Press, 1992), 5–23, 77–82.

48. Anderson, *Crucible of War*, 17–18, 24–32.

THE LONGHOUSE DIVIDED

1. William N. Fenton, *The Great Law and the Longhouse: A Political History of the Iroquois Confederacy* (Norman: University of Okalahoma Press, 1998), 496.

2. Quoted in Jon Parmenter, "L'Arbre de Paix: Eighteenth Century Franco-Iroquois Relations," *French Colonial History* 4 (2003): 71.

3. D. Peter MacLeod, *The Canadian Iroquois and the Seven Years' War* (Toronto: Dundurn, 1996), 47–54; Parmenter, "L'Arbe de Paix," 69–71 (quotation).

4. John Sullivan, et al., eds., *The Papers of Sir William Johnson*, 14 vols. (Albany, NY: University of the State of New York, 1921–1965), 2:705 [hereafter cited as *SWJP*].

5. Ian K. Steele, *Betrayals: Fort William Henry and the "Massacre"* (New York: Oxford University Press, 1990), 24; Parmenter, "L'Arbe de Paix," 71–73.

6. Francis Jennings, *Empire of Fortune: Crowns, Colonies, and Tribes in the Seven Years War in America* (New York: Norton, 1988), 80; Steele, *Betrayals*, 21–24.

7. E. B. O'Callaghan, ed., *Documents Relative to the Colonial History of the State of New York, Procured in Holland, England, and France*, 15 vols. (Albany, NY: Weed, Parson, and Company, 1857), 6:788 [hereafter cited as *NYCD*].

8. Jennings, *Empire of Fortune*, 80–81; Steele, *Betrayals*, 24–25.

9. *NYCD*, 6:869–870.

10. Jennings, *Empire of Fortune*, 81–83; Steele, *Betrayals*, 25–27; Richard Aquila, *The Iroquois Restoration: Iroquois Diplomacy on the Colonial Frontier, 1701–1754* (Detroit, MI: Wayne State University Press, 1983; reprint, Lincoln: University of Nebraska Press, 1997), 105–112; Fenton, *The Great Law*, 468–476; Fred Anderson, *Crucible of War: The Seven Years' War and the Fate of Empire in British North America, 1754–1766* (New York: Alfred A. Knopf, 2000), 78–85.

11. *SWJP*, 9:203–206 (quotation); Steele, *Betrayals*, 32–34; Fenton, *The Great Law*, 476–480; Anderson, *Crucible of War*, 91–92.

12. *Betrayals*, 40–44; Anderson, *Crucible of War*, 108–118.

13. Steele, *Betrayals*, 44–47; Anderson, *Crucible of War*, 118.

14. *NYCD*, 10:316–318, 1013–1015; *SWJP*, 9:231; Steele, *Betrayals*, 47–50; MacLeod, *Canadian Iroquois*, 71–74; Anderson, *Crucible of War*, 118–119.

15. *NYCD*, 6:1011–1013 (quotation); Steele, *Betrayals*, 51–54; Anderson, *Crucible of War*, 119–123.

16. *NYCD*, 10:560–561 (quotation); *SWJP*, 1:803–806; 2:80–86, 125–128; Steele, *Betrayals*, 54; Fenton, *The Great Law*, 497–499.

17. Jennings, *Empire of Fortune*, 261–262; Anderson, *Crucible of War*, 275–276.

18. *NYCD*, 7:57.

19. Jennings, *Empire of Fortune*, 396–403; Anderson, *Crucible of War*, 205–207, 275–279.

20. Isabel Thompson Kelsay, *Joseph Brant, 1743–1807: Man of Two Worlds* (Syracuse, NY: Syracuse University Press, 1984), 62; Jennings, *Empire of Fortune*, 353–368; Anderson, *Crucible of War*, 241–264.

21. Fenton, *The Great Law*, 509–513; Anderson, *Crucible of War*, 330–333.

22. Brian Liegh Dunnigan, *Siege—1759: The Campaign against Niagara* (Youngstown, NY: Old Fort Niagara Association, 1985), 57–60; Ian K. Steele, *Warpaths: Invasions of North America* (New York: Oxford University Press, 1994), 216–217; Anderson, *Crucible of War*, 335–336, 787n4.

23. Dunnigan, *Siege*, 93–98; Steele, *Warpaths*, 217; Anderson, *Crucible of War*, 337–338.

24. Kelsay, *Joseph Brant*, 65–66; Anderson, *Crucible of War*, 404–406, 467–469.

25. Richard White, *The Middle Ground: Indians, Empires, and Republics in the Great Lakes Region, 1650–1815* (New York: Cambridge University Press, 1991), 256–260; Gregory Evans Dowd, *War Under Heaven: Pontiac, The Indian Nations, and the British Empire* (Baltimore, MD: The John Hopkins University Press, 2002), 54–89; David Dixon, *Never Come to Peace Again: Pontiac's Uprising and the Fate of the British Empire in North America* (Norman: University of Oklahoma Press, 2005), 73–81.

26. Gregory Evans Dowd, *A Spirited Resistance: The North American Indian Struggle for Unity, 1745–1812* (Baltimore, MD: John Hopkins University Press, 1992), 33–35; White, *Middle Ground*, 260–263, 277–287; Daniel K. Richter, *Facing East from Indian Country: A Native History of Early America* (Cambridge, MA: Harvard University Press, 2001), 191–201; Dowd, *War Under Heaven*, 90–105; Dixon, *Never Come to Peace Again*, 92–98.

27. Michael McConnell, *A Country Between: The Upper Ohio Valley and Its Peoples, 1724–1774* (Lincoln: University of Nebraska Press, 1992), 169–170; Fenton, *The Great Law*, 520; Dixon, *Never Come to Peace Again*, 71.

28. Samuel Hazard, ed., *Colonial Records of Pennsylvania, or Minutes of the Provincial Council of Pennsylvania*, 16 vols. (Harrisburg, PA: T. Fenn, 1838–1853), 8:767; White, *Middle Ground*, 271–272; Dixon, *Never Come to Peace Again*, 99.

29. McConnell, *Country Between*, 171–172; White, *Middle Ground*, 271–273; Dixon, *Never Come to Peace Again*, 85–88

30. Nicholas B. Wainwright, ed., "George Croghan's Journal, April 3, 1759 to April 1763," *Pennsylvania Magazine of History and Biography* 71 (1947): 410.

31. SWJP, 10:291 (quoation); Dowd, *War Under Heaven*, 105–107; Dixon, *Never Come to Peace Again*, 88–93.

32. NYCD, 7:532–533; SWJP, 10:871–872; Anthony F. C. Wallace, *The Death and Rebirth of the Seneca* (New York: Random House, 1969), 115; Kelsay, *Joseph Brant*, 90; White, *Middle Ground*, 286–287; Dixon, *Never Come to Peace Again*, 147.

33. Dowd, *War Under Heaven*, 127; Dixon, *Never Come to Peace Again*, 147–148.

34. Dowd, *War Under Heaven*, 127–128; Dixon, *Never Come to Peace Again*, 149–150.

35. Wallace, *Death and Rebirth*, 116; Dowd, *War Under Heaven*, 137; Dixon, *Never Come to Peace Again*, 210–211.

36. SWJP, 10:754; Kelsay, *Joseph Brant*, 94–96

37. Kelsay, *Joseph Brant*, 98–102; Dowd, *War Under Heaven*, 151–153; Dixon, *Never Come to Peace Again*, 220.

38. SWJP, 11:316–324; Dowd, *War Under Heaven*, 153–154; Dixon, *Never Come to Peace Again*, 219, 228.

THE LONGHOUSE IN FLAMES

1. E. B. O'Callaghan, ed., *Documents Relative to the Colonial History of the State of New York, Procured in Holland, England, and France*, 15 vols. (Albany, NY: Weed, Parson, and Company, 1857), 8:623–624 [hereafter cited as *NYCD*].

2. *NYCD*, 8:617–620.

3. *NYCD*, 8:621–624 (quotation); Barbara Graymont, *The Iroquois in the American Revolution* (Syracuse, NY: Syracuse University Press, 1972), 70–74.

4. June Namias, ed., *A Narrative of the Life of Mary Jemison, by James Seaver* (Norman: University of Oklahoma Press, 1992), 98.

5. Anthony F. C. Wallace, *The Death and Rebirth of the Seneca* (New York: Random House, 1969), 130; Graymont, *Iroquois in the Revolution*, 82–94.

6. Graymont, *Iroquois in the Revolution*, 33–40, 69–71; Isabel Thompson Kelsay, *Joseph Brant: Man of Two Worlds* (Syracuse, NY: Syracuse University Press, 1984), 161–175; Max M. Mintz, *Seeds of Empire: The American Revolutionary Conquest of the Iroquois* (New York: New York University Press, 1999), 12–15.

7. John Burgoyne, *A State of the Expedition from Canada* (London: J. Almon, 1780), x–xi.

8. *NYCD*, 8:689.

9. Graymont, *Iroquois in the American Revolution*, 94–100 (quotation on 99); Mintz, *Seeds of Empire*, 20–21.

10. Wallace, *Death and Rebirth of the Seneca*, 132; Kelsay, *Joseph Brant*, 182–196; Graymont, *Iroquois in the Revolution*, 104–106, 108–113; Colin G. Calloway, *The American Revolution in Indian Country: Crisis and Diversity in Native American Communities* (New York: Cambridge University Press, 1995), 33; Mintz, *Seeds of Empire*, 15–20.

11. Wallace, *Death and Rebirth*, 131–132; Graymont, *Iroquois in the American Revolution*, 120–122; Thomas S. Abler, ed., *Chainbreaker: The Revolutionary War Memoirs of Governor Blacksnake, as Told to Benjamin West* (Lincoln: University of Nebraska Press, 1989), 65–69; Mintz, *Seeds of Empire*, 21–22.

12. Abler, ed., *Chainbreaker*, 75.

13. Abler, ed., *Chainbreaker*, 74.

14. Graymont, *Iroquois in the Revolution*, 122–128; Kelsay, *Joseph Brant*, 198–199; Abler, ed., *Chainbreaker*, 70–80; Mintz, *Seeds of Empire*, 22.

15. Richard S. Ketchum, *Saratoga: Turning Point of America's Revolutionary War* (New York: Henry Holt, 1997), 64–88; Mintz, *Seeds of Empire*, 20–21.

16. *NYCD*, 8:721; Marinus Willett, *A Narrative of the Military Actions of Colonel Marinus Willett*, ed. William M. Willett (New York: Carvill, 1831; reprint, New York: Arno Press, 1969), 50; Mintz, *Seeds of Empire*, 23–29.

17. Burgoyne, *State of the Expedition*, lxxvii–lxxviii.

18. Abler, ed., *Chainbreaker*, 128 (quotation); Graymont, *Iroquois in the Revolution*, 134; Mintz, *Seeds of Empire*, 32–33.

19. NYCD, 8:725–726; Graymont, *Iroquois in the Revolution*, 134–136; Mintz, *Seeds of Empire*, 34–35.

20. Abler, ed., *Chainbreaker*, 128.

21. Willett, *Narrative*, 55–59; NYCD, 8:721–722; Graymont, *Iroquois in the Revolution*, 138-146; Mintz, *Seeds of Empire*, 37–44.

22. Namias, ed., *Mary Jemison*, 100.

23. Graymont, *Iroquois in the Revolution*, 142–143; Calloway, *American Revolution*, 33–34; Mintz, *Seeds of Empire*, 42, 44–45.

24. *Iroquois in the Revolution*, 146–147, 149–155 (quotation on 155).

25. Quoted in Mintz, *Seeds of Empire*, 46.

26. Wallace, *Death and Rebirth*, 136–137; Mintz, *Seeds of Empire*, 45–48, 50.

27. C. Hale Sipe, *The Indian Wars of Pennsylvania* (Harrisburg, PA: Telegraph Press, 1931), 537–549; Edgar W. Hassler, *Old Westmoreland: A History of Western Pennsylvania during the Revolution* (Pittsburgh, PA: J.R. Weldon, 1900; reprint, Bowie, MD: Heritage Books, 1998), 68, 119–121; Mintz, *Seeds of Empire*, 49.

28. Graymont, *Iroquois in the Revolution*, 167–169; Abler, ed., *Chainbreaker*, 97–98; Mintz, *Seeds of Empire*, 56–57.

29. Graymont, *Iroquois in the Revolution*, 169–171; Abler, ed., *Chainbreaker*, 98; Mintz, *Seeds of Empire*, 57–61.

30. Wallace, *Death and Rebirth*, 137–138; Graymont, *Iroquois in the Revolution*, 171–172; Abler, ed., *Chainbreaker*, 98; Mintz, *Seeds of Empire*, 61–63.

31. Graymont, *Iroquois in the Revolution*, 172; Calloway, *American Revolution*, 110, 123–124.

32. Hugh Hastings, ed., *Public Papers of George Clinton, First Governor of New York* (New York and Albany: Published by the State of New York, 1899–1914), 3:377–378, 402–414, 413 [hereafter cited as CP]; Graymont, *Iroquois in the Revolution*, 165–166; John C. Dann, ed., *The Revolution Remembered: Eyewitness Accounts of the War for Independence* (Chicago: University of Chicago Press, 1980), 288–291; Kelsay, *Joseph Brant*, 216–217; Mintz, *Seeds of Empire*, 50–51.

33. CP, 3:475–476, 555–559, 581–582; Graymont, *Iroquois in the Revolution*, 174–175, 178; Kelsay, *Joseph Brant*, 223–224.

34. CP, 4:39, 47–49, 53–55, 80–83; Graymont, *Iroquois in the Revolution*, 178–179; Mintz, *Seeds of Empire*, 66.

35. CP, 3:742.

36. CP, 4:163–164, 185, 222–228; Graymont, *Iroquois in the Revolution*, 181–182; Calloway, *American Revolution*, 124–125; Mintz, *Seeds of Empire*, 66–68.

37. Samuel Hazard, ed., *Pennsylvania Archives*, 9 Series, 120 vols. (Philadelphia and Harrisburg: State Printer of Pennsylvania, 1852–1935), 6th ser., 7:5–8; Graymont, *Iroquois in the Revolution*, 180–181; Abler, ed., *Chainbreaker*, 101–103; Mintz, *Seeds of Empire*, 68–70.

38. Graymont, *Iroquois in the Revolution*, 182–187; Kelsay, *Joseph Brant*, 229–233; Mintz, *Seeds of Empire*, 70–73.

39. *CP*, 4:267, 286, 364; Graymont, *Iroquois in the Revolution*, 187–190; Kelsay, *Joseph Brant*, 231–233; Mintz, *Seeds of Empire*, 73.

40. *CP*, 4:364.

41. Graymont, *Iroquois in the Revolution*, 190–191; Calloway, *American Revolution*, 125–126; Mintz, *Seeds of Empire*, 70–71.

42. John Fitzpatrick, ed., *The Writings of George Washington from the Original Manuscript Sources, 1745–1799*, 39 vols. (Washington, DC: United States Government Printing Office, 1931–1944), 14:199; 15:189–193.

43. Mintz, *Seeds of Empire*, 78–83.

44. *CP*, 4:702–703; Albert Hazen Wright, ed., *Sullivan Expedition of 1779: Contemporary Newspaper Comment and Letters* (Ithaca, NY: Cornell University Press, 1943), 41–43, 59–63; Graymont, *Iroquois in the Revolution*, 196; Mintz, *Seeds of Destruction*, 83–85.

45. Otis G. Hammond, ed., *The Letters and Papers of Major General John Sullivan, Continental Army*, 3 vols. (Concord: New Hampshire Historical Society, 1930–1939), 3:95–100 [hereafter cited as *SP*]; Mintz, *Seeds of Empire*, 103–114.

46. Hazard, ed., *Pennsylvania Archives*, 7:589–592, 597–598; Graymont, *Iroquois in the Revolution*, 199–204; Kelsay, *Joseph Brant*, 250–252; Mintz, *Seeds of Empire*, 118–120.

47. Mintz, *Seeds of Empire*, 121–123.

48. *SP*, 3:107–113; Graymont, *Iroquois in the Revolution*, 211–213; Kelsay, *Joseph Brant*, 259–262; Abler, ed., *Chainbreaker*, 108–110; Mintz, *Seeds of Empire*, 123–129.

49. Louise Phelps Kellogg, ed., *Frontier Retreat on the Upper Ohio, 1779–1781* (Madison: State Historical Society of Wisconsin, 1917), 55–66; Mintz, *Seeds of Empire*, 115–116.

50. Graymont, *Iroquois in the American Revolution*, 215–216; Abler, ed., *Chainbreaker*, 109–113; Mintz, *Seeds of Empire*, 129–138.

51. *SP*, 3:131; Graymont, *Iroquois in the Revolution*, 216–218; Dann, ed., *Revolution Remembered*, 292–296; Abler, ed., *Chainbreaker*, 113–114, 140–141; Mintz, *Seeds of Empire*, 140–145.

52. Mintz, *Seeds of Empire*, 145–154.

53. Joseph R. Fischer, *A Well-Executed Failure: The Sullivan Campaign against the Iroquois, July-September 1779* (Columbia: University of South Carolina Press, 1997).

54. Quoted in Mintz, *Seeds of Empire*, 157–158.

55. Graymont, *Iroquois in the Revolution*, 220–222; Calloway, *American Revolution*, 58–59, 135–139; Mintz, *Seeds of Empire*, 154–156.

56. Calloway, *American Revolution*, 140–141, 144; Mintz, *Seeds of Empire*, 158–159, 162.

57. *NYCD*, 8:796; *CP*, 5:883–884; Graymont, *Iroquois in the Revolution*, 233–235; Calloway, *American Revolution*, 141.

58. Graymont, *Iroquois in the Revolution*, 234–237; Mintz, *Seeds of Empire*, 151–152, 164–165.

59. Graymont, *Iroquois in the Revolution*, 242–244; Calloway, *American Revolution*, 53, 58–59, 101.

60. Graymont, *Iroquois in the Revolution*, 252–258.

EPILOGUE

1. Colin G. Calloway, *The American Revolution in Indian Country: Crisis and Diversity in Native American Communities* (New York: Cambridge University Press, 1995), 141, 153–155.

2. Max M. Mintz, *Seeds of Empire: The American Revolutionary Conquest of the Iroquois* (New York: New York University Press, 1999), 173.

3. Anthony F. C. Wallace, *The Death and Rebirth of the Seneca* (New York: Vintage Books, 1972), 239–337; William N. Fenton, *The Great Law and the Longhouse: A Political History of the Iroquois Confederacy* (Norman: University of Oklahoma Press, 1998), 601–706; Bruce E. Johansen, ed., *Enduring Legacies: Native American Treaties and Contemporary Controversies* (Westport, CT: Praeger, 2004), 45–134.

4. William H. Armstrong, *Warrior in Two Camps: Ely S. Parker, Union General and Seneca Chief* (Syracuse, NY: Syracuse University Press, 1978); Carl Benn, *The Iroquois in the War of 1812* (Toronto, Canada: University of Toronto Press, 1998); Laurence M. Hauptman, *The Iroquois Struggle for Survival: World War II to Red Power* (Syracuse, NY: Syracuse University Press, 1986); and *The Iroquois in the Civil War: From Battlefield to Reservation* (Syracuse, NY: Syracuse University Press, 1993).

Index

About the Author

DANIEL P. BARR is Assistant Professor of History at Robert Morris University, Pittsburgh. His research interests include American Indian history and the early American frontier. He is editor of *The Boundaries Between Us: Natives and Newcomers along the Frontiers of the Old Northwest Territory* and author of *The Ends of the American Earth: War and Society on the Pittsburgh Frontier*, both forthcoming.

Printed in the USA
CPSIA information can be obtained
at www.ICGtesting.com
LVHW020258300823
756703LV00004B/207